Ed Douglas has been climbing around the world for 20 years. He writes regularly for *The Observer* and *The Guardian* on mountains and mountaineering and is editor of the *Alpine Journal. Chomolungma Sings the Blues* was awarded The Jury Prize at the Banff Mountain Book Festival and The 1998 Outdoor Writers' Guild Award for Best Book.

Praise for *Chomolungma Sings the Blues*

'I had no prior interest in Everest or mountaineering until I read Ed Douglas' *Chomolungma Sings the Blues*. Well written, it is particularly insightful on the damaging effects of adventure tourism in Nepal and Tibet.'

Russell Celyn Jones, *The Times*

'Author Ed Douglas presents an aspect of Everest that is very rarely considered.'

Geographical

'A wise and useful book which has been asking to be written ever since Hunt's successful expedition in 1953 or, for that matter, the first forays by Charles Granville Bruce in 1922 and 1924. Douglas is a first class journalist.'

David Craig, *Literary Review*

'Douglas's book is very refreshing and honest, an excellent geo-political travelogue that takes the reader under the surface of the happy smiling trekking holiday. He is a thoughtful and informed observer.'

Roger Payne, *High*

'The authority and balanced judgement of this book will make it essential reading for those contemplating a trek to Tibet and Nepal.'

Terry Gifford, *Yorkshire Post*

D1147586

CHOMOLUNGMA SINGS THE BLUES
Travels round Everest

Ed Douglas

ROBINSON
London

Constable and Robinson Ltd
3 The Lanchesters
162 Fulham Palace Road
London W6 9ER
www.constablerobinson.com

First published in the UK by Constable and Company Ltd, 1997

This paperback edition published by Robinson,
an imprint of Constable and Robinson Ltd, 2001

ISBN 1-84119-400-X

Printed and bound in the EU

Contents

Introduction

It feels like a heartbeat and not five years since I was tramping around the Khumbu region of Nepal with my Sherpa friend Dachhiri. It has been transfigured into a golden time in my memory, weeks where one perfect day led seamlessly into another. Of course, it wasn't like that; all I have to do is skim through this account to remind myself that I was sometimes ill and often weary. The nostalgia I think is for a time when it was still all new for me, when each bend in the trail brought a fresh discovery.

I wasn't, and still am not, an expert in those areas that I wanted to investigate around Everest. The truth is that a mixture of ignorance and curiosity drove me out to Nepal and Tibet. I felt that there was an unanswered question about Everest, about the impact that so much obsession could have on a landscape and a people. As I discovered, and continue to discover, there are scores of experts both inside Nepal and around the world who have dissected the rare combination of culture, geography and history that make the Everest region so rich and compelling.

I never intended to write anything comprehensive or especially insightful. What I wanted to achieve was a snapshot, something fresh and light that would offer an accessible introduction into dry and complex areas and provide a glimpse of the region as it was then. Everest is usually presented as being all about the triumph of the human spirit, the overcoming of impossible odds. And in a way it is, but I discovered in 1995 and 1996 in Tibet and Nepal that ordinary lives hold those qualities in abundance and that going to climb a mountain can show their absence as much as their presence. If I've shown that in this book then I've succeeded.

The self-aggrandisement and egotism that I saw among mediocre mountaineers at Everest then has grown steadily in the last five years to the extent that I no longer have much interest in what happens on the mountain. I think speed records by Sherpas like Babu Chhiri, who died so tragically in the spring season of 2001, are impressive, but much of what goes on lacks the imagination and ability of previous generations. When mountaineers have to resort to paying twenty, forty or sixty thousand pounds to struggle up a mountain, relying on Sherpas to carry their gear and oxygen, with the odd injection of steroids to keep them going, then I hardly see the point. I know good climbers who have climbed Everest in the last few years, quietly getting to the summit without issuing a press release or even talking about it much. But they seem the exception now. Climbing has moved on, and Everest is now firmly the stuff of headlines, no longer a true part of the Himalayan mountaineering that I grew up admiring.

One of the things that struck me as both hilarious and infuriating in my research was the proliferation of clean-up expeditions. (Some of them did excellent work of course; I am thinking more of the automatic and generally approving coverage these expeditions receive.) With the increase in recent years in the number of climbers on the mountain, environmental pressures have grown, but they are as nothing compared to the pollution overwhelming Kathmandu, a city I have come to love above, I think, all others. There have been some successes. The electric rickshaw project I saw in its infancy in 1996 has now flourished and the most heavily polluting rickshaws are banned. Recent visitors may not believe it, but the air in Kathmandu is actually getting better, although the petrol is still cut with kerosene and increasing vehicle numbers mean that any gain will be short lived.

In some areas of the city, Kathmandu's globally important

architecture and cultural life has been shored up, especially in Patan where the new museum and programme of renovation has added a fresh lustre to its exquisite Durbar Square. But the rush of development continues unabated, and Kathmandu's planning controls, systems that we in the West take for granted, seem incapable of responding. While people remain hungry, as they do in many parts of Nepal, then the question of garbage on Everest, or even of garbage on the streets of Kathmandu, will inevitably preoccupy governments and agencies less urgently.

You can still cycle out into the country surrounding Kathmandu and watch farmers threshing by hand as they have done for millennia, and then turn and glimpse a wide-bodied jet take off from the airport. But I can see in the future the bowl of the Kathmandu Valley built over, the farms forgotten, the land lost, as migrants from the country, victims of Nepal's spiralling population growth, look for work in the capital. These problems deserve priority.

That is not to say that I don't think anything needs to be done for Chomolungma's environment. It is the most famous mountain on Earth, and if we cannot protect it, then other mountain areas around the world have an even bleaker future. When I travelled to Tibet in 1995, I felt that even though the south side of the mountain, the Khumbu, attracted many more visitors, the openness of Nepal to foreign media, the ease of travel and the region's high profile would actually work in the environment's favour. In Tibet, where local people have been allowed fewer benefits from tourism by the Chinese, there is less momentum to create the kind of environmental awareness that has proved so beneficial among Sherpas in the Khumbu, and the state of base camp has worsened considerably. But while I support those projects working on either side of Everest to ameliorate the damage done by trekkers and climbers, and I wish them well, I still believe that the most pressing issues lie elsewhere.

Since I wrote this book I have returned to Nepal half a dozen times and travelled the length and narrow breadth of this beautiful country. My understanding of its politics and culture has deepened, and the freshness that I felt writing about this journey has faded somewhat as I have recognised the flaws and shortcomings under the surface. But on cold winter mornings in England, perhaps out walking in the Peak District, I'll catch the smell of wood smoke or hear a cock crow, and feel a powerful twist in my memory. Now, for me, Nepal feels like home . . .

As I write this, barely a month after my latest visit, the country is facing its greatest crisis in modern history. The brutal murders of King Birendra, a thoughtful and kindly man much loved by the Nepali people, his wife and many members of his immediate family, coupled with the continuing Maoist insurgency that was just underway in 1996, has left the very survival of the nation in question. Violence, political instability, corruption, economic stagnation and environmental failure are what the people of Nepal face ten years on after the introduction of multi-party democracy.

Climbing mountains, even the biggest on Earth, seems inconsequential in the face of these problems. But the Nepali people are a resilient and joyful people. During the last years of the oppressive Rana regime, the poet Lakshmiprasad Devkota wrote the poem *Jhanjhaprati** : *Bholi hunchha dhauta gagan pavan nirmal santa, / Ritu basanta haaschha madhur, sisir hunchha anta.* Tomorrow the sky will be clear, the breeze will be pure and peaceful. Spring will smile tenderly, winter will come to an end.

Ed Douglas
June 2001

*Jhanjhaprati = To a rainstorm

Acknowledgements

I am grateful for the assistance of many people and a number of organisations for their time and advice in writing this book. Without a travel fellowship from The Winston Churchill Memorial Trust the travelling and research I did in Nepal and Tibet would have been impossible. In Nepal I received help and advice from the journalist Liz Hawley, Steve Webster and Lisa Choegyal of Mountain Travel, Ruth Hall of the American Embassy, Kanak Dixit of *Himal* magazine, the hotelier and environmentalist Karna Sakya, Narayan Belbase of the IUCN and Colonel Jimmy Roberts. I travelled through Tibet with the Bristol trekking outfit Himalayan Kingdoms whose clients were wonderful company, even in the worst circumstances. For those who wish to protest against the Chinese occupation of Tibet, I encourage you to contact the Free Tibet campaign in London. Thanks to Forward Publishing for permission to quote from Dominic Sasse's poetry. I am also grateful to Audrey Salkeld for sharing her deep knowledge of Everest and its history and offering advice, and to the following who provided information and support during the years this book was in gestation: Chris Bonington, Steve Bell, Sue Carpenter, the late Mal Duff, Bernard Newman, Nick Banks, Jim Perrin, Tom Prentice, Paul Rogers, Sean Smith, Jon Tinker, Mike Westmacott, Robbie Barnett and Bill Wright. The debt I owe my wife for dealing with the consequences of my long absences and accepting me back at the end of them is axiomatic. Finally, I owe a great deal to Dachhiri Sherpa who was an excellent companion in the mountains and a patient and tolerant guide.

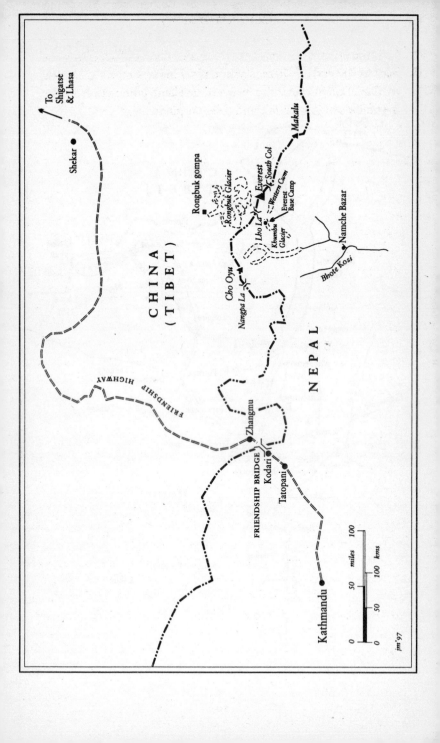

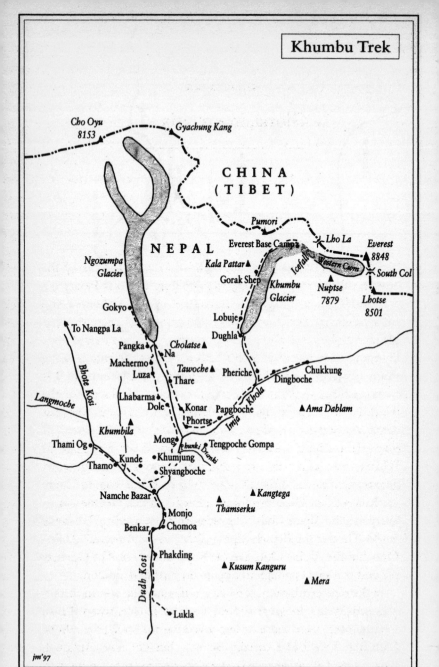

Khumbu Trek

CHAPTER ONE

Gloria, in excelsis . . .

North of the glass canyons of the City of London and east of the crowds of shoppers streaming along Upper Street is Hoxton, a forgettable range of offices converted from warehouses and modern council flats. Except for a strange twist of chemistry that blended Bohemia and low rent, Hoxton would have stayed non-descript but in recent years it's achieved a certain fame housing more artists than anywhere else in Europe. But it's not art that takes me down there, at least not in the conventional sense of the word. It's an anonymous brick building on a narrow lane that spans the arteries of Great Eastern Street and Old Street. It houses the Alpine Club, not as prestigious a name perhaps as White's or as fashionable as the Groucho. Social advantage won't get you admitted and there's none to be gained if you do. There are, however, qualifications for membership which exclude almost everyone; the Alpine Club is the oldest mountaineering club in the world. There is the French Alpine Club and the American Alpine Club, but the Alpine Club, like the Royal Society or The Open, is old and confident enough to require no further definition.

In the nineteenth century, when mountaineering was an acceptable activity for the great and the good to pursue, when British mountaineers were more or less inventing the sport, the Alpine Club may have had a certain cachet – but not now. Although today's members are relieved to be without that sort of nonsense, its exalted past does beg the question of what the Alpine Club is doing in scruffy little Hoxton. The Royal Geographical Society sits in faded splendour on Kensington Gore in a redbrick pile of high ceilings and sweeping staircases with a large auditorium that is regularly full to bursting for lectures on the few parts of the planet that remain obscure, at least to the Society's fellows. The Alpine Club, on the other hand, has stripped itself down for the twenty-first century, is more utilitarian linoleum than plush carpet. It used to occupy grand premises in Mayfair but the Alpine Club has often proved canny in the management of its assets and sold the few years of its lease before the price of property collapsed at the end of Mrs Thatcher's decade. Its lectures, concerning themselves with obscure mountains in the obscure regions covered by the geographers, attract at best a few dozen cognoscenti brought to order by the president striking a heavy oxygen bottle of 1920s vintage like a gong, a gently ironic relic brought home from the slopes of Everest to show to the faithful. I suspect that the Alpine Club secretly prefers this understated mood.

At the head of a narrow flight of stairs through painted doors is a collection of photographs of all the presidents since the club's foundation in 1857. There are sequences of faces like this in boardrooms, schools and associations all over the country, the austere and bearded jowls of the last century giving way to gruff, clipped moustaches following the Great War and then the clean-shaven, more open and relaxed faces of the 1950s. Few of these men have been more than dedicated amateurs; most excelled at something other than mountaineering. Leslie Stephen's mournful and pinched face appears early in the sequence. The photograph was taken after he had given up the mountains to look after his daughters Virginia and Vanessa and work on the *Dictionary of National Biography*; the youthful exuberance of his Alpine memoir *The Playground of Europe* has vanished from his eyes. Edward Lisle Strutt seems even more severe and without Stephen's melancholic introspection. Strutt was president of the club when Hitler sent the Wehrmacht back into the Rhineland, and fought his own little war against the Third Reich, writing waspish editorials in the *Alpine Journal* against the fanaticism that had crept into German mountaineering and which found its greatest expression in the death-or-glory antics played out in public on the 'Mordwand', the North Face of the Eiger. A few photographs down the line and past the war is the patrician figure of Leo Amery, educated at Harrow and Oxford and Secretary of State for India and Burma in Churchill's wartime cabinet. In his obituary notice in the club's journal of 1956 Geoffrey Winthrop Young wrote that when Amery was offered the presidency during a period of 'much grave preoccupation, it was with hardly a smile that he said that of the two ambitions, he believed he had always set it above the premiership'. Amery's preoccupations, politely ignored by Young, included the loss of his seat in Birmingham after thirty-four years in the Commons and the trial and execution of his son for treason after he collaborated with the enemy.

The most striking thing about this collection of interesting and occasionally eccentric men is how many of them this century were involved in attempts to climb the highest mountain on earth. Overcoming Everest might seem the obvious challenge for any mountaineer but climbers know better than anyone that size isn't everything. When the mountain was finally climbed in 1953 the stylish and now legendary Eric Shipton – another president of the Alpine Club – looked forward to everyone getting back to some real mountaineering. To Shipton Everest was a side-show freak whose gross bulk drew attention away from the main entertainment of wandering across blanks on the map and climbing mountains whose appeal was aesthetic or sporting but certainly not famous. His hope was in vain because the struggle and legends behind the several attempts on the mountain in the 1920s and 1930s had dominated the public's interest in climbing. Everest had become a distorting mirror in which the world saw the whole point of mountaineering. Climbing it was as much about the glory of the Empire as sport; it was the perpetuation of a myth begun by Livingstone, Scott and Shackleton which continued seamlessly to the mountaineers of the 1920s in their tweeds and Chamonix caps, appearing in George Bernard Shaw's phrase 'like a picnic in Connemara surprised by a snowstorm'. However much Shipton resented Everest's squat mass settling on his life of careless exploration, the public's interest meant that nothing else would get the same attention.

There have been other reasons for the continuing obsession with Everest. When plans were first mooted for expeditions to the world's highest mountains to follow the Empire's glorious polar achievements, the Royal Geographical Society had the necessary political clout to secure permission and the Alpine Club offered the expertise. The two organisations were yoked together to form the Mount Everest Committee under the chairmanship of Sir Francis Younghusband. He told the Royal Geographical Society, or the 'Jog' as he called it, that 'whilst climbing Mount Everest will not put a pound into anyone's pocket, it will take a good many pounds out, [and] the accomplishment of such a feat will elevate the human spirit.' Younghusband was wrong in this, as he was about so many things. Everest continues to offer governments, businessmen and adventurers alike a ready source of income, the biggest milch cow on earth. The price of a permit to climb the mountain from Nepal now begins at $70,000, the name Everest sells everything from mineral water to double glazing. And while there are thousands of unclimbed mountains and difficult routes still to be explored, finding new ways of reaching the summit of Everest captures the interest of sponsors ahead of any other project.

As for the elevation of the human spirit, Younghusband's prediction has proved just as naive. The Alpine Club's library and archive is full of evidence that Everest often inspires overreaching ambition and corrosive obsession. Charles Bruce, who led expeditions to Everest in 1922 and 1924, told the *Daily Mail*, rather appropriately, that 'there is no finer school for the manhood of our country than mountain climbing'. Maurice Wilson would have agreed with Bruce. After the tortured former soldier and

4

businessman had recovered from severe mental and physical illness through fasting and prayer, Wilson told the world that his newly discovered spiritual strength could overcome the most arduous of challenges, including Everest. In 1933 he set off in a Gypsy Moth he renamed *Ever Wrest* on his year's odyssey to fly to India and then trek to the mountain that had defeated some of the best mountaineers Britain had to offer. His body and the journal of his attempt on the mountain was found by Shipton and Charles Warren in 1935. They buried him in a crevasse and brought his journal home. The small notebook is now in the Alpine Club and you can follow the deterioration of Wilson's handwriting in a pathetic echo of his loss of realism and judgement. Wilson hasn't been alone in thinking erroneously that self-belief is enough to get you to the summit of the world. His sun-bleached bones and scraps of clothing which are occasionally rediscovered on the ever-changing glacier below the mountain serve as one of many reminders to those contemplating an ascent.

Wilson wasn't alone in seeing the route to the summit of Everest as his salvation. Raymond Greene, with brothers Hugh and Graham yet to achieve success, pompously wrote to his mother that going to Everest in 1933 might 'yet save the situation for the whole family'. George Mallory told his father that 'it would look rather grim to see others, without me, engaged in conquering the summit' before he left in 1924 for his fatal last attempt to climb the mountain. Maurice Wilson, who appears as the basis for Graham Greene's character Richard Smythe in *The End of the Affair*, is a melancholy footnote; George Leigh Mallory appears through the mists that swept over the mountain to capture him forever as a romantic hero who paid the ultimate price for his ambition. There is not as much difference between them as we would like to think. Perhaps it was for the best that it was the native Tenzing Norgay and the down-to-earth New Zealander Ed Hillary who finally 'knocked the bastard off'. They both used the achievement to better effect than a dream-filled Englishman might have.

The first ascent of Everest was so obviously a singular achievement that the completion of the task was seen as the end of something, not the beginning. What would fill the void, the anticlimax after the triumph? The newspapers were ready to speculate as soon as plans to climb the mountain were announced in 1921. The *Pall Mall Gazette* suggested that explorers would turn their attention to the bottom of the oceans, while the *Glasgow Citizen* rather more presciently favoured the exploration of space. Neil Armstrong and Ed Hillary have in common an understanding of what it is to have done something unique. But the moon is out of reach to the humdrum masses while Everest is approachable, even climbable given sufficient resources. The *Evening News* warned against this in 1921. 'Some of the last mystery of the world will pass when the last secret place in it, the naked peak of Everest, shall be trodden by those trespassers.'

Nobody, however, considered what would happen to the people who lived around the slopes of the mountain*, how their lives would change when the last mystery was lost. They were a foreign, distant race on the fringes of the Empire with a slight and largely academic interest for those viewing the adventure from afar. Even today many still think the word Sherpa is a local description for a porter, or coolie in the archaic vernacular, rather than the name of a tribe. The obsession with Everest would have an impact on these people that wasn't imagined in the corridors of the Royal Geographical Society.

Myths the size of Everest get people's attention. My father, like many now in their fifties and sixties, can remember the excitement and wonder of the news that the mountain had been climbed just before the coronation of Queen Elizabeth II, although his uncomfortable position sitting in a trench in Malaya might have contributed something to the memory as well. John Hunt's successful team sent a wave of interest in mountains and mountaineering across the world and many were caught up sufficiently to try it for themselves.

* known to them as Chomolungma

Others have since perpetuated that interest, like the most recent president of the Alpine Club, Chris Bonington, whose expeditions to the mountain in the 1970s answered the question 'What next?' in an emphatic way. His successful expedition to Everest's South-West Face in 1975 was the first to subtitle the mountain: Everest, the hard way. Others imitated his epithet by climbing Everest without oxygen, in winter, alone, anything to renew interest. Climbers from nations without an Everest summiteer scrambled to be first; women climbers repeated the exercise. As each record fell, new and increasingly unusual claims were staked: first amputee, first ski descent, first traverse. And then, as restrictions on access to the mountain were relaxed and increasing numbers reached the summit throughout the 1980s, those with money but little experience or expertise began to see Everest as an attainable dream. They could pay experts to lead them in the steps of those who created the myth and share in its glory and tragedy.

Far from fading into obscurity, newspaper and television editors have come to expect an Everest story during the peak climbing season of May and with so many on the mountain each spring they are rarely disappointed. This level of obsession, the expense and loss of life, have become increasingly unattractive to a public who see the mountain's image as tarnished. And the question is repeatedly asked: 'Why?'

The roots of something as bizarre and compelling as mountaineering are often obscure but are laid down early. Pablo Picasso got me started. The first thing my parents bought after they were married was a print of 'Acrobat and Young Equilibrist', a striking work painted in 1905 during Picasso's Rose Period. It features a thickset and muscular gymnast sitting on a square block of stone with the 'equilibrist' balancing delicately on a stylised ball. I spent a lot of time as a child studying this painting, perhaps because to my infantile mind the solid male figure looked a little like my father, and the feminine balancer like my mother. What gripped my imagination however was the background to the painting, a pale brown wasteland punctuated by the figures of a mother and child with a dog, and a horse grazing in the wilderness. A series of stepped ridges disappeared into the limitless horizon. There wasn't country like this in the suburbs of Birmingham and its aesthetic austerity snagged in my memory like a net caught on a rock. No matter how hard I've tried to shake it free, it seems lodged for good. I remember crossing Dartmoor on the way to beach holidays in Devon, sitting between my sisters in the back of my father's Triumph, looking out at the land stripped clean of trees and buildings, hedges and crops, seeing the landscape in my mind matched by reality.

After that, building sand-castles was never the same. Like John Ruskin, mountains became for me 'the beginning and the end of all natural scenery' and all I could think of was getting to them, to recover that feeling of innocent amazement that the things you could imagine actually existed. Going to school in Leicestershire, a county that Ruskin once described as being not worth the trouble, may have contributed to this burning desire. Other boys chased girls, but mountains required few social skills while remaining more or less constant and this suited my painfully self-conscious adolescent character rather well.

So much for aesthetic appeal but it's a big step from walking through such places to climbing up sheer slopes of steep rock and ice to their summits. Ruskin never grasped the point and at first I couldn't see it either. A boy at school had a promotional poster of Bonington's 1975 expedition on his wall with inset photographs of all the team members and a picture of the huge and dramatic South-West Face.

'He's dead,' he told me, stabbing with an inky fore-finger at one of the men. 'He disappeared near the summit. And he was killed in an avalanche skiing in Switzerland. And that one died in an avalanche on K2 a couple of years ago.' Within two more years a fourth would be dead, returning with Bonington to Everest for another new route. What possible reward could justify such alarming odds? What secret lived up there in that scintillating frozen world of the high mountains that could provoke such commitment? Looking around at the embryonic lawyers and bankers I saw every day in the class room, I began to understand. There had to be more to life than the price of shares and weekends in the country. Going climbing at my school was like admitting I was a republican. And then, once my little act of rebellion was made, the compulsion of the thing itself took over, a feeling of complete and brilliant existence. You couldn't get anything this good from pills or money.

After ten years or so of total obsession I fully understood that climbers were as prone to the same narrow-minded ambition and self-flattery as the rest of the world. I also discovered that I was never going to be very good at it. It was in this mood of cynical realism I took my first steps towards Everest. For years, writing anything substantial about the mountain never crossed my mind; it was so familiar, there was nothing more to say about tired old Everest that hadn't been said a thousand times before. Then I was sent by a magazine to report on the reunion party of the 1953 team celebrating the fortieth anniversary of their first ascent. They gathered near Snowdon outside the Pen y Gwyrd Hotel, where they had met years before to prepare for the expedition, a group of pensioners who could have shared the same shop floor or war-time billet but for whom Everest just happened to be their defining experience. There was an easy friendship, an innocent pleasure in their shared history that belied the scale of their achievement as they lined up to face the cameras. Ed Hillary appeared as one of a team, no more and no less, as though it was forgotten that it is he who is most often remembered, that it's his head printed on bank notes and stamps. Meanwhile, the news-papers were full of stories describing the ruination of the moun-tain they climbed, the garbage on its slopes and the queues of pseudo-mountaineers paying to be dragged up to its summit for no other reason than to say they had done so. Everest was reduced by the clichés that had been heaped on it. There was a gulf between this quiet and comradely group and the spoiling of a national myth.

One thing, however, hadn't changed over the seventy years people had climbed on Everest. The fate and circumstances of those who lived around the mountain still seemed of peripheral interest. Columns of print used Everest to show how the optimism and spirit of the New Elizabethans had dissipated to be replaced by cynical self-interest. The changes faced by local people, however, which the obsession with climbing Everest had brought, were skimmed and marginalised. Typing the word Nepal into a database of newspapers, the first five selections displayed on my computer screen outlined two stories on Everest, another about a mountaineering accident on a different mountain, one about the abominable snowman and another about cheese, where Nepal was featured only incidentally. A nation of twenty million people, wearied by social problems and with long and important links with my own country, was reduced in the national consciousness to the exploits of a few mountaineers and a mythical beast. There had to be more to it than that. There had to be a way of showing how the summit wasn't the end of the story, just the start of another chapter. I wanted to understand how our – my – obsession could fracture or improve the lives of those caught on the fringes of something so consuming as climbing Mount Everest. I wanted to see for myself whether it was Chomolungma and the people who worshipped her who had changed, or just us.

CHAPTER TWO

Tripping with Kafka and the tsampa-eaters

We don't mind trippers and scouts and ramblers.
They can come and stand in the rain all day.
They give us money and beer and a right good belly-laugh.
Then they go away.

Jake Thackeray

Outside the whitened gatehouse a Nepali policeman stood in the middle of the road holding a hose pipe, his thumb pressed over its end, spattering water over the Friendship Highway. Each afternoon from the north, from Tibet, a fine silvery dust blew down the valley, coating everything and so ensuring he would have something to do next and every day. There was no reason for this place. Few people lived here and the border with its guards was still several miles up the road. This didn't seem to bother the policeman. He put down his hose as he saw us approaching and smiled and we all Jucked into the cool air of the checkpoint's office. The sign on the desk read 'Amidistration' and the policeman, the 'amidistrator', sat behind it and took my passport. He examined it closely. Holding the last page up to the light, he carefully wrote in his dusty register. 'Ebenezer W. UK. 1995.' Then, looking up from his labouring hand, he smiled. 'Where you have come from please?'

'The mountains,' I said, pointing behind me, back up the road.

'Ah,' he said and returned to his ledger. 'Nowhere.'

Nowhere in the lawman's book was the Jugal Himal. The itinerant curmudgeon Bill Tilman had been the first European to tramp his way through this slim portion of the Himalaya in 1949, travelling south from Langtang to Panch Pokhari and then west to the

Helmu, grumbling about skinflint shepherds and sleeping in damp hovels at night, maybe dreaming that he was seventeen again and back in a trench on the Somme. He wouldn't like those districts now with their tea houses and apple pie and I doubt he'd like this road either. None of it was there in the 1940s. In those far-off days the Ranas still ruled from their palaces in Kathmandu and the Dalai Lama looked over his people from the Potala in Lhasa.

Mountains, of course, are not really nowhere, they're more in between, keeping people and their various warring gods apart. To the south of these mountains is the gargantuan democracy of India scrubbed clean every year by the monsoon. To the north is the can-do autocracy of modern China transplanted most unwillingly to the arid, anhydrous brown-ness of Tibet. Squeezed between the two are people on the fringes, washed up on the steep slopes of the Himalaya, pushed back by road-builders and inquisitive tourists. When change floods the valleys and plains, the last remnants of the old ways are found up here, among the glittering peaks.

A mile or so beyond the amidistrator's checkpoint was the village of Tatopani, perched between the road and the river. If taking the road into Tibet had ever sounded exotic, then sitting in one of Tatopani's street-level eateries changed my mind. Attempting to combine the fashionable with the pastoral, the owner had pinned a poster of an Indian movie star wearing a little black dress and scrawled 'No1 Indian Hiroin in Movies' next to her head. Beside this was a picture of an ordinary English house, apparently in Surrey, set in a green garden with a pond. Perhaps his nirvana was a combination of the two; the Indian Hiroin would be waiting on the patio. Outside, a little girl waddled up the dirt track on bandy legs, the first case of rickets I'd seen in Nepal. She turned and smiled. Another child had a belly swollen by malnutrition. He ducked into the café wearing only torn and dirty trousers to watch us eat. An albino dog trotted past, followed by two men who were mentally handicapped in some way. Others had deformities. Trucks and buses honked their way past, full to the brim on their way from Zhangmu, scattering the chickens which pick their way through the garbage filling the gutters.

'You would have to do something pretty bad to be reincarnated as one of these chickens,' Sandy said and then took another swig from her San Miguel.

'I'm not so sure,' I replied. 'Maybe to come back as a Tatopani human you would.' Poultry and child jumped for the gutter as another truck rushed past. The cheap streamers hung from the roof for the recent new year celebrations lifted in its slipstream. I ordered another beer. The good-looking boy at the next table pushed his long black hair from his eyes and smiled at us.

'Where you from?' We were more interested in him, the best dressed man we'd seen in days. He was waiting in Tatopani for a lift across the border to Tibet. 'I am a trader,' he told us. 'Import, export. Shoes. I bring Chinese shoes from Zhangmu to Kathmandu. And clothes.' He grinned at us so we could see his gold tooth.

'What else?' I asked him and he tipped back his elegant head and laughed. Gold and other commodities are brought across the border, and probably a great deal else besides. There is a strong trade in endangered species across the Nepali–Tibet border, traffic that is often run by Tibetans.

Sandy glowed pinkly from our visit to the public open-air showers. There are lots of villages called Tatopani in Nepal; it translates as hot water. The *tato pani* at Tatopani was searingly hot, as you might expect of water drawn from the earth's immersion heater, but not so hot that you couldn't bear to stand in front of the steel pipes that siphoned the stuff from whichever crack in the ground it emerged from. After the dust of the highway and a week in the mountains, water like that was a gift from the gods. We'd stood under the water as long as we could, the boys' section coyly separated from that of the girls by a crumbling wall, even though nobody took their clothes off since they were always washed at the same time. Ennervated by the heat of the water we sat drinking beer.

Donald appeared at the end of the street from the direction of the showers, his white hair bobbing above the brown children who gathered round him, his towel tucked under his arm.

'Ahhh!' he said in his stentorian voice, drawing back a chair. 'Beer.' Donald was a Yorkshireman living in Scotland where he had taught music until retiring. He had a fascination with mountains which matched my own. We sat drinking for a while and then Sandy and I escorted Donald back to our campsite on the edge of town. The beer allowed his eccentricities free expression. The band of small children he'd collected were bemused to be regaled by a tallish, white-haired old man with a passion for eastern European composers responding to requests for pens or money by greeting them in a range of languages. 'Guten Abend!' or 'Hoots, mon!' Donald shouted, and the children backed away with a confused smile or laughed nervously. Half a mile beyond the village we were reunited with the rest of our group sitting around a table set up in front of our tents.

It is disappointing to be the prosaic, packaged inheritors of travellers like Sven Hedin or political adventurers like Frank Younghusband. Both men fretted over Tibet, alluring and inaccessible, the country Younghusband's biographer Patrick French described as the 'missing square on the imperial chess board'. But blank spaces on the world's maps get filled. It is in the nature of things. Unblinking satellites track across the wastes of Central Asia, dissecting and reducing the landscape to reference points. Where is the romance in that? What space is there for heroes on the twice-weekly flight from Kathmandu to Lhasa among the holidaying business people from Europe in their neatly pressed safari shirts? (They hunt the exotic and are armed with video cameras.) I thought of Alexander Kellas being dragged through Tibet on a stretcher in 1921, exhausted by dysentery and dying from heart failure as the first Everest expedition rode from British-controlled Sikkim. Everest's first victim didn't even reach the mountain. In the expedition's official account, Charles Howard-Bury described his loss in coolly practical terms. 'His death meant a very great loss to the Expedition,' wrote the Irishman, capitalising their venture, 'as he alone was qualified to carry out experiments in oxygen and blood pressure which would have been so valuable.' A modern Kellas would have been pumped with drugs and bottled oxygen, lifted onto the back of a Chinese truck and driven not to Sikkim but down this road and put onto a flight for the hospitals in Bangkok. Already in that spring of 1995, eleven expeditions had driven up the Friendship Highway like armies in the field, their logistics organised on computer, their communications in place, their first-aid kits bulging with powerful drugs, hermetically sealed units rushing to the mountain.

And yet, in our own unremarkable way, following though we were in the footsteps of pretty much everybody, we were part of a struggle; we contributed to a political process. The Chinese lured us forward, dangling our romantic notions of the old Tibet to spend our currency in the new one. We were there to add a fresh gloss to the peeling and cracked walls of their propaganda. 'See,' they whisper, 'it can't be so very bad here if so many liberal westerners are persuaded to come.' Claim and counter-claim, so many hundreds of thousands killed or not, religion suppressed or encouraged, the labyrinthine twists followed by the leaders of Tibet and China are not roads for the literal mind. Just how much was an average citizen of the free world expected to know? Yellowing documents from half-forgotten meetings of the United Nations are not standard reading on long-haul flights to the remoter parts of the world. Luckily, the Dalai Lama was on my side. 'The Dalai Lama has announced publicly that it is beneficial for foreigners to witness the oppression in Tibet,' read a leaflet from the Free Tibet Campaign in London. 'Tourism is thought to be a source of encouragement to Tibetans to have any form of contact with the West, when the only alternative is to be confined within the boundaries of the Chinese empire. Reports by responsible travellers of their own experiences are an important source of information to the outside world.'

The last sentence provides a wonderful frisson for those instinctively outraged by the misery of the Chinese occupation. Not only, they think, do we get to see one of the most remarkable countries on earth, we also get to do our bit in exposing a monstrous regime. Moral dilemmas don't get any easier than this. Younghusband had the weight of the Empire at his back, modern tourists rely on natural justice. Waiting at the border next day at Kodari, an even more desperate place than Tatopani, I felt the weight of anticipation. Trucks choked the road as officials picked through their contents and drivers slipped them wads of rupees. Beyond the fragile barrier was the Friendship Bridge, a crisp sentry post at the far end to contrast with the affable chaos of Kodari, the merchants of Nepal sticking like molluscs to the hull of China's prosperity. The deep olive gorge below the bridge, the mint-green Bhote Kosi rushing over rocks at its base, were hardly typical of the Tibet I had read about, but then this region had only been ceded to Tibet following the war with Nepal in 1792. Along with it went the small trading post high above the river, looking down the valley. Zhangmu was the Chinese name, Khasa the Tibetan. I have no idea what the Nepalis called it. That's the problem with borders. They won't sit still.

Finally our truck was waved through and we drove across the bridge. The gorge had been swept by floods in the 1980s requiring several of the bridges to be rebuilt. They are impressive structures, capable of withstanding the heaviest of traffic – tanks, for example. The Chinese have been generous in supplying the Nepali people with the Friendship Highway, although south of the border its name changes to the Arniko Rajmarg, and they also gave Kathmandu its own orbital, making the trip to India comfortable and fast. Poor Nehru. Constantly out-manoeuvred by Chou En-lai, the road must have seemed like one more nail in the coffin of his foreign policy after the war between India and China in 1962. Nehru described that war as a stab in the back from his old friends in the Chinese Communist Party, but Chou En-lai stabbed nobody in the back. He just persuaded them to shut their eyes and cover their ears while he stabbed them in the chest.

Just across the bridge representatives of Mao Zedong's greatest legacy, the People's Liberation Army, shuffled uncomfortably in their oversized uniforms. They really did look like schoolboys. I stood up in the back of our flat-bed truck to get a better look at this outpost of the Chinese empire and instantly regretted it. The driver gunned the engine and swung the truck up the steep track on the other side of the river. The road was now unmetalled, throwing up clouds of dust as we swung round an apparently endless succession of hairpin bends with perpendicular views of the bed of the gorge hundreds of feet below. I scanned the valley floor for ruined vehicles but could see none. Those would start appearing later.

At passport control a thin-faced Han Chinese woman flicked through our documents. The one advantage of signing up for a coach tour to the roof of the world is that the bureaucrats get off your case. We were waved through, our bags with their regulation contraband of photographs of the Dalai Lama and my illegal map of Tibet showing the sites of various Chinese atrocities, were thrown after us. A round-faced, clean-shaven man in his late twenties approached to introduce himself. The initial surprise was that he was a Tibetan whereas most guides working for the China International Tourist Service are Han Chinese. The second surprise was that Lobsang was bright and helpful with an encyclopaedic knowledge of his culture; we had expected a nanny, not a tutor. The biggest surprise of all was that Lobsang would act as an accurate interpreter when there were only Tibetans present.

At his back were three enormous Tibetans, the kind of men who probably saw yak-wrestling as light entertainment. They wore their long hair coiled on their heads and wound with a red scarf in the traditional way of Khampas from the east of Tibet. Their faces were black with grease, even blacker than their clothes, and a pungent, woody odour drifted behind them, like the smell of an illegally strong smoked cheese. They smiled like the pirates they probably were, but in that moment I could see why the Chinese would eventually lose control of Tibet, as they always had in the past. It's not just that they are wrong; that's rarely stopped anyone before. It's simply that the Tibetans are better at making friends than the Chinese.

Throughout my charabanc ride from Kathmandu to Lhasa, I didn't meet a single Han Chinese who made me feel welcome, let alone made me laugh. For the meantime I reserved judgement; passport control officials are usually discourteous people from London to Irkutsk. But you might have thought it politically shrewd to smile and say something positive like: 'Welcome to China, have a great stay and don't believe everything you hear.' Perhaps when Mao started the Cultural Revolution and declared war on the four 'olds' of culture, ideology, custom and habit he scribbled an addendum to his memo suggesting they abandon politeness, empathy, humour and niceness at the same time.

The best example of this followed close on the heels of passport control. The Zhangmu Hotel has, as far as I can tell, been established for all those friends of the former Soviet Union who struggle to find a hotel quite as laughable as those they grew used to in remote Siberian coal-mining towns. Oscar Wilde once said that only fools don't judge by appearances, an apposite epigram in Chinese hotels built to hoover up the tourist dollar flowing into Tibet. They look awful and they are. It's not that the rooms are dirty, or at least not as dirty as some of the flop houses in Kathmandu. It's not that the plumbing is despicable. It is, but if you complain aggressively enough they move you to another room that isn't ankle-deep in shit. I cannot fault the food, or at least I can't fault the dinner, which had plenty of fresh vegetables and lashings of soy sauce. We'll get to breakfast later. It wasn't the extortionate charges made by the Chinese in a state-owned hotel that employed, as far as I could tell, only Chinese staff. I knew what I was doing when I signed up, although these things stick in the throat.

There are two things which make this hotel, and others of its kind in Tibet, the worst hotels in the world. First, the service is loathsome. It's the closest one human being can get to hurting another without an arrest being made. The interaction between waiter and diner is like the course soldiers are sent on to see if they meet the standard required to resist interrogations when they are captured by the enemy. The second failure is the apocalyptically bad taste employed to decorate the rooms. After dragging my bag down miles of pleasantly retro-seventies corridors with distressed orange carpets and worried chocolate brown walls that achieved the effect of a Smarties tube, I arrived at my room. This first attempt at securing a bed for the night ended at the door. A stench of urine and excrement rushed out from the bathroom as though it were pleased to leave. I left my bags upwind and trekked back to the desk. Ten minutes later the hotel's plumber arrived, a lethargic, spotty youth who couldn't stop yawning. It was clear that his appointment had not been considered promotion. It was my turn to have Lobsang, so at least I could understand the few words the plumber spoke.

He stared into the bathroom and tried the light switch. Mercifully, it didn't work. He extended a cheap plimsoll towards the inch of water slopping round the plastic floor and patted it gently two or three times, clearly pleased with the smacking noise it made. 'The toilet's broken,' he said finally and returning his spanner to his bag led the way to the next room. For a second time we were disappointed, although the problem here was a lack of water, not a surfeit. The sink was green with dried slime, ditto the bath and toilet. I couldn't help myself. 'There's no water in the taps, there's no water in the bog and there's only a bleeding lizard in the bidet,' I shouted at the plumber who looked back at me aghast and then started inching towards the door.

'Please, Mr Ed, what is bidet?' Lobsang looked worried.

'Don't worry, mate. Just my little joke. Or rather Monty Python's. Let's go and find another room. And please don't call me Mr Ed.'

Finally, I settled for a room with water in the cold tap and a little puddle in the toilet bowl. Of course, the toilet wouldn't flush, but

...ded the hotel could deal with the consequences. The inter-
... of the room was breathtaking, every egregious detail worked
... badly from the plastic flowers in the plastic vase beside the
bed, to the plastic flip-flops which fell apart in my hands when I
took them out of their plastic wrapper. I sat down on the orange
nylon bedspread and switched on the television. John Cleese
appeared in wobbly, fuzzy lines across the screen, barking in
demotic Mandarin at his waiter from Barcelona whose agonies
seemed even greater now he was obliged to speak bad Spanish
English in Chinese. These little ironies are supposed to make travelling fun but I didn't feel like laughing. There's little reason to
laugh when *Fawlty Towers* metamorphoses from comedy to documentary. There's little reason to laugh in a country that persuaded
Rupert Murdoch to drop the BBC's news output from his Star TV
satellite service because they didn't like its coverage of the massacre at Tiananmen Square. I scanned through the channels and
found a range of asinine quiz shows and karaoke slots all merging
into each other so that you lost track of which channel was which.
It was fifth-rate American cable-standard junk except the toothy,
coiffured clones talking breezily into microphones had yellow
skins and narrow eyes. Nevertheless, it gave off a certain artificial
charm, like watching a fat pink flower bursting garishly from its
puce head. Modern Chinese culture is brightly coloured plastic
garbage blowing across a television screen to catch the eye and
hold it there long enough for thought to lose interest and drift
away. It must help in running the country.

My guidebooks were upbeat about the village of Zhangmu
itself, creating an impression of cosmopolitan energy and material
wealth. This is pushing things. Zhangmu is not quite the most
desperate place I have ever been, but it I bet it has a similar post-
code. The houses were more neatly planned than a modern Nepali
town and more robust, but there was also a stronger feeling of
dilapidation and indifference. Threads of grey cloud worked
across the green slopes above the town. Garbage was piled everywhere, even more than the worst towns in India. The stench of

excrement poured from the gutters and filtered through the shoddy kiosks selling 'kwality' goods brought in trucks from the east. Tracksuits with cod English logos, plastic trainers whose colour was already fading, dreadful cassette players like the one your mother bought you for Christmas in 1978 which slap music around a bit on its way through the speakers. All the stalls had one of these machines on all the time releasing into the community the artistic offering of a range of post-pubescent Chinese pop stars who all sounded exactly the same, playing chirpy sub-standard Bucks Fizz numbers or lugubrious ballads squawked by Whitney Houston wannabes with their managers' hands apparently round their throats. Pushing this dross to the back of the mind is a challenge, but once I'd managed it I began to see what the guidebook writers were reaching for.

Along the switchback streets of Zhangmu was a bewildering sweep of human beings. Narrow-nosed and pale brown Nepali traders jostled with broad-faced, mahogany-skinned Tibetans. Chinese merchants thumbed through wallets stuffed with yuan, while a group of tall unshaven Israeli tourists looked for somewhere to sell them beer. Our group joined them in a gloomy restaurant at the top of the village. An American girl was eating noodles. She was, she said between mouthfuls, an acupuncturist on her way to Lhasa and then Yunnan where she was studying. 'When I finish, I'm gonna live on a beach in Thailand and open a Chinese medicine clinic,' she said. She told us of a landslide twenty kilometres further up the Friendship Highway that would keep the road closed for weeks. The road has been constantly closed and reopened in this way since its course was blasted into existence. The Israelis said they were looking for transport to take them up to the slip so they could walk across and arrange a lift on the other side. We were packaged tourists, we said, and couldn't help. Flotsam has to look out for itself on the Friendship Highway. Walking back to the hotel for dinner we passed a pool table set up on the street with bricks wedged under its downhill feet to keep it level. A Chinese youth shouted at us and grinned when he had our

n. In his hand was a mop handle. On the table was half a
. He made an exaggerated cueing movement with the mop-
dle against the brick and it slid a few inches across the tattered
beize. He looked up again and laughed some more. Then it started
to rain.

Breakfast at the hotel stretched even Donald's optimism. He
pushed a group of stale peanuts around his plate with his
forefinger before sighing deeply and taking another sip of tea.
Eating when you get up is a new one on the Chinese but where had
they learned that decadent westerners start their day with stale
crisps and peanuts, spam and brick hard rolls? Gloomily, we
stepped outside to the bank next door. An official watched us
approach the metal-barred gate and promptly locked it when we
got close. 'I've got to get out of here,' I told Donald. Lobsang
appeared with a bitter-faced Han in a cheap leather jacket. He
would be driving us to the landslide, we would walk across the mud
and stones and then climb aboard our luxury coach waiting, as he
spoke, on the other side. All of us piled into the Han's diminutive
pick-up. I found a comfortable position wedged between the cab
and our luggage and we chugged up through the village along the
switchback road, cheered beyond reason to be on our way. As we
reached the edge of town an oil line fractured in the guts of the
little truck and sprayed hot black oil over the racing engine. Huge
billowing mushrooms of thick smoke engulfed the back of the
pick-up. Choking in the smoke, we spilled off the truck and I sank
to my knees by the gutter and coughed and vomited until my chest
burned. Two Khampas drinking tea at a roadside stall came over
to slap me on the back and have a laugh. It was a great start to the
day.

The stoatish driver killed the engine and stepped out of the
truck. He stood in the filthy street, his hands stuck into jacket
pockets, watching a pool of arterial oil congealing under his
vehicle which fed a small rivulet running down the hill towards
Nepal. He spoke sharply and nervously to Lobsang who shouted
back. There were problems with a refund. A flat-bed truck

charged up the hill and parked behind the pick-up. A PLA officer, pistol at his waist, climbed down from the cab and spoke to Lobsang who was running his hand through his hair and looking worried. The officer then spoke to the pick-up driver who suddenly remembered that a refund was, after all, absolutely possible and would the officer like some money? Donald, Sandy and the rest of us stood along the edge of the street watching our holiday unfold. You don't get this in Mallorca. The Khampas hauled our gear off the pick-up and onto the army truck and we climbed up after them. Tourists, guide, soldiers and assorted Tibetans then continued, leaving the pick-up bleeding to death on the street and its owner staring after us. At the edge of town a group of soldiers were standing in the raised bucket of an earth-mover fixing a garish message in Chinese characters above the highway.

'What does it say, Lobsang?' I shouted across the back of the truck.

'It say, "See you in Zhangmu again real soon!"'

I thought of Larkin. In a pig's arse, friend.

This section of the Friendship Highway is a spectacular gorge, lush with huge crags towering above the road. The narrow grey thread through this monstrous landscape is an extraordinary feat of engineering but is threatened almost everywhere by loose stones glued on with mud perched above it, just waiting for someone to breathe. This road is the sudden link between green Nepal and brown Tibet, the gorge a geographical conjunction. This twenty-mile stretch is where the last gasp of the monsoon dissipates and the edge of the wind-whipped arid plateau tumbles down. The truck crunched to a halt before the landslide where three men were sitting morosely in the dirt, a pile of shovels discarded on the road beside them. They watched us for a while as we hauled our bags off the truck before returning to their card game. The road had once curled round a spur and around the back of a gully but it wasn't just blocked. It was gone. Nothing would get through for weeks, even if the army started using dynamite. At the base of the cliff, leaning drunkenly towards the spinning water in the base of the gorge, were the bodies of two crushed trucks, one on its back, the other upright on crumpled axles. We hauled our bags down and picked our way through the rubble to the other side. Lobsang's driver was waiting with our vehicle, a coach perched on a truck's chassis. We crawled up the highway until the gorge grew shallow and then disappeared altogether, the trees and greenness thinned and disappeared. The air hardened and our perspective deepened. And then there was the dust, thrown up by everything that moved and blown by the wind. Even inside the bus I kept a silk scarf across my mouth against it. At night I'd find it in my underwear or languishing in my camera bag. There was no escape. Dressed like bandits, we drove towards Everest.

It was hard to miss him. As I stepped off the bus to visit the monastery at Phegyeling, he stood by the door with his hand outstretched. His whole face was a running sore, as though it had been dipped in boiling water and the blistered skin had sloughed away. There was a score of other ragged-arsed children to grab your hand and drag you away to the monastery but always from the corner of my eye I could see the smiling ruined face of the little boy and always the same question. How can you live like that and smile? None of the children asked for money. All they wanted to do was stroke our soft white skin with their rough brown paws.

The Chinese economic miracle hadn't arrived here yet but the people weren't starting a revolution about it. They were getting on with planting that year's barley crop to grind into tsampa flour in the autumn and picking up what they could get from the tourists who pulled off the highway to see the cave. A long time ago, the poet-saint Milarepa had propped this up with his back while his favourite pupil Rechungpa slid a rock under the roof to keep it in place. Pilgrims come to run their hands over the imprint of Milarepa's hand and shoulders and the black rock is smooth and greasy. Tibetans believe that just being in a holy place takes away sin so maybe the soldiers who drove the hundred of monks out and smashed the monastery, or gompa, to pieces during the Cultural Revolution got some absolution for their sins. Milarepa spent all his life in this district, meditating and teaching in isolated caves. He followed an ascetic Buddhist mysticism called Kagyü, a yogic system that frees the mind of its duality to reach nirvana in the space of one lifetime. Milarepa lived on the borders of his dreams, between death and rebirth, and the legends of his magical powers and deeds are still popular. He died an old man of eighty-four at the hand of a jealous lama, Geshe Tsakpuwa, who persuaded his mistress to give the teacher poisoned curd. Like Judas, both were forgiven by their victim. After handing the last of his few possessions to his disciples, the poet had nothing left to give or take. At sunrise on the fourteenth day of the twelfth month in the year of the wood hare Milarepa passed into nirvana.

All this happened during the time of the Norman conquest, in the days when sea shells were still used as currency in Tibet. The Chinese have brought the road and hundreds of strange white people who have trouble concentrating on a newspaper, let alone the teachings of a great man like Milarepa or Jesus Christ, and there may now be pieces of paper called yuan instead of shells, but the land doesn't get any easier or the mountains any smaller. There are around thirty monks living in the monastery now, allowed back after Mao died and the Cultural Revolution dissipated. There's been some restoration, although as far as the authorities are concerned, it's just something to show the tourists. I thought about the market at Zhangmu and the plastic detritus on offer, about how the Chinese had put their faith in Mammon, the one 'old' that Mao couldn't do anything about. And I thought of the shadow of Milarepa in the cool black cave beneath the monastery and his inheritors still scratching a life from the heavy brown land and living in their dreams.

Donald should not have raised his camera to his eye, but retired music teachers are rarely experts on espionage. Lobsang saw him first, the olive figure half-running from the checkpoint across the brown dirt towards the bus. Lobsang turned his back on Donald and pulled open the door. The soldier stood at the foot of the steps breathing hard, the collar of his uniform hanging loosely from his throat and his delicate hand sweating round the stock of his rifle. His face held the fragile anger of a petulant child as he twitched the muzzle at Donald to get him off the bus. Lobsang moved forward instead, holding his clasped hands in front of him, the sleeves of his black leather jacket sliding from his wrists as he extended his arms towards the Chinese sentry. He kept up a constant *sotto voce* petition on Donald's behalf. The two men stood in the dust of the Friendship Highway, Lobsang's moon face pricked with sweat, the Chinese soldier's eyes swivelling in panic, his hands tighter and tighter around the rifle. We sat there and stared without any inkling of what to do or how to behave.

Finally the sentry jerked his rifle towards the checkpoint and turned on the heel of his plastic running shoes. Lobsang climbed one step onto the bus and quietly asked for our passports. He still held his hands in front of him, his face pale, sweat pasting his hair onto his forehead. For us the worst fear was deportation. For Lobsang, whose father had been in prison for ten years, who talked of self-imposed exile, fear was the most constant thing in his life. He smiled weakly as he stepped back off the bus and walked slowly towards the checkpoint. For two minutes we sat in silence. Donald stared out of the window, somehow diminished by his indiscretion, his chin on his fist. He hadn't, he finally admits, even taken a shot of the checkpoint and now all his pictures of Everest's still distant form would be lost.

'Give me your camera,' I told him. 'And a blank film.' He passed the Olympus. 'Look out of the window. Watch him.' I released the film and started winding.

'He's coming back.' I kept winding without looking up. 'He's still coming.' Donald's voice had an edge as he realised I didn't have time. I flipped open the camera and swapped the film in my hand with the finished cartridge. The soldier was in the doorway.

At his back were four or five Tibetans who had been waiting by the wall of the checkpoint, squatting in the dust until we became too interesting. Sandy stood behind them. I hadn't seen her get off the bus but it didn't surprise me that she would want to irritate the sentry further.

'He wants the camera,' Lobsang said quietly.

'Here, take the film. Take it.' The spent cartridge stayed tucked behind my back as I held out the other hand with the Olympus and the fresh roll in my palm. The sentry looked at me, still scared and angry, and reached out to take only the film. He climbed off the bus, his back to the Tibetans, Sandy to one side. He stared at me. Sandy responded by putting her thumb on her nose and waggling her fingers. The Tibetans roared with laughter and the sentry spun round. Sandy looked blankly at him and the Tibetans looked at the floor. He took a fresh grip on his rifle. And walked towards the checkpoint.

As we drove under the barrier there was no sign of the boy in a uniform. The group of Tibetans were working with shovels by the road. They stopped to look at us again as the bus ground past in low gear, their faces blank again, no laughter or fear discernible as they stood to watch us disappear into the dust, on the road to Shekar.

We queued outside the store in Shekar for bottles of 'Himalayas Magical Water' which offered to cure three hundred and sixty acute diseases and four hundred slow ones, promote bone growth, improve circulation, prevent goitre and whet the appetite. When I got mine I waited outside with Lobsang for the others. The bus cooled itself in the shade of a willow tree, waiting to make the long drive to Everest. In front of the hybrid village – half Chinese, half Tibetan – was the fairytale mountain that gave the village shelter and its name, meaning white crystal. In the rich morning sunlight it is more honey than white crystal. Shekar is a good place for one of those impressive before-and-after photographs, like when a bridge collapses or a town is hit by earthquake. In 1921 Charles Howard-Bury took a photograph of several of the monks at the gompa. They hadn't seen a camera before, although they'd heard about them and were intrigued. Copies of his shot of the gompa's abbot were highly prized and used at altars as something the monks could worship. He also took a picture from his expedition's campsite on the plain below Shekar Dzong, not far from where I was standing. It's an impressive sight, something to be imagined not created. Before Tolkein started his epic about a heroic age of sorcery and demons set against fantastic castles in the air and tribes of horsemen crossing the huge plains, the real thing was alive and well in Tibet. Of course, it's gone now, as the photographs taken by me and every other tourist who passes this way show. The soaring fortifications are holed and gap-toothed. The monastery has a fraction of the number of monks Howard-Bury found. A MIG bomber did for that dream-like world at roughly the same time as the Americans were trying to send Cambodia back to the Stone Age. It was impossible to tell from the scheduled, whistle-stop experience most tourists get in Tibet, but religious intolerance was on the increase again after years of relaxation. Orders were coming once more from Beijing to tighten the Communist Party's grip.

A group of Tibetans were at work on a new building on the same block as the village shop and I walked over with Lobsang. Would he talk to them for me? It seemed surreal to be worried about talking to the people I was on holiday to visit. A PLA officer was walking away from the workers, wheeling a bicycle behind the row of buildings. Another soldier stood across the street talking to a civilian Chinese outside the village's restaurant. Through Lobsang I asked the nearest Tibetan what he and the other dozen men and women were doing.

'We're building a restaurant for the Chinese.'

'And how much will you get paid?' As Lobsang translated this they burst out laughing.

'They say they will get nothing,' Lobsang said.

'Do you think they're telling the truth?' I asked him and he looked back at me as politely as he could.

'Ask them if they're from Shekar,' I told him but suddenly the soldier across the street was looking at us and the officer was striding towards the Tibetans from behind the shop. We turned away and Lobsang whispered, 'Yes, I think so.'

Compulsory labour is widespread throughout Tibet, generally on infrastructure projects like roads or irrigation channels. This isn't always done grudgingly since such projects often benefit a local community but, as more Chinese arrive in Tibet as part of Beijing's policy of immigration and assimilation, resentment is growing. Chinese workers on such projects are paid, while Tibetans aren't. It's just one more example of how the Chinese occupation chisels away at Tibetan identity, another way to make Tibetans feel like second-class citizens in their own land. We met a group of Americans the night before in our hotel on the edge of town. They were travelling west towards the border at Zhangmu and had met a similar gang working on the road. When they stopped to take pictures the work party's military escort had thrown stones at their bus. It seemed as though the package tours designed by the Chinese to strip hard currency from foreign visitors just weren't packaged enough.

The old woman sat beneath the chorten at the Rongbuk monastery watching the trucks drive by on the way to Base Camp, thumbing through her rosary, her face tipped slightly towards the sun that had, over the last seventy years, turned her skin to leather.

'What's she saying, Lobsang?'

'She says they never stop and she wants to know what they're for.'

'The trucks?'

'Yes, the trucks.'

Donald wanted to know her age which we'd guessed at around ninety. When Lobsang translated he realised he was not much younger. Donald, tall and white-haired with his broad mix of Scots and Yorkshire accents, and the sun-dried Tibetan, like a raisin, tiny beside him. She had spent her life in this valley, seen the monastery destroyed and then partially rebuilt, watched her people starve when the Chinese forced them to change their crop from barley to wheat. She even had a distant memory of the first group of tall, white-faced men to come and try to reach the top of Chomolungma. In those days there was no road; that came when the Chinese took up mountaineering and needed to supply their army of climbers in much the same way as they'd built roads to supply their armies of conquest.

I couldn't think of a more dramatic approach to a mountain, forgetting for a moment that it's the biggest mountain of all. Before 1921 no European had been so close. George Mallory's description of the walk from the small village of Chobuk to the south up to the thriving monastery is still the most precise:

> To the place where Everest stands one looks along rather than up. The glacier is prostrate; not a part of the mountain; not even a pediment; merely a floor footing the high walls. At the end of the valley and above the glacier Everest rises not so much a peak as a prodigious mountain-mass. There is no complication for the eye. The highest of the world's great mountains, it seems, has to make but a single gesture of magnificence to be lord of all, vast in unchallenged and isolated supremacy.

Mallory is describing a stadium for heroes, a blank and savage canvas on which to write his name in VERY BIG LETTERS. Given the scale of the enterprise, it's not surprising that during the 1920s and 1930s the enduring leitmotif of climbing on the north side of Everest was failure. Seven expeditions, not including the inevitably doomed attempt by Maurice Wilson, failed to reach the summit. This cult of failure reached its apotheosis with the disappearance of George Mallory and Sandy Irvine in 1924. (Had all nationalities had the same kind of access as the British, then it's an uncomfortable truth that Everest may well have been climbed before the Second World War.) For much of the period following the war Tibet has been closed to foreign climbers but there has been a great deal of success, first from the colossal Chinese expeditions of 1960 and 1975. They held party meetings at 8000 metres and put their faith in Mao to keep them safe from avalanches. In complete contrast the Tyrolean maestro Reinhold Messner marched up the East Rongbuk Glacier in 1980 and climbed the mountain alone, in the monsoon and without bottled oxygen – the best style ever managed on Everest. In 1995, soon after I left, sixty-six people climbed Everest from the north, one of them twice. This is success in spades but the mood has subtly altered, some of the glamour is gone, despite all the satisfied customers. The Irish writer Dermot Somers put his quizzical finger on it, describing the north side of Everest as like a 'drive-in movie'. And that's what it is. All those trucks the old woman watched crunching along the dirt road up and down the valley were supplying some vast Hollywood dream factory. Climbers have a community memory, just like everyone else, and Everest is their proto-myth, starring courageous men in tweeds in an age before jet aeroplanes and four-wheel drives. Those early books and photographs have bred more books and films. Those around the world who couldn't share in that summer's expeditions could watch them unfold over the internet. But they are grasping at something which is no longer there.

The old woman wanted something from us. Westerners always had something to give, even if they were all a little mad. The instinctive response was money but she had nothing to spend it on so we gave her some sweets instead. It was already too late for her teeth. Inside the monastery a monk sat in the sunshine having his hair cut by another. They seemed to be the only people around. We asked to see the abbot but were told he was away in the Khumbu, visiting the monastery at Tengpoche. Buddhism on the south side of Everest owes its survival, perhaps even its origin, to monks on the north side. When Mallory marched up the Rongbuk

Valley, Buddhism there was enjoying a resurgence. The current monastery at Rongbuk was founded at the start of the century and over five hundred monks and nuns lived there in its boom years under the inspirational teaching of Ngawang Tenzin Norbu, its head lama. His influence extended into Nepal where he established four monasteries before his death in 1940.

A small part of his monastery has been restored since the destructive excess of the Cultural Revolution but I couldn't escape an impression that the integrity of the gompa and the region itself had been fractured. The pre-war Everesters travelled on foot and horseback and stayed in local villages on their way to the mountain. They left their world behind them. Modern expeditions stay in state-owned hotels, pay permit fees to the Chinese authorities and ferry small bubbles of technological isolation to the mountain to keep them in touch with home. We'd driven through villages below the monastery that we would have loved to explore and understand a little better, but always the schedule prevented us. Men and women would straighten up from their work in the rough square fields to wave as we passed, looking on through the dirty windows. Small boys would chase after the bus, some of them in ragged western t-shirts. But facilities and transport were too closely controlled for any except the most hardy of individual travellers to escape. The local yak-herders, hired to ferry supplies from Base Camp to the Advanced Base on the East Rongbuk Glacier, were given only a percentage of the total fee, the rest going as commission to the Chinese.

There were eleven expeditions camped below the mountain as our bus pulled into Base Camp's parking area. Together they contributed hundreds of thousands of dollars to the government, a significant percentage of their total tourist income. Most of those living in this expensively tented village shrugged their shoulders at the injustices and got on with the business of climbing the mountain. A hundred tents were gathered around a huge bank of moraine above the parking lot like a nomad army camped for the night. Yaks rested in the afternoon sunlight and climbers shuffled round them on their way to the concrete shit-house or for afternoon strolls. On top of the moraine bank was a low concrete hut built by the Chinese to house liaison officers appointed to each expedition. I could see them sitting inside watching television sucked out of the sky by dishes set up at the back of the building, but I was blocked from entering by a representative of the China Tibet Mountaineering Association.

I tried to look through the doorway but he stood in front of me. 'Hi! Ha-ha. How are you?' I asked him but he stared me out and I slunk down the back of the hill of stones. Standing outside a mess tent on the other side were two women whom I thought I recognised.

'You'd go anywhere for a story,' said the slightly taller one when I was still some distance away. I recognised her. It was Alison Hargreaves. She was down from the mountain resting before her attempt to climb Everest unsupported and without bottled oxygen, something no other woman had done before. The other woman was Mandy Dickinson, a former champion sky-diver who was working on a film about an amputee called Tom Whitaker who was also trying to climb the mountain. I was sat down in their mess tent, its shelves groaning with exciting food, in front of a scrubbed vinyl table. A group of mountaineers were already sitting down, dressed in polyester and down clothing, all looking whippet fit and tanned. I scratched my beard and tried to keep a low profile.

It's interesting being on the outside the goldfish bowl but having occasional opportunities to get inside and look out. I had neither the dedication nor the ability of these climbers but I felt I knew enough to understand the tension and problems they were dealing with. In contrast, the others on my package tour were all in love with the high country but found the atmosphere of Base Camp oppressive, the climbers surly and uncommunicative. They seemed locked into something. I mentioned this to one of the climbers round the table I'd met before, the Australian Greg Child, now living in Seattle. Over the years Child had climbed K2, the second-highest mountain in the world, and a host of other steep and difficult peaks. That he was still alive after so many dangerous expeditions was impressive in itself.

'They're like that,' he said flatly, 'because most of them are out of their league. They're too gripped to enjoy it.' Child had recently been at a camp on the North Col where an American mountaineer had become distinctly territorial about the lines of rope his expedition had fixed on the mountain. He had warned Greg that his tents would be slashed and destroyed if he encroached on his expedition's space. This had not impressed him. There were upwards of a hundred and fifty climbers attempting the same route on Everest and, while it's a big mountain, it gets very crowded at key points. He compared the consequence to putting too many laboratory rats in the same cage. Greg was also on Everest with Tom Whitaker. The ex-patriate Welshman had lost his lower right leg in a car accident in Idaho in 1979, ending a promising climbing career, although by the next summer he was climbing again, albeit at a much reduced standard. He unstrapped his prosthesis to illustrate how he would be keeping his stump warm high on the mountain. Anticipating a great deal of wear and tear, he had brought three spares.

This loose-knit group all had different designs on the mountain. Mandy wanted her film, Tom wanted to show his disability was no handicap, Greg wanted Everest off his to-do list, Alison saw an opportunity to break new ground and make her reputation. Somewhere on the mountain was George Leigh Mallory's grandson, also called George Mallory, who would be one of the many to reach the summit that summer. After crossing the terrain from which his grandfather disappeared George saw the possibility that he wasn't the first Mallory to reach the top after all. Even though the mountain was no longer a blank canvas, its image wouldn't stop being reinterpreted, even subverted; in another mess tent, a different team had hung two large portions of a dried goat carcass for cold storage, one called Mallory, the other one Irvine.

There wasn't much here for us trippers, though. We made a tour of the memorial cairns and blundered about the Rongbuk Glacier for a while, discovering jewel-like pools of melt-water among the crumbling moraine and ice, taking pictures of each other with the mountain as a backdrop, as though it were the Blackpool Tower. But doing anything in the anaemic air took time and effort. Few coach parties make the long and tortuous drive to this cul-de-sac and it's left pretty much to the climbers whose attention is fixed firmly ahead and above them. There were plans to change all that by building a small hotel in the lee of the moraine bank with a restaurant and souvenir shop but the idea had been excoriated by western mountain conservationists. Looking at the vast pyramid of shit under the toilet block which had been hastily dug to cope with the huge increase of climbers, I wasn't sure it was such a bad thing. At least it would deal with the human waste in an intelligent way.

The project had been launched by Russell Brice, a forthright mountaineer from New Zealand who returned to the Rongbuk Valley year after year to guide expeditions. Greg, Tom and Alison had all found it convenient to buy a place on his trip and let him worry about the logistics of running Base Camp. The way Russell saw it, he was already running a hotel with its own communications centre and kitchens, it's just that the hotel wasn't permanent. He had commissioned elegant designs from an architect in France and found a discreet location at Base Camp to realise them. Brice's guiding principle was putting something back into the local community which had been so neatly by-passed by the Chinese.

'You're prepared to walk away,' he told me in his office-tent, 'and say those people look nice in my photographs but let's not do anything to help. I'm trying to give them a better deal so when groups come they buy postcards and souvenirs. Let the Tibetans have the chance to build shops and tea houses and make money out of the tourist trade.' Everybody else was, especially the Chinese, so why not the people we waved to from our bus? I wondered how he squared his political conscience. 'I don't necessarily agree with the Chinese being here but then I could sit in London and say 'Free Tibet!' as much as I like. It's not going to help these people in this valley.' Plenty of Tibetans made regular trips to the Khumbu and had seen for themselves the money to be made from the uniquely large lump of rock and ice at the head of their valley and Russell's image of a local crafts shop was rather encouraging. But the cynical voice in the back of my mind warned that one day the Chinese could refuse Brice a visa and appoint some indifferent retired PLA officer to run the hotel and to fill the shop with souvenirs that read 'Made in Beijing'.

In the morning we packed our tents back onto the bus for the long haul to Shigatse and Lhasa hundreds of miles east down the Friendship Highway. Before leaving, some of the friends I'd met gave me letters to their families to take home with me, like notes from soldiers on their way to the front. The bus bumped its way down the rough track and the little colony of tents receded in the mirrors. I thought about the people in the villages watching so much wealth driving past their houses every year. I thought about the Dalai Lama encouraging tourists to come and experience what the Chinese were doing to Tibet and her people. And I wondered how much of this you could see with Everest in the way.

CHAPTER THREE

All Englishmen cannot be gentlemen

> To complain of the age we live in, to murmur at the
> present possessors of power, to lament the past, to
> conceive extravagant hopes of the future, these are
> the common dispositions of the greatest part of
> mankind.
>
> Edmund Burke

Sher Bahadur Deuba, prime minister of the kingdom of Nepal, was having a bad week. Critics accused him of vaccillation, enemies conspired his downfall. Deuba's coalition partners, the Rastriya Prajatantra Party, were split down the middle. Some of its members of parliament favoured a new alliance with the Communist Party, others argued they remain in government with Deuba's Nepali Congress Party. A motion of no confidence in the coalition had been tabled in an attempt to bring down the government and as the margin between success and failure narrowed, each member's influence increased. Political nonentities were suddenly finding the confidence to walk out of meetings and issue threats of non-cooperation. It was too close to call. Kathmandu breathed in speculation and exhaled rumour.

If Deuba survived then he could return to the shattering problems facing the people his government represented. Nepal has an annual per capita income of $180, an adult literacy rate of around 65 per cent, a child mortality rate of 12 per cent before the age of five. In some areas this rises to more than 30 per cent. The country imports four times as much as its few industries export and, if favourable export quotas to the United States end, this situation will worsen. From being net exporters of food after the war, the Nepalese, 80 per cent of whom are subsistence farmers, have become net importers. The country's population is growing at more than 450,000 a year and is expected, at the current rate of increase, to double within thirty years. As much as 30 per cent of Nepal's annual budget is already provided by other countries. Sher Deuba had a lot of bad weeks.

I put down my newspaper and summoned the waiter. The Northfield Café, shaded by trees and set back from the street, allows its patrons to step away from the mercantile frenzy of Thamel. My guidebook described it quite accurately as a 'place for serious breakfast devotees' which is why I was there. Beyond the doddery brick arch of the Northfield's entrance I could see the dust rising from the street, a crumbling Toyota taxi nosing its way through a stream of girls in printed cotton dresses and sandalled feet which moved aside as it passed. Inside the garden, Bach's cello suites hummed through the fresh morning air.

Coffee appeared at my elbow and I continued reading. In the spring of 1996, Deuba's problems, labyrinthine and gigantic as they were, did not end at Nepal's frontiers. Under news that the prime minister might soon be spending more time with his family was a warning for him from the Chinese ambassador to continue supporting China's position in Tibet at the United Nations. The ambassador added that proposed commercial links with Taiwan could have a political cost for Nepal. It made me wonder whether Deuba wanted to lose. I shouldn't have blamed him if he had. More perplexing was why so many others wanted his job in such uncertain times.

Pauline stepped through the arch, an armful of brochures under her arm, and looked round at the tables and the few tourists still breakfasting. She sat down opposite me and smiled.

'What you need, darlin',' she said, 'is a rafting holiday.' I flicked through her brochure. It was full of sunny photographs of muscular young people straining with paddles against mountains of frothing green water or gathered smiling around campfires with cups of rum punch. Pauline had abandoned her job as a barrister with Her Majesty's Customs and Excise to sell this invigorating experience to tourists like myself. It was her route to a life on the river. It was an exciting idea but Sher Deuba probably needed it more. Besides, I had plans.

'I was thinking of going back to Tibet after I get back from trekking in the Khumbu,' I told her. Since getting back to London from my bus trip through Tibet the previous year I had thought of little else beyond returning.

'Wow. Tibet. I've heard it's terribly hard there. And dusty.' I looked at her brochure again and acknowledged she had a point. I could feel the white sand beneath my feet, the sun on my back, the cool green water on my face. 'And the politics. I couldn't handle the politics. That's what's so good about Nepal. You've got none of that stuff to worry about here.' She gathered up her brochures and moved on to the next table.

I watched her move among tourists like myself, flicking her long brown hair from her eyes, laughing at jokes she made and heard a dozen times each day and found myself agreeing with her. It seemed as though the city shifted before my eyes, changing shape to present an image of whatever it was I wanted to find. Each time I returned I found my memories of the place weren't exact, that the streets had subtly altered to reveal prospects and ideas I hadn't seen before. Kathmandu's political future was everything and nothing, depending on what you thought you saw in the narrow streets or by the banks of the poisoned Bagmati.

These shifting perspectives were visible on the faces of the other travellers in the Northfield Café, expressing paranoia, cool, experience and shock, while all looking broadly similar. Conversations ranged from just passing the time of day to nervous discussions about the symptoms of giardia. A Belgian, in the process of establishing yet another non-governmental organisation for the benefit of the Nepali people, sat reading the *Kathmandu Post*, his briefcase on the floor beside him. Like many before him, his world had been fractured by the discovery of people living and dying in abject poverty. He was determined to help at least the street children who slept in the doorways of the cheap restaurants in Thamel. Charitable donations were even now trickling into a Brussels bank account as he moved from ministry to ministry in the heat of the day seeking permissions.

Three unnervingly clean Americans sat in the shadows flicking through the guidebooks and discussing the cheapest daily rate they had enjoyed on their round-the-world journey – Madagascar is apparently good value. They looked tired and harassed and talked of Thailand and lying on a beach. The conversation moved to restaurants and which were least likely to make you ill. 'It's so dirty here,' complained the red-headed girl who had just arrived. 'And so hot. I feel so hot and dirty here. Don't you? Don't you feel that, too?' Pauline barely hesitated at their table and was too late for the next. The middle-aged couple from Seattle looked up at her and smiled but their adventure had been pre-booked weeks in advance. They sat reading fat airport novels, waiting for their flight in-country. Each wore matching fawn pants and t-shirts provided by their expedition's organisers. I shifted my chair further into the shadows of a rubber plant to read the legend on their chests:

STOKE the dream
FIRE the imagination
IGNITE the journey

A ghastly image flashed across my mind of adventure tourists being strapped to huge fireworks and blasted towards the mountains to burst in a shower of brightly coloured sparks. Underneath this explosive slogan were details of the company which had organised the adventure. Kathmandu was the local colour promised in their brochure as a prologue to the experience of a lifetime. I left them to it.

Out on the street the heat was quickly building. Fresh young faces moved among the booksellers and photo developers, the souvenir shops and the restaurants. In early March the spring season is barely underway, but already there were reports in the papers of another increase in the numbers of tourists and Thamel is where, sooner or later, most of them come. It is not so much a district as an organism, growing and changing to meet the needs of the tourists who give it life. It has little to do with the real Kathmandu, whatever and wherever that is, and its boundaries aren't fixed. Hoteliers, anxious to attract custom, ensure that contiguous neighbourhoods are quietly absorbed. If Thamel is where the tourists go, then the place they occupy will become part of Thamel. What I could never fully grasp is whether the souvenir-sellers provided the tourists with the things they wanted or whether the tourists bought the things the shopkeepers sold because that's what you buy in Kathmandu. The result is clear, even if the logic isn't; girls and boys taking a year off before university, dressed in cotton pantaloons and negligible vests embroidered in the shop of origin with the all-seeing eyes of Buddha; sleek trekkers with branded t-shirts and bright rucksacks buying postcards of mountains they have walked beneath; and all of them offered anything they could want from trips to the temples and palaces of Durbar Square by the sinuous rickshaw-drivers to blackmarket currency deals or heroin from the hustlers and dealers that fringe the narrow streets and call softly from the shadows. Tourists look down from the roof terrace bars, greet each other with hugs and kisses that used to shock the woman selling cigarettes outside the Kathmandu Guest House but now is just another part of the weirdness of round-eyed strangers. It's a scene that provokes those distressed that something is being lost from Kathmandu to talk of cultural pollution, the corruption of values that the money and attitudes of these people affects. Looking down the street towards Chetrapati I had to acknowledge that none of this would be here without the tourists. But then in among the white faces were plenty of brown ones, some of them street children, serving tea, selling souvenirs, organising air tickets and getting paid for doing so. It also occurred to me, watching the way white and brown faces called at each other, even just to refuse an offer to buy, that at least they were talking.

From behind me came a distant shout, regular and slowly growing in volume. Then I could make out a second, more metallic shout which was being taken up by the first. One voice was prompting many, growing louder and louder until round the chicane in the street just up from the Northfield came a column of protestors, perhaps a hundred in total, carrying bright red flags with emblems making it clear that these were Communists marching. The tourists drew back to the margins of the street to watch in amazement as the earnest faces of the marchers swept by, a short, moustachioed figure at their centre with a loudhailer. I checked my camera and followed them towards Chetrapati. Two policemen dawdled at the back, occasionally talking into their radios.

Soon the column had left the tourists to their shopping and swept into a series of narrow streets, staring ahead and shouting slogans. The faces that watched them pass were now all brown, and the souvenir shops gave way to market stalls selling vegetables and rice. There seemed a dislocation between the determination of those who marched and those who stood aside to watch them, not so much indifference as a recognition that what those shouting wanted held little promise of change or improvement in the lives of those who remained silent.

Whichever tradition you follow, Buddhist, Hindu or plain old rationalist, the Kathmandu Valley was created by cataclysm. The sword of the Buddha Manjushri searching for the lowest point on the rim of the valley and splitting the rocks to drain the lake behind, Krishna hurling his thunderbolt through the Chobar Gorge, an earthquake in pre-history, whichever – the people of the valley are used to seismic acitivity of one sort or another, turning things upside down, breaking down the old. In between the people have prospered on the rich black earth, the richest, some say, in all of South Asia.

When tourists complain that they wish they could have seen Kathmandu as it used to be, I wonder which Kathmandu they mean. Wang Hsuan Tse, on a diplomat's mission to India, described the city in the seventh century with a jewel-encrusted palace and tiered temples so high 'you would take them for a crown of clouds'. Is this the place? Or the Kathmandu whose Malla kings competed with those of the neighbouring valley towns of Patan and Bhaktapur not just in war but in the scale of their architecture, the magnificence of their festivals. Gorged on the silver they raised as duties on trade between Tibet and India they bickered through centuries of stability which become stagnation which in turn prompted the next thunderbolt to free another tide of change.

The latest fracture was still fresh in the minds of the demonstrators, urging that the momentum of revolution be carried forward and not allowed to dissipate. Throughout the 1970s and 1980s, the Panchayat one-party system, managed by the king and his advisers, had lost direction under the weight of change as aid agencies and tourism poured money into Nepal. Where was the need for enterprise or reform when wealth arrived regardless? Kathmandu's elite has regularly failed to improve the welfare of its people, preferring to build palaces before sewers.

In 1989 Nepal's Trade and Transit Treaty with India expired. Instead of extending it while a new treaty was negotiated, the Indian government imposed a trade embargo on Nepal and crucial supplies, particularly of fuel, ceased. The growing disquiet about the Panchayat system and demands for multi-party democracy were focused by India's intervention; there are some who believe India actively attempted to destabilise the *ancien regime*, although it seems unlikely that the revolution could have succeded in 1990 without the active support of most of the population of the Kathmandu Valley.

On April 6th, as the King and his advisers struggled to preserve the status quo, half a million people took to the streets. At first the police who swarmed throughout the city did not interfere and the crowd gathered at Tundikhel to demonstrate. But when some of them moved north to Durbar Marg, towards the Royal Palace itself, chanting slogans against the King and his Rana wife, troops opened fire with automatic weapons. The BBC reported more than fifty killed, other estimates put the number at more than a hundred. In all, throughout the course of the revolution, more than three hundred are thought to have died. There have been many violent changes of government in Kathmandu, but none before had the support of so many ordinary people. And in the late twentieth century aid agencies and tourists are impressed by popular movements. While King Birendra misjudged his political future, both of these fundamental resources were threatened. After almost two centuries of isolation, Nepal needed the outside world. The Panchayat gave way to a parliamentary democracy and the monarchy became merely constitutional.

Six years on from the revolution antipathy had returned, the gilded promise of democracy chipped and faded. The marchers continued towards Ratna Park but I gave up the effort. Retracing my steps, I found the streets unaffected by the march, as though nothing had passed at all. A group of Buddhist monks were arguing with a street vendor about the price of underwear, the sleeves of their robes falling back from their arms as they argued. Bicycles wove around the ditches that were slowly filling with garbage. Four scruffy boys came towards me pulling faces at the camera. An old man pushed a cart loaded with oranges, a contrast to the ubiquitous green of chillies, cauliflowers, beans. The houses sagged around their inhabitants, while traders watched from the shadows of their open-fronted shops.

If any party could have championed the interests of these people it should have been the Communist Party of Nepal. The Communists had enjoyed a brief period of power but in-fighting and factionalism undermined its success in bringing politics to the people. Nor was its cause helped by the almost surreal divisions within the Communist movement itself. You weren't Communists unless you had a set of brackets to let the voters know which nuance of Marxist-Leninist-Maoist theory you favoured this week. The Communist Party of Nepal (Marxist Leninist) together with the CPN (Marxist) had combined to form the UML, and this has had the most representatives in the Pratinidhi Sabha, Nepal's parliament. Voters could also choose the CPN (Masal), the CPN (United), the Communist League, the CPN (Marxist Leninist Maoist), the Nepal Majdoor Kisan Party, the CPN (Maoist) and the CPN (Unity Centre). Outside Kathmandu, in places that don't feature in the guidebooks, some of these groups, like the Maoists, had abandoned the political process altogether in favour of terrorism. Groups like the United People's Front, with a set of bracketed splinter groups all its own, issued statements about the failure of the revolution and waging a people's war.

I walked back to Thamel, disappointed that so much energy could have drained away without much to show for it. Corruption in the civil service had worsened, most agreed, and many expatriate westerners said that the fall in environmental standards had quickened since the first elections were held in 1991. Others told me that the old Panchayat system had acted as a brake on consumerism and now people were free to spend. As a consequence an acquisitive middle class had emerged which wanted things, not ideas. It was obvious that the government's crisis was its own affair and ordinary people had slipped back into resignation.

I stopped at the desk of the Kathmandu Guest House to collect my key and climbed the narrow stairs to my room. This took longer than it should, as it often did, since I had to stop regularly to say hello to various members of staff, from the manageress to the laundry man. People have time for each other in Nepal and this is so overwhelming to most westerners that they miss the undercurrents of frustration that many Nepalis feel which led, eventually, to revolution. I knew climbers and travellers who made several visits to Nepal throughout the 1980s but were still shocked by the events of 1990. The poverty most people endured was obvious but there seemed a tolerance of it. Their typical western understanding of Hinduism suggested that people accepted their fate, not protested to change it. Despite the city's problems and the continuing daily struggle made by most of its people, I spent months on my own in Kathmandu without feeling isolated or lonely. Hospitality is one thing the World Bank can't teach you to develop.

The Guest House is not as fashionable as it once was. Many climbers and trekkers stay in quieter districts like Patan and the well-heeled opt for the five-star hotels on Durbar Marg. The air and water are cleaner, the risk of an infection that would ruin a holiday less likely. Nevertheless, the Guest House is often full during the season and its lobby crowded with those leaving for the mountains or just returning. I would sit here for hours, partly to watch cricket on the communal television and partly to earwig conversations. It was obvious, watching the American Cable News Network whenever there was no cricket, that the introduction of television has had a profound effect on Nepal. Tourism is often cited as having a major cultural impact but in many ways television has proved just as influential. The revolution in Nepal occurred at a time when countries from eastern Europe to China were undergoing profound political change. Seeing ordinary people taking their fate into their own hands was a liberating idea for those Nepalis with access to television. Those without could listen to All India Radio, Voice of America and the BBC. These foreign broadcasters were used by opposition politicians as the only outlet for their message and offered the Nepali people an alternative view to that promulgated by the state-owned media.

Unlike the newer hotels that have crowded round to share in its success, the Guest House is no overnight brick sensation, but a former palace, albeit a small one. It had belonged to Kumar Narsingh Rana, the first civil engineer in Nepal, who set to work adding similar palaces for other members of his family before the Great War. Not that the Ranas were short of palace space. Chandra Shumsher Rana, prime minister from 1901–29, began his reign by building the vast Singha Durbar at a cost of five million rupees. Despite the fact that the complex occupied a large part of Kathmandu, his sons were soon agitating for palaces of their own. So the prime minister sold his palace to the state – in effect to himself – and used the proceeds to start building more palaces. Chandra, who has something of a reputation as a reformer, waited until his palace was finished before considering any expenditure on the people: a water supply constructed for Patan in 1904 at a fraction of the cost of the Singha Durbar.

Rana palaces stud the Kathmandu Valley like fat paste jewellery. Had I been running the revolution I'd have dynamited the lot in a fit of rage. But while somebody, according to rumour, burnt down much of the Singha Durbar in 1974, the other palaces have been subsumed by the modern era. Some are hotels, others have been turned into ministries. The Ministry of Education and Culture belonged to Kaiser Shumsher Jung Bahadur Rana until his death in 1964 and was then left to the government. The irony being, of course, that when the Ranas were finally overthrown in 1951 hardly anybody in the country could read.

Like the ministry, the Guest House is littered with echoes of the Ranas' century of dominance. There are scores of photographs of short men in uniform with luxuriant beards and moustaches, usually standing behind a dead tiger or rhinoceros. The pictures of Kathmandu show a city before the rash of development spread across its face. I examined one picture of Pashupatinath, the Hindu temple complex on the banks of the Bagmati, and judged from the lack of buildings around it that the photograph must be very old indeed, perhaps from the last century. And then I noticed the caption 'Pashupatinath – 1974' written at the bottom. It had changed almost beyond recognition in only twenty years.

The Ranas came to power in 1846 following the massacre of Queen Lakshmi Devi's coterie in the Kot Arsenal off Durbar Square at the hands of Jung Bahadur and his six brothers. Jung assumed the name Rana and the title of Maharaja to give his obscure origins a little dignity and the title became hereditary. For the next one hundred years Nepal was run as the personal treasury of the Rana family. Jung Bahadur was a capable and energetic man who lived in violent times. Laurence Oliphant, who accompanied Jung to Nepal when he returned from his celebrated visit to

London, wrote in 1852: 'The power of the Prime Minister is absolute until he is shot, when it becomes unnecessary to question the expediency of his measures.' Jung was more successful than any of his predecessors at avoiding this fate, which was regularly attempted, and if his behaviour was extreme, then his position demanded it.

They were brutal times. The fifth king of the Shah dynasty, Rajendra, poisoned his infant son and then punished the physicians who failed to save the child's life. The senior doctor was a Brahmin and so excused execution but was 'burnt on the forehead and cheeks until his brain and jaw were exposed'. The junior doctor was a Newar and so impaled in Rajendra's presence and his heart ripped still beating from his chest.

Even the Ranas thought this period particularly grim. Jung's son Padma described life at court in the first half of the nineteenth century as a 'sink of iniquity with all, from the Queen down to the humblest maid, engaged in love intrigues.' The palace held a thousand concubines with five hundred working, according to Padma, a two-week shift before the other five hundred clocked on. So when the gutters of the Kot ran red with blood it was more catharsis than *coup d'état*.

The consequences of Jung's rise to power reverberated all over South Asia; even the fledgling sport of Himalayan climbing was affected. When the British and Nepali authorities signed the Treaty of Segauli in 1816, a relationship was formed which effectively kept Nepal isolated from the rest of the world and gave the British access to some of the best troops in the sub-continent. It also realised a long-standing ambition of the British to station a Resident in Kathmandu, a position held most notably by Brian Houghton Hodgson. Hodgson lived in Kathmandu from 1820–43 but the activities and movement of the Resident were strictly controlled and, wherever he went, Hodgson would have an escort with him. Nevertheless this sensitive and astute man made a detailed study of everything that he had access to and while many British accounts of life in Nepal in the nineteenth century are rather flat and superficial, Hodgson was an acute observer, publishing four volumes and scores of papers on subjects ranging from Hinduism to the physical geography of the Himalaya. (This didn't prevent him, as we shall see later, from failing to identify Everest correctly.) Hodgson was ultimately dismissed from the job he loved so much but continued to have a significant influence on policy in India and was made a Fellow of the Royal Society for his contribution to botany.

The Resident was initially a marginalised and unpopular figure in Kathmandu society but, partly through Hodgson's influence, when Jung Bahadur came to power the British had a stronger position. Jung wanted to understand the British more fully, this neighbour who 'crushes thrones like potsherds', so in 1850 he crossed the sea to England. He spent £10,000 on his travel arrangements to Southampton and carried with him presents valued at the vast sum of £250,00 to impress his hosts. London society was agog to meet the first high-caste Hindu ruler to travel to Europe and stories of his blood-thirsty rise to power gripped the capital, something which Jung found rather tiresome. Queen Victoria was convalescing after giving birth to Prince Arthur, Duke of Connaught, so in the meantime Jung exchanged visits with the Duke of Wellington who greatly impressed the Maharaja. When Wellington died in 1852, Jung had a shot fired from the guns of Tundikhel for each of the Iron Duke's eighty-two years. When they finally met, Queen Victoria awarded Jung Bahadur the Knight Grand Cross of the Order of the Bath which meant, as far as the people of Kathmandu were concerned, that the Queen and the Maharaja had shared a moment's intimacy in the royal bathroom.

During his visit Jung Bahadur developed a deep respect for the British rule of law and the organisation of her still expanding Empire. With a friendly buffer state between Russia and China and the East India Company, the British were content to leave Nepal a largely autonomous nation. Jung Bahadur's intervention in the Indian Mutiny by contributing loyal Gurkha battalions at a critical moment gained him the tolerance and gratitude of the British. The arrangement was cold realpolitik for both countries. In 1922, as Britain and Nepal prepared to sign a new treaty confirming Nepal's independent status, Sir Arthur Hirtzel, Under-Secretary of State for India, observed that 'it was mainly because of the Gurkha element in the Army that we value the friendship of Nepal.' During the Great War, Nepal contributed over 100,000 Gurkhas to the Empire's armies, leaving old men and women to work in the fields. These soldiers fought on the Western Front, at Gallipoli, in Egypt and Palestine and throughout the entire theatre of war with great distinction.

Part of the deal for this contribution of manpower was that foreigners would be kept out. Prithvi Narayan Shah, the first of the Gurkha dynasty who captured Kathmandu in 1768, believed that 'first the Bible, then the trading stations, then the cannon' would be the consequence of contact with Britain and could threaten his position. No doubt he would have added tourism to the list had it existed. The British Empire was content to stay away if Nepal's most precious asset – her people – kept joining her armies. Countless travel writers have pointed out that in 1950 Nepal was a country largely unknown to Europeans. The irony is that Europe was much better known to the Nepali people who had lived and died defending its borders and interests.

Everest is a footnote to all of this, although an interesting one. In 1905, as he neared the end of his period as Viceroy of India, Curzon wrote to the writer and mountaineer Douglas Freshfield, renewing his interest in the idea of an expedition to Everest. Most interested parties felt that access through Tibet offered the best chance of success, following Colonel Francis Younghusband's military expedition there in 1904, but Curzon, who had visited Nepal in 1899, believed he had some influence in persuading the Maharaja Chandra Shumsher to let a party of mountaineers in.

'It has always seemed to me,' he told Freshfield, 'a reproach that with the second highest mountain in the world for the most part in British territory and with the highest in a neighbouring and friendly state, we the mountaineers and pioneers par excellence of the universe, make no sustained and scientific attempt to climb to the top of one of these mountains.'

The other peak was K2, attempted for the first time in 1902 by a party which included the diabolist Aleister Crowley and which failed in some ignominy. As for Everest, Curzon over-estimated his influence and had not counted on the objection of Lord Morley, the Secretary of State for India. London had always viewed Nepal's status as more independent than the administration in Calcutta believed it to be, and Morley had no hesitation in pouring cold water on the idea of climbing Everest from any angle, not least because of his disapproval of Curzon's decision to send Younghusband into Tibet. It would, argued Morley, offend the Russians and, anyway, the Nepalese had forbidden visitors. Presumably Morley didn't include Raj officials who fancied a spot of tiger shooting.

Sir George Goldie, president of the Royal Geographical Society, wrote to *The Times* enclosing his correspondence with Morley, a man whose cabinet colleagues referred to as Aunt Priscilla and who Campbell-Bannerman once called 'a petulant spinster'. *The Times* thought the issue worthy of a leader: 'There certainly is some piquancy in the fact that it is not merely a Liberal Government but one of its most distinguished 'intellectuals', a scholar and a student as well as a man of affairs who is thus presented as the enemy of enlightenment.' Alas for the mountaineers, *The Times* concluded that Lord Morley may have had a point. 'A still more weighty argument may lie in our diplomatic relations with a certain Great Power.'

The Royal Geographical Society persevered, awarding a fellowship to Chandra Shumsher when he visited London in 1908, but such ingratiation was in vain, according to minutes of his meeting with the petulant spinster.

'Last year,' Morley began, 'a very important society, the Geographical Society demanded a pass from me to explore Everest. I refused it. Is it not as you wish me to do?'

'It was so good of Your Lordship,' replied the Maharaja. 'My object in keeping my country isolated is so that the Gurkhas may continue to respect the British as they have been doing so far. I think I am right when I say that their respect of the British official in their cantonment equals, if is not greater, than their respect for their sovereign. But if we agree to let a party into our country others will gradually follow and all Englishmen, Your Lordship, cannot be expected to be gentlemen. If unfortunately there may be a quarrel between the British subjects and the Nepalese subjects and if there be frequent associations between them in the hearth and home of the Gurkhas, it may breed contempt and they may not respect the British in the same manner as they do now, which would be a dangerous thing for the interest of Nepal.'

The implication of this exchange is that permission was denied initially not by the Maharaja but by Lord Morley and in his history of Himalayan exploration, *Abode of Snow*, Kenneth Mason suggests that the authorities in Kathmandu were prepared to give their assent. At least Curzon got some compensation for his trouble. The Survey of India records that its servant Natha Singh was given permission to explore the valley of the Dudh Kosi which flows from the Khumbu region below Mount Everest. He was the first outsider to approach the base of the mountain, reaching the hamlet at Lobuje from where he made drawings of the snout of the Khumbu Glacier. The visit was made at the request of the Resident in Kathmandu, Major Manners-Smith, a holder of the Victoria Cross from the Hunza Campaign of 1891 and an old friend of Curzon, Younghusband and the eventual leader of the Everest expeditions, Charles Granville Bruce. But no European mountaineer reached the Khumbu until 1950.

In the courtyard of the Guest House, the evening rush was starting. The waiters in their short-sleeved pink shirts, brown trousers and natty chocolate bow-ties hurried between the tables. A group of Yugoslavian climbers with permission for Everest were still sitting at the same table they had occupied all day with an impressive collection of empty beer bottles spread before them. I had met their leader the day before while I was arranging a flight to the Khumbu. He carried a briefcase, as most Everest expedition leaders are forced to these days given the paperwork involved, and looked worried. His expedition had been on and off for years as political and financial problems at home caused the team to delay and then cancel permits. Now money they were counting on from Yugoslavia, tens of thousands of dollars, had not arrived and the team was stuck until it did. In the meantime the expedition languished. They spent the time videoing each other for the expedition film and playing back the results on the Guest House's video player. One evening they watched their departure from what I assume was Belgrade airport. Images of their wives and girlfriends kissing and then waving them goodbye appeared on the screen. They fell silent and the room was still for a moment. But then to mask their sadness or embarrassment they roared abuse at each other and ordered more beers.

It emerged that they were Montenegrans which explained why they were prepared to call themselves the 1996 Yugoslavian Everest Expedition. The discovery left me wondering how they would get on with the Slovenian expedition who were also expected on the mountain that year. Rival expeditions from the same country often have enough trouble getting on – I recall a robust exchange between the first two Chilean teams who reached the summit of Everest some years ago at roughly the same time – let alone those countries which are a product of a recent divorce.

Pauline was hosting a rum-and-coke evening to attract potential clients, so I decided to reconsider the possibilities of a rafting holiday. Arriving at her office, I found a projector and screen set up outside and a small number of slightly bemused travellers waiting for things to start. Three Israeli girls were flicking through a portfolio of dramatic rafting pictures with a growing sense of unease until they laid the book gently down, drained their plastic cups and crept back into the shadows.

After Pauline's slide show, I started chatting to Cate – 'with a "C"' – and Clarkie, two English dentists who were seeing something of the planet before returning to get married, and to a British soldier called Gary who had been working near Tumlingtar in the east of Nepal, visiting welfare centres established for the Gurkhas. He described meeting a ninety-two-year-old ex-Gurkha who each week made a three-day round-trip to collect his pension. The old man had fought at Tobruk and spent three years in a prisoner of war camp. Gary's eyes glowed with respect. He then took a swig of rum and began a diatribe about a non-governmental organisation he had come across during his travels. I added him to the long list of people I met in Nepal who believed aid agencies should leave Nepal alone.

There are no right answers to questions about the aid programme, only answers that are less wrong. Before King Tribhuvan opened the doors to foreign aid donors there were a few hundred primary schools in Nepal and now there are thousands, raising the literacy rate from a figure some had put as low as two per cent. But then the hundreds of millions of dollars that the United States alone poured into the country has developed a dependency culture which the hierarchical social system in Nepal fell upon like a lost brother. The elite in Nepal were happy to abdicate reponsibility for improving the living standards of ordinary people to representatives of western governments willing to do it for them. I had heard and read stories of huge bribes being required to 'release' funds to the projects they were allotted to, sometimes as much as fifty per cent of a total budget. Some Nepalis took it for granted that involvement with an aid project would be a personally enriching experience and not in the spiritual sense. Equally, dedicated Nepalis, working for non-governmental organisations (NGOs), were demoralised at having to work alongside westerners who were paid perhaps a hundred times their salary and yet had no more expertise and certainly not the local understanding they did.

One story I had read a couple of years before was a succinct and bleak illustration of how the West had interacted with Nepal in the last thirty years. The *Kathmandu Post* had carried a report of a debate in the lower house of parliament on drug trafficking. A member had complained that a local representative of an NGO which had been working in Kathmandu with drug addicts had been 'deprived of opportunities for foreign trips'. Thomas Gafney, a long-standing campaigner on drug rehabilitation in Nepal, was outraged by this cynicism. 'Priorities are hopelessly out of order,' he wrote. 'The moral discord between unsparing fulfilment of social assistance to the needy, and selfish pursuit of personal benefits might be more worthy of parliamentary consideration.' He raged against the greater interest shown by officials in their social position than in the improvement they were appointed to bring. 'The drug control section *has* no drug experts, or any personnel experienced in the problem or the nature of addiction. It has administrators. It is unknown that any member of the drug control office has ever visited any drug treatment centre except to preside at functions.'

Clarkie the dentist's vocal moral outrage at this kind of corruption and bureaucracy which was holding back the development of Nepal attracted the attention of an American man in his late forties. He was, he said, working for an impoverished NGO south of the city, researching something to do with animal diseases. He had a narrow face and long, grey-black hair swept back into a pony tail. A pair of wire-rimmed spectacles perched on his nose and he leaned forward as he spoke, adding to his intensity. From the deepening shadows he spun a tale of corruption, deceit and bureaucracy so monstrous that at times I gasped with surprise. How much of it to believe in this city of rumours? Then he lowered his voice still further.

'Man, did you hear about the Italian?'

'What Italian?'

'The Italian that was murdered.'

'Murdered?'

'Yeah. Murdered.'

'Where?' I asked. He glanced to his left.

'*Here*, man. In *Thamel*.'

I nodded slowly and then recovered my natural attitude of scepticism. 'It wasn't in the paper.'

'It wasn't in the paper because *they kept it out*. They don't want you to know.'

I had to acknowledge that the murder of a tourist might be bad for business, although similar tragedies hadn't stopped people visiting Miami. The conversation had moved on before I could mention this.

'When I came here first in '71 you could only book a hotel through Yeti Travels. And who owns Yeti Travels? The King, man, the King. And the Annapurna. In fact, he owns a lot of those first tourist businesses.'

This I knew to be correct. In 1971 Mahendra was still on the throne. Mahendra is my favourite among Nepal's recent monarchs, despite the fact he ended the country's first attempt at multi-party democracy after arresting the prime minister Bisheshwar Prasad Koirala in 1960 and taking back control of government. The fact remains that, like Koirala, he had a vision for his country and believed that the Panchayat one-party system could deliver it. And to be fair, under his direction the country made some progress. My respect for him was secured after I toured the museum dedicated to his memory in the Basantapur Tower of the old Royal Palace, the Hanuman Dhoka in Durbar Square.

The guidebooks to the Valley are strong when it comes to describing the enchanting pagoda architecture of Kathmandu, Patan and Bhaktapur but have missed the post-modern ironies of Mahendra's museum, openly hinting that it is boring. This is far from the truth. Mahendra seems to have been born with a pair of Ray-bans clamped over his eyes and he never took them off, even when jetting round the globe to hob-nob with other world leaders. The museum is full of photographs of the King looking like a jazz musician meeting President Tito or Queen Elizabeth. There are also scores of uniforms on display, designed for every state occasion in any location and at any time of year but all with fat epaulettes and lots of trimming. He listened to music on an enormous, coffin-sized music centre and a plaque on the wall behind it testifies to Mahendra's love of the arts.

The centrepiece of the exhibition is a wonderful recreation of his office. The motif is plastic, mostly in a dark chocolate. Plastic brown office chairs, brown accessories and filing cabinets, brown carpet, brown walls, a cream telephone – there is one item on the desk that isn't brown, something like a pencil sharpener or a gonk, but it only serves to illustrate the unmitigated brownness of it all. I imagine that this may not have been so alarming to a man who always wore sunglasses. As I left the museum a boy jumped off the steps of one of the nearby temples and shouted after me.

'Hello mister, I am one sexy guide.'

'I'm sure you are,' I replied, 'but I have a rickshaw to catch.'

Cate was now deploring the traffic in the city, most particularly the pollution it caused. It was widely recognised as being one of the reasons that tourists were spending less time in Kathmandu. It was sadly ironic to read the signs in Thamel advertising 'eco-trekking' through a haze of exhaust fumes. The aid agencies, according to the animal husbandrist, were as much to blame as anyone else. 'You should go down to the UN compound, man, check out the 4WDs. These people need 4WDs maybe once a year.' He spoke sadly about his first stint in Kathmandu in the days when personal transport meant bicycles. Now those cyclists had bought mopeds and two-stroke motorcycles. It wasn't progress – if any city should be given over to the bicycle it is Kathmandu – it was the triumph of consumerism. The same cynical exploitation of self-interest that has swept through parts of eastern Europe since their revolutions has arrived in Nepal.

The obvious solution was to get drunk. We walked up the street to Old Spam's and sat in the garden drinking beer. At other tables young Nepali men – never women – sat with young western tourists dressed in the same clothes, drinking the same drinks and listening to the same music. The liberal sexual attitudes of western women dressed in very little must be intoxicating to young men constricted by the rigid social mores of Nepali society. And beautiful, brown-skinned boys clearly make an impression in the other direction. People don't go on holiday to be puritans, after all.

Thamel and its equivalent, Lakeside, on the shore of Phewa Tal in Pokhara in Central Nepal, are obvious illustrations of how tourism can pollute a culture, not least because young people will insist on testing boundaries. And they offer rich pickings for travel writers trying to make the point that superficially attractive but shallow western culture is undermining a more ancient and stable tradition. I suppose there are bars like Spam's or Tom and Jerry's just down the street everywhere, from Corfu to Goa, and it's easy to imagine that the whole world will end up drinking Coke or Budweiser and watching Rambo videos. But the more time I spent in Nepal the more I felt that far from the world growing smaller or more homogenous, its differences were becoming greater and greater. Seventeenth century Englishmen would, I've no doubt, have more in common with Nepalis than I do – the same fear of disease and the loss of infant children, the same lack of education, the same reliance on subsistence farming and the same practical attitude to human relationships. More importantly, the rhythm of their lives would be the same. Nepal won't be rich enough to indulge in the kind of social fragmentation the West has for decades, so the cycle of birth, marriage, procreation and death, the pattern of festival and community celebrations, the daily rituals of puja or prayer will continue for a little while yet. Thamel, for the time being, is the exception that proves the rule.

That is not to say that western behaviour can't be a malign influence. Walking back to the Guest House after dinner one evening, I glanced into a shopfront and saw a blonde woman in her twenties running a straw shoved up her nose along a line of cocaine. This would be pretty radical behaviour on even the worst streets in Britain, but the police in Kathmandu tend to leave tourists alone, so they get away with it. It's not really the drugs I objected to, more the attitude that she could do in public something many Nepalis find objectionable and not care. Many of the tourists in Thamel are budget travellers, inheritors of the hippie tradition that rushed to Kathmandu in the late 1960s. They dossed on a road off New Road that became known as Freak Street and got deported just before King Birendra's coronation. Budget travellers are usually young and have wonderfully liberal values and so give money to street children. But they are also broke and so haggle over a few rupees with rickshaw-drivers. If someone had just spent three years' worth of your wage flying to your country and then skimped on paying you a fair price for something you would be outraged. The Nepalis, even after two or three decades of this, can still manage to smile. Of course, it's never so straightforward. Those in authority in Nepal have exploited ordinary people for centuries. That Nepali society – parents, villages, government – can still allow as many as 200,000 girls to be sold into prostitution in India, that tens of thousands return home infected with HIV to continue working in Kathmandu, shows a continuing moral failure somewhere. Thamel is quite a mellow place when seen in the context of Bombay's so-called supermarket brothels. Perhaps part of the problem is that western writers have portrayed Nepal as Shangri La for too long and are shocked – and guilty – to discover elements of the tawdry flourishing.

I arrived back at the Guest House and climbed through the small gate that is left open for late-nighters like myself. The gate keeper saluted smartly and I returned the gesture but with a little less panache. Crawling into bed I could hear the Yugoslavian expedition still at their post in the courtyard. They began to sing, softly at first in low dark tones but then louder and louder. As I drifted towards sleep I could hear their refrain over and over again, and for some unfathomable reason they were shouting it in English: 'We are Serbs! We are Serbs! We are Serbs!'

CHAPTER FOUR

Kathmandu, mailo Kathmandu

Every morning I walked the short distance from the Northfield Café to the stand of bicycles just outside the Guest House where the same tall boy of thirteen or fourteen would rent me a mountain bike. The Guest House itself offered bicycles for hire but they were old sit-up-and-beg models with such poor brakes and gears they would be better described as sit-up-and-pray. If I got to the stand early, I was assured of a new model with excellent brakes; if I was late, then I had to take my chances.

'Today is good bike,' the boy said. 'You bring before six. Where is going today?'

'I'm meeting Karna Sakya,' I said.

The boy stopped fiddling with the padlock and looked up at me with new interest. He seemed impressed.

'He is very rich man,' the boy said. 'He own many hotel.'

I climbed onto the bike and set off through the crowded lanes of Thamel. Cycling within Kathmandu is hugely exciting but requires a steady nerve and some kind of breathing apparatus as protection against the fumes. Weaving among the auto-rickshaws and taxis along Tridevi Marg, I turned north along Kantipath and parked my bike outside the Hotel Ambassador, set on a corner near the British Embassy. It was a new building of quite attractive red brick and better designed than the majority of hotels that have suddenly sprouted throughout the city.

Karna was sitting at a desk in the lobby reading aloud from a Nepali newspaper to an elegantly dressed man in his thirties whose mongoloid features suggested he was a Bhotia. When he finished and stood to offer me his hand he was still excited. 'This political business is terrible,' Karna said as he showed me into his office. It was elegantly decorated with wood panelling in the Newari style found all over the older parts of the city. Karna immediately launched into an impassioned attack on the Rastriya Prajatantra Party and their political cynicism in vacillating between Deuba and the Communists. I asked him whether he felt that government corruption was on the increase.

'Possibly,' he answered. 'But it's not like India. There just isn't the kind of money here to allow that scale of corruption. You know, it's more a matter of incompetence than anything else.' Karna, now in his early fifties, had spent his early years abroad. Educated in Dehra Dun, he had studied forestry in Australia and national park management in the United States and had travelled all over the world. On his return to Nepal he had played an important part in establishing national parks in the Langtang and at Chitwan. He told me about his childhood in Thamel, then called Thahiti, of walking to school and watching in shame as people squatted in the street to relieve themselves. His family had bought what would become the Kathmandu Guest House from Kumar Narsingh Rana and his father had maintained and restored it. 'He was carried away by colonial art,' Karna said. 'He bought all kinds of things from Calcutta.' When it became Karna's responsibility to manage the house he turned to his experiences as a traveller to open a twelve-room hotel. 'I was terribly impressed by the Manila Hotel. You know, where General MacArthur stayed.'

Karna's problem was that his hotel was in an unfashionable part of the city. Freak Street, as the hippies called it, just off Durbar Square, was the established haunt of budget travellers, while expensive hotels like the Annapurna and the Yak and Yeti were opening on Durbar Marg. To secure regular occupancy, Karna persuaded the American Embassy to send Peace Corps workers to the hotel for their orientation courses and then struck a deal with an overland travel operator to extend their trips from India to Nepal. It was the start of what has become known as adventure tourism, a term which has always struck me as a contradiction in terms but which seems to meet a need. He thought of clever hooks to attract attention, making his telex address 'Kathouse'. He instructed his staff to be polite but not servile. Guests were required to collect their own clean sheets and towels and the savings allowed Karna to charge only $2 a room. By 1973 the Guest House had forty-eight rooms but it still struggled to survive. So Karna tried a different tactic.

He invited friends to open businesses – restaurants, book shops and even other hotels – and the area's influence began to grow. 'I wanted an atmosphere where tourists felt they were in the right part of Kathmandu,' he told me. And he succeeded. Every building in Thamel has a business, and often several, dedicated to tourism. Karna has gone on to open other hotels and was opening his fourth that week at Nagarkot, a popular viewpoint in the Valley from which to see the mountains. He no longer manages the Guest House – that is left to his daughter-in-law – and they change the sheets for you these days but he remains unable to leave things alone. 'My mother always used to say I had ants in my pants,' he said.

Karna's attitude to tourism's development was paradoxical in some ways. 'Tourism was developed first and planned after,' he complained to me but from its organic structure it is clear that Thamel had grown up on a wave of entrepreneurial fervour, largely instigated by Karna himself. He is by training a conservationist but with a flair for business. And yet if he has got the balance wrong sometimes, at least he understands the value of preservation. Thamel disgusts some people but it provides jobs, even for the street children and, compared to environmental disasters elsewhere in the city, cultural pollution is merely an uncomfortable consequence.

Karna's latest project is establishing a cancer hospital in

Kathmandu. 'Do you know there is no oncologist in Nepal?' he asked me, as though this was just another factual illustration of how far Nepal has to travel. It was more personal than that. Karna's wife and one of his daughters had both died of cancer in 1986. They had been forced to go abroad for treatment. Those without Karna's considerable resources do not even have that option.

I cycled back along Kantipath towards Patan, two or three miles to the south, choking on the fumes from the overloaded lorries and buses. This part of Kathmandu depresses those who have known the city for a long time. Development has spread like a disease, often without planning and without any architectural sensibility. Most of the buildings are ugly and with no feeling whatever for the past; bleak cement boxes shuttered to the ground. Some have concrete frames jutting from the roof, waiting for building regulations to change so owners can add an extra storey at less cost. There are countless towns like this all over South Asia but that is little comfort in a city that was once as beautiful as Kathmandu.

I thought of Dervla Murphy's closing words in *The Waiting Land*, her account of travelling in Nepal during 1965:

Perhaps nowhere in Asia is the contrast between a dignified past and a brash, effervescent present as violent as in Nepal; and one knows that here too, eventually, the present will have its shoddy triumph. Yet even when the Nepalese way of life has been annihilated the Himalayas will remain, occasionally being invaded by high-powered expeditions but preserving an inviolable beauty to the end of time.

The present would appear to be enjoying its shoddy triumph and I wasn't even sure that the beauty of the Himalayas was so inviolable. The collapse or destruction of old houses, the spiralling real estate prices and inappropriate development aren't just aesthetically disappointing. Land designation changes and thoughtless construction are undermining the religious and cultural traditions of the Kathmandu Valley. People cannot follow many of the customs they once did because the city has effectively changed beyond recognition. I crossed the Bagmati and wearily pedalled up the hill towards Patan, my ill-maintained bike clanking and my ill-maintained lungs wheezing from the smog. Patan was the largest of the mediaeval kingdoms of the Kathmandu Valley but when the Shah dynasty was established and Kathmandu became its capital the town sagged a little in its fortunes. A traveller at the end of the nineteenth century described Patan as a city 'much too large for its inhabitants'. Now the town is bursting at the seams and the coherence of Patan's mediaeval plan is breaking up. Its Durbar Square is still enchanting, there are plenty of bahal left, the small two-storeyed houses built around a square, despite the crass development, but something is being lost here as it has been in Kathmandu. Of the three great city states of the Valley, soon only Bhaktapur will be left to remind the people of Kathmandu and Patan of the beauty they once shared.

I propped my bicycle against a wall just beyond the Patan Gate and asked around for the office of *Himal* magazine. After ten minutes spent following contradictory advice I sat down to rest and drink. Across the street was a small temple I'd walked past half a dozen times already and not noticed. Its walls sagged, its shrine was smeared with tika, scuffed and worn. Religion in Nepal is not just a ceremony or practice, it is simply one of the things you do to live, like eating or breathing. The day begins and ends with the gods, or with Buddha, and temples and shrines are sewn through the fabric of the city like jewels. We turn on breakfast television, the people of Nepal refresh their souls. Perhaps when ordinary people understand that the city's agonising changes threaten this part of their lives as well as their income from tourism or their history, there will be the kind of popular support for conservation that is needed.

Handing back my empty Coke bottle, I asked the street vendor for directions. He pointed to a man in uniform standing by a gate where I could find Kanak Mani Dixit. 'Up!' said the security guard. 'Up!' and pointed at a concrete staircase. At the screen door Kanak greeted me in an open-necked shirt and socks. I kicked my shoes off and followed him inside. *Himal* magazine, despite a narrow market and lack of investment, had managed to raise awareness not just in Nepal but throughout the Himalayan region of the problems brought by development and exponential population growth. Patan was Kanak's home and he had watched it change with horror and anger but not, it seemed, despair.

'We thought Kathmandu would stay like that forever,' he said. 'It was largely intact until around 1980 but now it's going fast. I don't mind the garbage. Tomorrow we can clear it up. What I am worried about is that Kathmandu had a unitary ambience which is lost. The Newar culture preserved something of the urban culture of India two thousand years ago. There are still parts that are old and if you preserve them you can earn tourist dollars forever.' Kanak knew where the blame lay. 'I am worried that the super-elite in Nepal has no concern for their communities, for their country. They are only really in it for themselves. Something will happen but only if the elite realise it has to. Otherwise we will become a Calcutta of the Himalaya.'

He has no shortage of ideas for turning things round, including converting some of the extant Newari houses, whose elegantly carved wooden windows and ageing brickwork characterise the Valley, into guest houses for tourists. I had visited a restaurant in Thamel housed in a restored Newari building and been impressed. Kanak talked about bed and breakfasts off Durbar Square. It is the kind of low-key, individual activity that could save the Valley's architectural heritage but wouldn't attract the kind of backing from the World Bank that a hydro-electric scheme might get. Kanak had serious doubts about the continuing aid programme. 'Any government that said to hell with foreign aid would fall the next day but it's the direction we should move in,' he said. 'As a result of aid the rich in Kathmandu get richer and with all that money sloshing about real estate prices soar. Aid hasn't been a catalyst, it's been a blunderbuss that sprays money around and removes initiative. There have been worthwhile achievements: family planning, an improvement in child mortality rates and the eradication of malaria. But if anything it's debilitated us.'

Kanak organised an exhibition in 1994 called Kathmandu, Mailo Kathmandu – *mailo* means dirty or soiled – to try and shock not just the authorities but the people themselves into recognising what was being lost. One picture struck me in particular, of a tourist photographing a pig eating garbage in Thamel. I am fond of pigs and have no objection to sharing a street with them but I could understand how pigs eating garbage could be bad for business. When Lufthansa stopped flying to Kathmandu in 1996 the reasons it cited included the pollution of the city and the build-up of rubbish on its streets.

Kanak talked of instilling pride and a sense of responsibility in the Valley's citizens, of putting a new heart into Kathmandu. 'We have no parks for our kids to play in; there is no theatre. Sure, there's corruption here but the biggest problem is that there is no socialisation in how cities are run.' The people of Kathmandu are still paying for the exploitative isolation they endured under the Ranas.

I expected to find Kanak a depressed man, able to criticise but unable to halt the Valley's decline, yet despite it all he fizzed with ideas and energy. He sat quietly for a moment and then, as though dismissing any notion of pessimism, waggled his toes and leaned forward. 'You know, we could be on the verge of something great in this city. This could be Shangri La again.'

It was already mid afternoon when I retrieved my bike but I wasn't ready to pedal back to Thamel. Instead I made the long journey to Pashupatinath, close to the airport. The temple complex on the banks of the Bagmati is a good place to look for the soul of Nepal. It is dedicated to Pashupati, literally the Lord of Beasts, a benign form of Shiva and central to the identity of the Nepalis for two millennia. Even under the Communists, official proclamations ended with the words 'May Pashupati protect us all!' Its main temple is closed to western tourists, although thousands of Indian pilgrims visit each year, but there is so much to see and experience here that it remains one of the most visited sites in the Valley. Tourists are gripped by the cremations that start each morning on the ghats on the west bank but despite their dislocating presence, their video cameras and their retinue of guides and souvenir salesmen, they cannot puncture the mood of reverence and the rhythm of life and death.

I came here again and again to sit among the small shrines on the east bank and watch the cremation ceremonies and the monkeys splashing in the Bagmati. In early February the sadhus start arriving for Shivaratri, the festival celebrating Shiva's birthday, and they offer the tourists an even more exotic target for their cameras. Most sadhus are delighted at the chance to charge a modelling fee. I left my bicycle by the ring road and walked down the dusty track to the river as the evening shadows lengthened.

'Do you want a guide?' I looked round and then down at an impossibly small man.

'No. Thank you, but no.'

'Hashish?' A diminutive hand emerged from its pocket with a huge lump of hashish, perhaps the size of a deck of cards.

'No. I'm sorry, I have no money.'

'It's okay. You come with me for nothing.'

Mahendra introduced himself and we toured the temples, visiting the hospital where wizened men and women lay, listening to the crackle of the flames from the cremation ghats. Outside in the hospital's courtyard, women were washing in a stone-clad pool. We peered into the temples of Parvati and Vishnu and looked down from a balcony as another fire was set. The dead woman's sons circled her body with the priest. Inevitably the conversation came around to our families. My daughter Rosa was eighteen months old and I missed her.

'Oh, children are such trouble.' Mahendra said, walking on again. 'My son thinks I'm an idiot. He's fourteen years old. What does he know? And then in a couple of years he will come to me

67

and say "Daddy, I want to get married. I need money." Then who will be the idiot?' He stopped by a lingam and pointed.

'What's that?' he said.

'A lingam.'

'Yes, yes. In *English*.'

'Well . . . I . . . well, I don't . . .'

'Yes?'

'Um . . . I suppose we'd say penis.' I blushed and Mahendra giggled.

'And I'd call it a cock,' he said, 'but there you go.'

Lingams are an important feature at Pashupatinath and not all of them are carved from stone. Mahendra introduced me to some sadhus standing by a small shrine. One had a monkey on his shoulders, another stood by a huge rock. I felt a nudge in my ribs and looked down. Mahendra's eyes were crossed and he held his right hand under his scrotum. Then he started hopping up and down and giggling. The sadhu by the rock looked rather cross and came over to me, his back towards Mahendra.

'If you like I will lift this stone with my penis,' he announced. 'You like?'

'Um . . .'

'It weighs over eighty kilos.'

'How much money?' He gave me a price. 'I will give you half if you promise *not* to lift that rock with your penis.' Mahendra looked rather disappointed but the sadhu seemed relieved.

'It's a hard life being a sadhu,' he said.

We walked along a little and I asked to see Arya Ghat – where the royal family and those of high caste are cremated – and the house of the dying. Here, in 1959, the writer and journalist Dom Moraes found Nepal's greatest poet Lakshmi Prasad Devkota consumed by stomach cancer and in terrible pain. 'If the god Pashupati were to come,' Devkota told him, 'I would beg him to crack my skull. Pray for Devkota that he may die.'

Early in life Devkota had earned the hatred of the Ranas for trying to open a library and, although he graduated in law, he abandoned a career to write and teach and thus spent much of his life in poverty. He wrote love poetry and epics, satire and fiction and translated between several different languages, including a Nepali edition of essayists like Hazlitt and Swift. Too much of the West's understanding of Nepal comes from western writers so perhaps someone will do the English language the return favour of translating some Nepali poetry. Devkota had a prolific output but his life was beset with political difficulties. He spent two years in exile at Benares – Nepalis always seem to go to Benares when they are exiled – but when he died Koirala was prime minister and the Ranas were gone. 'It seems to me that I was made for miracles, born for strange wonders,' Devkota once wrote and given the times he lived through – earthquake, coup d'état and then democracy – his judgement seems correct.

Mahendra and I stood in silence as a group of tourists crossed the stone-arched bridge behind us. 'And over here, in this corner,' shouted the German guide to his charges, 'you will have an excellent photo opportunity.' We scurried back across the bridge and took up station on the opposite bank.

It is a good thing that Devkota did not live to see the current state of the holy Bagmati, although he could have usefully contributed some excoriating lines on the subject. Raw sewage and garbage, effluent from the factories and pesticides have all poisoned the river. Thirty miles south of Kathmandu the water is still filthy as it flows down to the Terai through the Chobar Gorge. Sand extraction for cement works has destabilised the banks of the river and there are fears that the poisoned waters will percolate through the exposed clay and ruin the city's drinking water even more. As one environmental campaigner wrote: 'The rape of the river is almost complete.'

The city's water and sewerage system is on the verge of collapse. During the monsoon when water levels rise, the leaky pipes of Kathmandu mean that sewerage and drinking water are mixed. In a dry report for the 1995 *Alpine Journal* from a medical expedition to Everest to research the physiological effects of high altitude, the authors included a succinct paragraph on the problems facing Kathmandu. 'The management of solid waste has, to all intents and purposes, ceased. It is generally accepted that all supplies used for drinking by the local population are contaminated – as the cholera wards testify.' The supply of safe drinking water is a more basic human right than democracy, but it is something that those with money or power in Kathmandu have failed to provide. During my research in the city I had been introduced to two environmental lawyers, Prakash Sharma and Narayan Belbase. Prakash, together with another colleague, was challenging development schemes that threatened the Bagmati in the courts, trying to make what little environmental legislation there was stick, but as Prakash told me, 'We have to have political and bureaucratic commitment or things won't change.'

Of course, if tourists are careful they can avoid the terrible consequences of a poisoned water supply. The best hotels have their own filtration systems and bottled water is widely available. But pedalling back to Thamel at dusk – a perilous business given Nepali driving standards – I was reminded that air pollution in Kathmandu is inescapable. By the time I got back to the Guest House my throat was raw from the fumes and my nerves in tatters.

The problem of traffic is a very modern phenomenon in Kathmandu. In November 1950 King Tribhuvan drove out of the palace ostensibly on his way to the countryside for a picnic. But as his motorcade sped past the Indian Embassy the car he was driving and that of his sons suddenly pulled off the road and slipped through the hastily opened gates which were then promptly shut in the face of his escort. The King was seeking political asylum and his action signalled the end for the Rana dynasty. If the King tried it now he would get stuck in traffic. In 1950 the royal family were almost the only people with cars. The only way to get them into Kathmandu was in pieces on the cableway built by Chandra Shumsher and on the backs of porters.

There were few roads in the Valley and none beyond it. When John Hunt led the first successful expedition to Everest in 1953 the only way into the city was by air or on foot. Now there are more than 80,000 vehicles of all descriptions in the Valley alone and the numbers are growing at a furious rate.

Like the water supply, fuel in Kathmandu is not as pure as it might be. To improve profit margins, it is cut with cheaper kerosene somewhere between the Indian border and the gas stations. Consequently, not all the fuel is burnt by vehicles during combustion and the smog that hangs over the city is even more noxious than it might be otherwise. This, of course, is illegal but the people doing it are too powerful to stop, largely because the distribution of fuel in Nepal is the responsibility of a state-owned industry. The government had recently tried to institute tests at petrol pumps throughout the city but the station owners went on strike in protest and the government caved in.

In 1991 Narayan Belbase was set to work by the first elected government drawing up environmental legislation that would limit emissions. It was finished but had still not passed into law when the Communists took over in 1994. The new government claimed to be equally committed to its passage but when the Nepali Congress regained control a year later the legislation had still not advanced. The new government decided that after so many years Narayan would have to start again.

There is some cause for optimism. Business-owners recognise that tourism will suffer if air pollution isn't tackled and the drift away from Kathmandu to other towns in the Valley continues. An American-backed aid project has tested electric vehicles in the city for a number of years; I had cycled behind the white Safa autorickshaws humming through Naxal on their way to the south of the city. It's a neat solution, since at night Kathmandu has a surplus of electricity generated by hydro-electric plants. Local people are holding their breath – almost literally – to see whether the scheme's promise is realised. If democracy is allowed to mature, then perhaps they will begin to appreciate that the politicians they elect are required to do something other than argue with each other.

That evening, still hacking from my extended bicycle trip, I wandered out from the Guest House to a garden restaurant close by in a small walled compound. I settled down beneath a huge rubber plant tree and ordered a buffalo steak. I'd barely started eating when a young Nepali man appeared at my side.

'Would you mind very much if I sat down,' he said in beautifully accented English. The restaurant wasn't particularly full but his polite approach disarmed me. Even if he was selling something I could hardly refuse. Far from being a salesman, Chandra was simply looking for someone to talk to; while he was Nepali, he had lived most of his life in Gothenburg. Chandra's family had lived in Chitwan but when his parents died he was put into an orphange in Kathmandu at the age of six and later been adopted by a Swedish family. He was to start university in the autumn but first wanted to meet his five brothers who he hadn't seen for fourteen years. He had been staying with the eldest of the five who was working at the bus park in Tundikhel selling tickets. He had been overwhelmed at how people had greeted him – 'It's very different from Gothenburg!' – but felt a little ashamed that he had forgotten his native tongue. His family seemed genuinely pleased that he had done so well. I asked him how much he remembered of his childhood.

'I remember one occasion in Chitwan. I had been looking after my father's cow but fell asleep and it wandered off. When I couldn't find it I was afraid and hid. My brothers came looking for me and I was frightened they would be angry. But they saw me crying and said it didn't matter and hugged me.' There were tears in his eyes as he told me this. 'I need to find answers to the questions in my head about who I really am,' he said. I asked him if he would return to live in Nepal and he hesitated. 'No. I don't think so,' he replied but it was clear that he felt more confused by his trip home than he had anticipated. He had also suffered the strange surprise of discovering that his true age was two years more than he had thought. I wondered whether the orphanage had lied to ensure that his Swedish parents would take him.

In the lobby of the Guest House the desk manager was watching television along with guests from almost every cricketing nation on earth. An angular American couple in tartan shorts paused briefly to shake their heads at the screen.

'There's a message for you,' said the desk manager, without taking his eyes from the game. Sri Lanka were playing and for some reason the hopes of this small, troubled country dominated by its vast neighbour struck a chord in the minds of Nepalis. More than anything, the desk manager said, he wanted Sri Lanka to win.

I took the note up to my room, the starched, threadbare sheets, the dripping shower-head, the smell of camphor, the tiny wooden chair at a narrow desk buried under trekking gear and cameras. Pasang Nima had written to say he would be coming tomorrow. This visit to Kathmandu was almost at an end.

Next morning I sat in the shadows of the courtyard drinking water and mud brown coffee. The Yugoslavs were in their regular spot drinking beer, waiting for their permission and their money. The Belgian, dressed inexplicably in a white kurta and pyjama ensemble, was holding a meeting with a Nepali couple. The Americans who had been stoking their dreams and firing their imaginations were about to ignite, their bags packed and propped against their chairs.

Pasang marched past the tables, his lips pursed and a pair of sunglasses hiding his eyes. He looked briskly round and then came over, the bulky figure of Dachhiri slightly behind him. The waiter shuffled over and they swigged quietly on bottles of Fanta. Dachhiri, untypically for a Sherpa, is heavily built with a barrel chest and a thick belly straining against his t-shirt. His small, wide-apart eyes, his thick, coarse hair and tiny, cupped ears give him the appearance of an amiable bear. But Dachhiri's most striking feature is his mega-watt grin, a smile of such dazzling brilliance that whenever it burst out from behind a cloud my lips would inevitably spread upwards too. At moments of intense hilarity, Dachhiri would cover his mouth to laugh – 'Sheesh! Sheesh! Sheesh!' – as though saving us from the worst excesses of his glittering smile.

Pasang was older and had an air of gravitas and competence. This could give way to a shy charm which fair-skinned women seemed obliged to encourage. He had organised my trek the year before, hiring Dachhiri and another Sherpa called Pemba. All three men came from the same village in Solu, the Sherpa region just south of the Khumbu. All were equally bad at cards which was an important advantage in hiring them. After five weeks with Dachhiri I finally discovered they were also cousins.

After returning from Tibet and the north side of Everest, I had travelled west to the Annapurna range with Pemba. We spent a week tramping around the most heavily trekked area in Nepal, though the season was now almost over and so the trails were empty. He used his good looks as a passport. When I asked him how he picked the lodges we slept in each night he grinned and told me that he chose those run by the most beautiful girls. He would sit in the kitchen and catch their eye as they made breakfast.

'I think I will marry a Gurung girl,' he said as we walked along the trail. I was slightly surprised at a Sherpa contemplating marriage into another tribe.

'You won't marry a Sherpani?'

'No way. They talk too much. And nag you. Gurung girls are very beautiful. Not like Sherpa girls.'

He would then start singing in his light tenor voice, a Sherpa song or one of the facile western pop songs he was devoted to, often something hopelessly out of date like Boney M. 'Brown girl in the ring, tra-la-la-la-laaa!' At regular intervals he would drop his sack under a tree and perch on a stone bench to smoke one of his foul Nepali cigarettes. His passion for tobacco was just one of many reasons that made Pemba a mediocre Buddhist and, at the same time, delightful company. Apparently, the Sherpas have a saying that if you smoke you will reborn in hell with an inextinguishably burning tree in your stomach. Pemba puffed away regardless.

I had tried to reach him through Pasang to ask him to come with me to the Khumbu but he had gone already, back to the Annapurna range with a group of French trekkers. Dachhiri, however, was available. He seemed uncomfortable sitting outside the Guest House, looking round impassively at the other tourists and keeping his smile well hidden. I didn't know then Dachhiri at all well and his English seemed less accomplished than Pemba's. Pasang relayed my questions but Dachhiri would just nod and sip his Fanta. His distant manner was unexpected and unnerving considering that we would spend at least a month together.

'Is he okay with this?' I asked Pasang.

'Yeah, sure. No problem.' I had no other option.

In the afternoon I cycled to Durbar Marg and the Yak and Yeti Hotel. There was a reception planned for an American expedition to Everest led by David Breashears. He and his team planned to make a film about the mountain shot in the vast IMAX format. As a journalist, I felt obliged to attend any function where I could drink and meet influential people at no cost.

The hotel is based upon another redundant Rana palace, although it has been extensively improved and enlarged. A two-night visit would cost the average Nepali a year's income. I hung onto this thought throughout the afternoon as the scale of the hotel's luxury grew more appealing. After chaining my bike in the car park, I walked up the hotel's steps. A brand new Landcruiser pulled up. On the driver's door were stencilled the words Agro-enterprise and Technology Systems Project. The Yak and Yeti is home to the Nepali branch of the World Bank, housed in air-conditioned comfort upstairs from where the family who once lived here took dinner. The dining tables are arranged on balconies around a sunken floor which had once been filled with water. A stage forms the back of the room from where the guests were entertained. On the ceiling is an incongruous zodiac painted in garish colours and on the walls the portrait of a fleshy and rather cruel Rana prime minister. The bank's carpeted offices and the ghastly excesses of Rana interior design seemed equally unreal.

In the garden of the Yak and Yeti I joined the Yugoslavs who were queuing to be introduced to the party's hosts. The hotel manager naturally assumed that I was one of them and so I spent much of the afternoon convincing people I wasn't Serbian. Breashears was keen to invest his film with the kind of depth that only experts can bring and so the party was full of them. I was introduced to Roger Bilham, the expedition's geologist, who had recently been issuing grave warnings about the imminence and probable consequences of the next great earthquake to hit Nepal. He was concerned that the authorities hadn't fully grasped the implications of his research. The general ignorance of building codes in Kathmandu and elsewhere will have tragic consequences. Roger had also been doing some work in the Khumbu and warned me that one of the most popular mountains in the region was under threat.

'Ama Dablam is going to fall over,' he said. It had never appealed to me as an objective but I was still alarmed.

'When?'

'Some time in the next four million years.'

'I'd better get on with it then.'

There were a number of anthropologists and environmentalists who looked on from a distance at the swaggering mountaineers. I recognised a woman I had met during a visit to the Kathmandu Environmental Education Project and who had lived for several years with the Sherpas. We discussed the role of KEEP, a body that was brimming with good intentions but was so difficult to find that only those already aware of the impact trekkers and tourists were having ever visited it. It was those with no interest in the issue who were most likely to add to the problem. Short of making a lecture on reducing their impact a compulsory requirement on their visa applications, it was difficult to see what could be done. She and those in her company were all agreed on one thing, that the Everest and Annapurna areas were already lost to tourism and that visitors should be kept away from more pristine areas or made to pay heavily. I couldn't help wondering for whose benefit – the local people, the government or the anthropologists.

The American and Yugoslav expeditions weren't the only climbers at the party. The Mexican Carlos Carsolio was there with two of his four brothers, all of whom climb, gossiping about a well-known mountaineer whose ambition regularly outstripped her capabilities. By the spring of 1996 Carsolio had climbed thirteen of the fourteen 8000-metre peaks, a high-altitude collection managed by only three others at that time. His remaining peak was Manaslu, just to the east of the Annapurna range and he intended linking up with other Everest climbers there after they had completed their climb. Seeing the different brands of expert – climber, scientist (social or otherwise) and environmentalist – gathered together was intriguing. They were all here for broadly similar reasons and had in common a passion for the same range of mountains. And yet there was an undercurrent of mutual suspicion that kept the groups largely apart. I knew Carsolio had a genuine respect for the Sherpas he had climbed with and a deep affection for the countries he visited but there is undeniably an exploitative quality to climbing big mountains, however small or sensitive the team. Professional climbers earn their living describing their own achievements, while those with a more long-term or scientific purpose can claim some benefit to mankind other than the realisation of ambition. It was clear, however, that they were prone to the same jealousies and quarrels.

I found myself talking to Brot Coburn who had lived for many years in Nepal, working initially for the Peace Corps in the early 1970s and later on a number of rural development projects. He had published a collection of photographs of an old Gurung woman he had lodged with together with her views and understanding of the world in a book called *Nepali Aama*. I asked him about the British writer Charlie Pye-Smith whom Coburn had guided to Namche Bazar during his research into aid projects for his excellent *Travels in Nepal*, a book whose comprehensible analysis of the success or otherwise of aid in Nepal had achieved considerable success. He told me the story of how Pye-Smith had to be lowered down the rocky slopes below Namche after he became overcome with vertigo. I then foolishly suggested that I was trying to do something similar but from a mountaineer's point of view. Coburn curled his lip.

'Climbers? I'll tell you about climbers, man. I went to this *Rock and Ice* magazine hero worship thing about the mountain environment. They brought this Rinpoche on the stage, this holy man surrounded by all these self-important climbers. And Reinhold Messner, he couldn't come because he'd bust his leg. So what does he do? He sends a video of himself. He's sitting in a chair with this leg in plaster pointing at the camera and he's saying: "Ve must do zis and ve must do zat for the environment." What does he know about the environment? What do *I* know about the environment? I mean, I've only lived here for *seventeen* years.'

I assumed he meant this to indicate that people shouldn't make conclusions without first spending a lot of time in the field, which was interesting, although if he expected people who make decisions to wait quite so long I was sure he would be disappointed.

'Doug Scott, man. He wrote this piece on portering in Himal. I write about one letter a year to that magazine. I let a lot – and I mean a *lot* – of things go but sometimes I am so *flabbergasted*,' at this he clutched his forehead and staggered around so that those not yet watching looked around, 'that I *have* to write a letter. He goes on about minimum wages and unions for porters working with tourists. But porters tell me, "Don't pay us more for tourist work! It screws up the market!" Like, ninety-eight per cent of portering is for the local people, not tourists.'

I asked him about the porters who had died in the Khumbu and elsewhere the previous autumn in a sudden and terrible storm.

Many of them were inadequately clad and uninsured, working for western tourists at altitudes they wouldn't otherwise visit.

'Well, that's a consequence of trekking with the Japanese,' he said and moved away, a little ragged from the afternoon's drinking. He may have been drunk but he also had a point. To judge what should or shouldn't be done in Nepal simply on the basis of a mountaineering career was superficial in the extreme. This wasn't what Scott was doing. He cared passionately about the local people he met on expeditions, gave time at his lectures to discuss the problems they faced and had with his Specialist Trekking Co-Operative tried to offer reasonable wages and contribute to the communities his clients visited. I had heard plenty of stories about porters being underpaid, of tips being diverted into the pockets of agents, and climbers like Doug who defended the porters from this kind of exploitation.

But I knew as well as Coburn that there are so many other climbers whose photographs of locals punctuated their articles and lectures to break up all those shots showing what heroes they'd been with a little local culture. Anthropologists and environmentalists must have a strong suspicion that most climbers and trekkers see local people as a human backdrop to their adventures. I almost admired the climber who told me that if he could go to the mountain in a bubble to avoid disease and arguments with porters, he would. At least he was being honest.

Breashears' project would cost $4.5 million, more than five times what is being spent on the electric vehicle project aimed at reducing Kathmandu's air pollution. The climbers included a handsome American and two beautiful women, one Spanish, the other Japanese, to broaden the movie's appeal. I didn't blame Breashears for covering the bases like this, but I couldn't help wondering why things always worked out this way.

As dusk fell I chained my bicycle just outside the vast stupa at Boudha and sat on a step near the entrance. A huge circle of people turned around the white dome, pulling at the prayer wheels set in the white walls surrounding its plinth. The rich scent of butter lamps and incense hung in the warm air. From the square harmika that sat on the dome, the eyes of Buddha looked out over the heads of the people, north to the mountains and Tibet, south to the plains of India, west to the city of Kathmandu and east to Nagarkot. I was surprised to recognise individuals in the stream that passed. A tall, elegant Tibetan woman in an emerald suit counted off beads on her rosary as she whispered the mantra. The day before she had sold me an airline ticket to the mountains. Then she passed the Boudha Gate and disappeared again into the mass of men and women, old and young, some prostrating themselves, many talking and laughing, some arguing, some dropping money on the maroon robes of the monks sitting cross-legged on the flagstones. They all turned on their mandala, their compass, their cross, a mixture of tribes but all one people, moving at their own pace but in one direction. There were few white faces left, the souvenir shops were closed. At six the sun left the golden tiers that crown the stupa and the darkness settled more heavily on Boudha. Only then, as the brown faces seemed to fade into the shadows, did I stand and brush the dust from my clothes and walk slowly into the circle.

CHAPTER FIVE

Rebel without a yak

Before dawn I locked my door at the Guest House for the last time and walked out into the deserted streets of Thamel. In the grey half-light they seemed more than ever like a theatre set. Empty of people and noiseless, I felt that if I walked too heavily, the buildings might shake. A single Toyota sat across from the immigration office and I hauled my rucksack into its boot. The city was drifting awake, mists clinging to the narrow streets as the taxi bounced and rattled along the back route towards the airport. A heavy log burned in the middle of a narrow lane and two men squatted behind it, holding their palms towards the glowing embers. The cab-driver shouted at them but they had the bovine look of the cows that ambled through the traffic on Kantipath and didn't stir. We got out of the car and dragged the log to the side of the road and the two shuffled after it. The taxi stopped again at the small temple at Baghwati Bahal in the heart of Naxal. A lot of Sherpas live here year round, moving from their villages in the mountains to be close to the trekking agencies who hire them. Dachhiri rented a small bedsit just to the north in Harigau for eight or nine dollars a month. I waited in the taxi half asleep, watching women fetching water, a young girl bringing a tray with flowers and tika for the shrine. Two men wearing topis passed the temple, touching their heads and hearts as they did so. An old woman stopped to face the points of the compass as she held her hands to her chest in a namaste. It was like a dream. Dachhiri loped out of the shadows with a huge smile on his face. '*Jaun.*' he said. 'Let's go.'

The airport had recently opened a new domestic terminal. I'd been rather fond of the old one which had lost half the roof and was in an execrable state of repair. Waiting for the early morning mist to lift and release a dozen stranded flights, monks and trekkers, Sherpas and aid workers would jostle for position. On one occasion I found myself sitting next to the pilot who would be flying our helicopter when the weather improved.

'When are we leaving?' I asked.

'Absolutely no idea,' he said in a pukka voice and then pulled at his collar. 'Gosh, it's warm in here.'

That chaos was gone now. In its place was a barn-like check-in hall and a shiny new lounge with plastic seats that weren't broken. When the desks at the front of the hall opened I was relieved to see the old entropy returning. A scrum of passengers pushed their luggage at the security man with his stick of chalk, while a larger crowd who had no obvious reason for being at the airport at all, not even to beg, surrounded them to watch. In the queue ahead of me for the Royal Nepal flight to Lukla were four Americans with gigantic rucksacks. The three men all wore bandannas and sunglasses, even in the gloom of the terminal. One who wore a trimmed goatee beard held a video camera to his eye and tracked across the hall, hoovering up the scene for later consumption. They spoke in monosyllables – 'Whoah! Hunh? Sure!' – and marked their ground with the smell of self-confidence. This buoyant mood continued even after we were airborne and the small twin-engine Otter slid and bucked through the air. Vast terraced hillsides drifted past the window. Everywhere I looked I could see smashed aeroplanes and me in them.

'Phaphlu!' said Dachhiri, pointing at a village and its airstrip below us. Most Sherpas are very Buddhist about flying and Dachhiri was no exception, sitting contentedly with his hands folded across his stomach and two tufts of cotton wool poking out of his ears to block the roar of the engines. Crossing the terrain that rushed beneath us on foot would – and later did – take days. John Hunt's team in 1953 needed to start walking from Bhaktapur a few miles east of Kathmandu but over the years expeditions to Everest have progressively got a little closer before starting to walk, first on the road to Kodari, then on the spur road to Jiri and then by aircraft to Lukla. It saves time but the leisurely approach is more thoughtful, it offers time to adjust and prepare. It engenders respect.

Suddenly the monosyllables of the four Americans became more urgent. 'Whoah! No way! Maaan!' I followed their line of vision through the windows of the narrow cockpit. We were flying straight at a green mountainside. Then we banked, sharply to the right, and were flying at another mountainside. My stomach dropped.

'There,' said Dachhiri. 'Lukla.'

I could see a grey strip carved into the mountainside which seemed impossibly short and steep. I imagine that pilots landing on the tilted deck of an aircraft carrier have a similar impression. I joined in with my own monosyllables.

'Aarghhh! Nooooo!' The plane sank lower until the end of the runway and the control tower, such as it was, were far above our heads. Wisps of cloud blew between us and the village, confusing me still further. I was so gripped by terror that I screwed my eyes shut . The pilot dropped the plane down lightly onto the runway and we bumped across the gravel and dirt. The engines roared and then stopped. I opened my eyes.

Dachhiri was already on his feet and those waiting for the return flight to Kathmandu crowded round the door. Still disoriented with adrenaline, I hauled my bag clear of the aircraft and followed Dachhiri up the steep slope behind the airstrip. Presumably this would be the final resting place of any aircraft that overshot the runway.

We stopped at a small lodge overlooking the village and sat on a low wall outside to watch the plane turn and take off. The airstrip had been carved out of the hillside in 1964 to bring materials in for the construction of schools, part of the work of Ed Hillary's Himalayan Trust. A by-product of its construction and improvement was to open Lukla for commercial flights, shortening the long approach from Jiri to Everest Base Camp by seven or eight days. For years after, flights to Lukla were the monopoly of the state airline but in the early 1990s private airlines were approved and a number now flew Russian Mi 17 helicopters to Lukla. These were less likely to be cancelled or delayed by bad weather, a regular problem for propeller aircraft in the cloudy valley below Lukla. The village had become a centre for trekkers with porters and yak herders touting for business and a rash of new lodges built to profit from the activity. In the days when bad weather might delay flights, hundreds would be stranded, adding considerably to the income of villagers. The development was hardly attractive, with a straggle of new lodges reaching out along the trail in the direction of Namche Bazar, but many had come to rely on the income it generated.

The establishment of private airlines and their use of helicopters had proved a mixed blessing for the people of Lukla. Their ceiling and power allowed the Russian helicopters to use the airstrip above Namche Bazar at Shyangboche. This had been built in 1972 to service an ill-starred Japanese venture to open a luxury hotel overlooking the Imja Khola with a distant view of Everest. The project had proved a failure, largely because of its cost, the high altitude – one tourist had died on the hotel's steps – and the area's unpredictable weather.

But now helicopters were flying to Shyangboche not with wealthy tourists but trekkers, thus shortening even more the traditional trek to Everest. As a consequence the lodge-owners in Lukla had suffered a dramatic loss of income. They felt that Sherpas from the upper Khumbu held too much influence in Kathmandu. Ang Tshering, a Sherpa from Khumjung who owns Asian Airlines, was planning to build a large lodge in his village, despite the chronic lack of water in the immediate area and the protests of Sherpas in Namche Bazar, since Khumjung is close to the airstrip while Namche lies at the bottom of a long, steep slope.

Sherpas in Lukla had already organised a demonstration which closed the airport to bring attention to their plight and would hold a similar protest soon after I left. The disparity in how the new wealth brought by tourism was distributed had created new jealousies and exacerbated old ones. My acquaintance from KEEP had been quite frank on the subject: 'Ang Tshering is a bastard.' Reluctant to do anything that might suppress the growth of tourism in the Khumbu, the Kathmandu authorities seemed content to allow the free market to take its course. Intelligent, alternatives, like a premium on flights to Shyangboche, would keep tourists spending money in the area longer and spread that income more widely but these suggestions have so far not been heard.

The Twin Otter started its engines and roared off down the runway, swooping into the grey void. As the dust from its engines settled, the door of the lodge opened and its owner appeared with tea. Dawa Gelgin Sherpa was from a village in Solu but ran the lodge in the season for the trekking company that employed Dachhiri most regularly. Pasang had flown in the day before to arrange equipment and porters for a group of English schoolboys he was taking up to Khumjung and we sat around playing cards. Like many in Nepal, Pasang and Dachhiri had developed a passion for a game similar to whist. We sat on stools and played a few hands but my head was confused by the moderate increase in altitude and I was soon dumped from the game as the worst loser. Dachhiri covered his mouth and laughed as I stood up to let a new victim take my place.

One of Dawa's four sons sat outside doing his homework. The eldest boy was away at boarding school in Kathmandu. Dawa himself was preparing lunch and I stood outside the kitchen drinking tea. Occasionally the airstrip's siren would sound and the card-players would pick up their stools and rush inside, slamming the door behind them. A distant sound of rotor blades thrashing in the thin air would grow louder and louder and then the fat body of a helicopter would swing into the head of the valley. As it landed clouds of dust would rush towards the lodge and then slowly settle. At that point everybody would move back outside.

There are four of five flights each day from Kathmandu and elsewhere to interrupt the cards and chase the small boys from their games of cricket on the runway.

Dawa's youngest son of about two years had grown bored watching the adults playing cards and worked himself into a rage. It was left to another boy, possibly another of Dawa's, to try and quieten him. I watched in case Sherpas had secret methods of subduing a frantic toddler that I could use on mine. The elder boy began by comforting him, hugging him to his chest, then laughing at him until the child lay on the floor and kicked out in a full-scale tantrum. A whole range of tactics followed, from ignoring him to shouting at him. None of them worked. Eventually, the older boy gave up and walked away and the toddler grew exhausted from his screaming and went to sleep in the sun. No insights there, then, I thought and went back to my tea. As I stepped over him on my way to lunch I noticed a small pendant around his neck framing a picture of the Dalai Lama.

Dawa served up the first of many plates of spinach, dahl and rice. A spoon was produced for me but Dachhiri and the others gathered lumps of rice in the fingers of their right hand and soaked them in the dahl before eating them. I was glad of the spoon. Being left-handed, I found the social requirement of eating with my right difficult to remember. (I had met a Sherpa in Pokhara once eating with his left hand. He sat alone and didn't welcome my expression of solidarity. So I stick to using cutlery.)

In the afternoon we picked up our rucksacks and started on the three-hour walk to Phakding, a little lower in altitude and further along the trail to Namche. There was hardly anyone else about, certainly no other tourists. Spring was just beginning to sweep up the valley of the Dudh Kosi with the lowest rhododendrons in bloom and fat white flowers on the hyacinth trees. The trail was bordered by thousands of primulas and the tall blue pines that leave the air heavy with their scent. After a couple of hours we stopped at a lodge for tea and slept in the sun. A middle-aged woman in her apron moved quietly around her house, while her husband washed clothes under a tap by a low barn.

Above my head the elegant fluted peak of Kusum Kanguru – a faintly comic name – ducked in and out of cloud. The mountain is one of eighteen picked from the thousands within Nepal designated as trekking peaks. The term suggests they are a straightforward walk but Kusum Kanguru is anything but. The idea behind this designation was to open lower, less popular mountains to more people by cutting back the amount of bureaucracy involved and so reducing the cost to expeditions. It was a good idea but it hadn't worked properly. Administration of the scheme was given to the Nepal Mountaineering Association and not the tourism ministry which usually issues climbing permits. There are scores of mountains that could be added to the list but there has been resistance to extending the role of the NMA and so nothing is done. A useful source of tourist revenue remains undeveloped.

By the time we reached Phakding I had started to feel light-headed and nauseous. I stepped onto the day's last suspension bridge across the Dudh Kosi and as it sank beneath my weight I felt my knees sinking with it. Dachhiri waited politely on the far side as I struggled to catch him up and we went inside the lodge. Sitting in the kitchen drinking tea, I thought optimistically about how I wasn't going to be ill. Two boys were making rice and dahl, while a young girl with an elegantly straight back and bossy manner made disparaging remarks about both her brother and the impossibly white tourist with his head on the table. Two Sherpas arrived, bringing the owner and his wife into the kitchen. They had a letter from Kathmandu to deliver and while the lodge-owner read it to his wife, she poured them all some chang. (This is the local beer made from rice or millet with a delectable sweet-and-sour flavour. It varies in quality and strength from household to household but is preferable to Coke and other sweet drinks. Chang features a lot in this story.) A third man, a Rai from down the valley, arrived to buy chang and was soon as drunk as the first two. My head started to spin and my eyes smarted from the kitchen fire's smoke. The lodge-owner's wife crushed a pan of boiled potatoes and then kneaded them into dough, while keeping up a hilarious monologue of which I understood nothing in a voice that was flint-edged and shrill. The husband took over and she was free to continue entertaining her guests. He would look up from to time to time to smile at his wife and offer his own quick-witted responses.

The banter was typical of many Sherpa marriages. There is no sense here of a man possessing his wife either economically or sexually. In fact, sex is not the central force in Sherpa marriages that it can be in many western countries. Marriages work through a sense of common purpose and friendship. Adultery happens – Sherpas are wonderfully curious, as a number of trekkers and climbers can testify – but is not the emotional disaster it often is in Europe or North America. Divorce also happens but not usually as a consequence of adultery. It is more simply that if a couple don't get on, then they separate, living in the same village on more or less good terms. Children can stay with either parent and, since village life is generally supportive, separations are not fraught with social consequences. It would be wrong to present Sherpa familial relations as ideal; they have problems just like the rest of us. But a strong sense of mutual respect and an impression of two people working to a common end were recurring elements in almost every Sherpa household I spent time in.

After staring blankly at a bowl of chicken soup for half an hour I carefully laid the spoon down and crawled into my sleeping bag in a dormitory upstairs. Some time in the night I awoke to the immediate premonition that something nasty was about to take place. Dachhiri snored happily on the next bed. Turning over, my hand fell on our aluminium cooking pot and almost at once I filled it with what was left of my lunch. Carefully placing the lid on top of the pan, I rolled over and went back to sleep.

Dachhiri shook my shoulder and looked in my face anxiously.

'You're very white,' he said. 'No blood. Heesh-heesh.' I struggled upright and looked out of the window. Black shadows were crawling down the hillside opposite into the depths of the valley, the trees lighting up as the sun touched them. I could barely think, let alone move. Dachhiri held up a cup of tea and I took it, along with a variety of powders and pills from my first-aid kit. Outside the air was still crisp and the ground hard from the frost. I picked up my rucksack and struggled after Dachhiri who was already some distance down the track.

I drifted through the next few hours as though through a dream, always seeing Dachhiri's thick legs and rucksack ahead of me. Just beyond a small barn a little girl looked up from a shockingly green pile of excrement she was in the process of laying down to smile a hello. A bubble of snot pulsed from her nostril as she breathed, her skirt in her hands. A mother walked towards us from the opposite direction, her hair tied up with a scarf whose end trailed behind her in the slight breeze. At first I thought the child on her back was screaming, then I realised that the woman was singing a high-pitched lullaby. At a small village called Benkar I lay down exhausted outside a lodge and watched the waterfall in a gorge above the houses cool the damp green moss on the rocks behind it. Dachhiri emerged from the house with more tea. I began to feel stronger.

The trail climbed up to the village of Chomoa and the Hatago Lodge, once owned and run by a Japanese called Mr Hagayuki who had lived as an illegal immigrant in Nepal for many years until the authorities got around to deporting him. I never found out what prompted them to do this after so many years. Charlie Pye-Smith had stayed there on his way to Namche Bazar almost ten years before and described the garden Mr Hagayuki had planted as the most beautiful he had seen in the Himalaya. The orchard and vegetable gardens still seemed to be thriving, despite his absence.

Another steep climb brought us to the entrance of the Sagarmatha National Park. Gaps among the trees just before the park boundary were strong evidence of how development of the Khumbu had damaged the area's ecology. This was the worst example of deforestation I would see while trekking in the Khumbu, although further south in Solu on the trek back from Lukla to Jiri the damage was much more extensive and little was being done to correct it. The determining factor is the park authority which regulates the management of the Khumbu's forests. People building lodges had come outside the boundary to cut trees for construction which was why the damage was so bad just here above the village of Monjo. There has historically been considerable friction between Sherpas and the park's managers who were heavily prescriptive in their early attempts to control deforestation. Since then the authorities have learned to work more closely with established local forestry practices. The whole subject of forestry is highly complex and controversial and evidence can and has been used to suggest that tourists are wicked, national government is wicked or that 'ancient' Sherpa forestry management practices – known as *shinggi nawa* – are not so ancient and were probably introduced by the Rana regime in the nineteenth century. Anyone who has an urge to understand the maintenance of this crucial resource has no shortage of material to go to. No environment or culture in the world has been picked over like the Khumbu.

It is clear that the nationalisation of the forests after the Rana regime fell had some negative effect on the Khumbu, but that this effect has been exaggerated. It is also clear that the Sherpas themselves started using a lot more wood in the 1960s and 1970s, before large numbers of tourists arrived, because their trading habits which took them away from the Khumbu for as much as five months during the coldest time of the year were disrupted when the Chinese invasion of Tibet closed the border. Ironically, news of the decision to establish a national park prompted many Sherpas to cut trees in large numbers because they feared access would be severely restricted in future years. Their fears were realised when in the early 1980s, soon after the establishment of the park, new regulations that banned all tree-felling, even lopping of branches, were enforced by a Nepalese army unit. There were those in the park's administration who understood that such draconian measures would alienate local people and the New Zealand advisors who helped in the park's establishment tried hard to include Sherpas in its management, consulting widely at village meetings and training Khumbu Sherpas in conservation and park management.

Part of the problem has been that the term 'national park' means different things to different people. In Nepal, to the Sherpas, it meant parks like Chitwan in the Terai or Rara in the far west of the country where people had been cleared from their homes. People establishing the parks had in mind such models as the Yellowstone in the United States where natural preservation is paramount. This may work in wilderness areas with no or very few local inhabitants but could not possibly in a region as settled and developed as the Khumbu where every scrap of land that can be used has been for the benefit of people. This concept of conservation and development is something more commonly understood in England and Wales since national parks there have had to wrestle with these problems since their inception.

The revolution in 1990 gave fresh impetus to Sherpas who wanted to re-establish their rights to managing land and forestry. The local panchayats were dissolved and two development committees, each covering several villages, were established to replace them. These changes also coincided with the appointment of a new chief warden for the park, Surya Bahadur Pandey, who proved sympathetic to established Sherpa ways of land management. He oversaw a range of changes which in effect created a two-tier system of control which reinstated shinggi nawa at a local level but left final authorisation with the park. The Himalayan Trust has established nurseries in the Khumbu and the Worldwide Fund for Nature has started work on improving those areas like Monjo that have suffered because they are just outside the boundary. These changes have improved the outlook greatly. What has become clear, however, is that nothing can be done for the long term without the co-operation of local people. At the same time, the importance of the environment to their economic future has to be stressed. Trekkers come to the Khumbu because it is beautiful and the income they provide is very sensitive to its maintenance. I was reminded of the continuing tensions between national and local opinion as I handed over the few hundred rupees permit fee to the park official. Where this money goes and what it is used for I still don't fully understand but I felt sure that it wasn't all going to the maintenance of the park.

From outside the office there was a burst of shouting and a German in his late forties appeared in the doorway, closely followed by a strutting, moustachioed soldier carrying a sten gun that looked like it was last fired in Burma in 1945.

'These idiots!' the German said to me. I saw his hands had been tied behind his back with red string. 'I know what all this is about. It was the pictures I took in Kathmandu, wasn't it? You're out to get me.' The German had been arrested coming out of the park with a video camera for which he lacked a permit. He would now be returned to Namche Bazar where there was a small garrison and the headquarters of the park.

His girlfriend, blond and severely beautiful, came into the office and stood a little behind him. There was blood on her hand and I asked if the soldier had injured her. She shook her head and turned her hand over and I saw that one of her fingers was notched, as though a wedge had been cut from it, almost to the bone. She had a voice that bled indifference. 'You know, it doesn't hurt me,' she said, looking at her finger as though it were a specimen.

Dachhiri, who looked at me and shrugged at this further illustration of European strangeness, led the way down the hill, back to the mint green waters of the Dudh Kosi and the flowering pink rhododendrons. Even relatively minor changes in altitude brought a change in the density and type of forest. It was as though you could move through place and time, from summer to spring, simply by walking up hills.

Ahead of us was the long climb to Namche Bazar, 700 metres in gain to an altitude of more than 3400 metres, and with my heavy sack it was hard work. There was a dramatic suspension bridge to begin with, whose boards had rotted badly. I could see the river rushing beneath where the wood had gone completely and the whole structure swayed alarmingly. Suddenly it began to bounce as well and I grabbed the thick wire that supported it to steady myself. Looking behind me I saw Dachhiri jumping up and down.

'Bridge not so good,' he shouted over the roar of the water. Dachhiri's English may have been limited, although not nearly as much as my Nepali, but he used what he had with considerable ingenuity. Things that were good – lodges, food, bridges – were ''s okay'. Things that were adequate were 'not so good, not so bad'. Things that were truly desperate and threatened disease or catastrophe were 'not so good'. His assessments were almost always correct. My biggest problem was keeping up with him. Dachhiri was formidably strong and loved to be on the move. On the long climb to Namche he would wait at a bend in the track as I gasped after him to greet me with a comment like 'I love to walk,' or 'Not so far now.' At the apex of a bend he pointed to a small subsidiary track and said 'Everesh!' I followed him for twenty yards and sure enough beyond a wooded ridge the black triangle of the mountain appeared, a long streak of snow blowing from its distant summit like spittle in the wind.

Finally, just as my weakened body seemed on the verge of calling it a day, we came over a rise and I found myself on the fringes of Namche Bazar, a town I had visited second-hand dozens of times before. I felt I knew it already. Bill Tilman was one of the first people from the West to see it and with his precise intelligence offered this impression of the town in *Nepal Himalaya*:

Namche Bazar lies at about eleven thousand feet on the ridge between the Dudh Kosi and the Bhote Kosi, facing westwards across the valley to the peak of Kwangde. The houses are detached as if the owners were men of substance. There are about thirty of these whitewashed, two-storeyed houses, with low-pitched shingle roofs. The ground floor serves as stables and stores, while above is the one long living room, with an open fire and clay stove against one wall, wooden shelves for fine copper ware and cheap china on another, and large trellised window frames set with five or six small panes of glass.

In several interviews I had read with Ed Hillary, he described the town as having been changed utterly by tourism and I was expecting to be disappointed. But the town's position, set in a huge natural amphitheatre with a stupa where the stage would be, gives a dramatic appeal which no amount of development could alter. There are more houses now than when Tilman came but not many more and they are constructed in similar fashion, although most now have metal roofs in place of the old wooden shingles. Some of the new lodges are three storeys, but there are plenty of old three-storey houses in Solu, two or three days' walk to the south. Few if any in the centre of town have a lower storey used as a barn any more but that is not to say that their owners don't have animals elsewhere. There was some garbage on the streets, but not a great deal and certainly less than I'd seen in towns of comparable size in other mountainous areas of Nepal.

Dachhiri led the way down a narrow, flag-stoned street, to the Kala Pattar Lodge – ''s okay' – and ducked through the low doorway. The Kala Pattar is a substantial building with three floors, granite walls, and rough pine beams and window frames. There was a fluorescent tube lighting the dining room and a tape machine blasting out Hindi music. Rugs on the walls and benches softened the room's appearance. Out of the window I could see other houses spreading round the hillside, the prayer flags and white trimming on the windows giving the village the appearance of a ship at sea, straining under the constant breeze.

In the mud enclosure at the back of the hotel a dozen men were hard at work building an extension, dressing stones and planing wood without ever seeming to stop. Until darkness fell, the sound of hammer on chisel on rock tapped away like a noisy clock. On the other side of the village, another lodge was nearing completion at a cost of some $25,000 for land and construction. I cannot imagine what the cost will be even in twenty years' time.

The only other guest was an Israeli who had alarmingly bucked teeth and the type of sunglasses which clip onto spectacles and can be levered up. This is how he always wore them. His guide was a Magar from Jiri called Rudra and he and Dachhiri compared notes in the way all Nepalis do, not just Sherpas: 'Where have you come from? Where are you going?' Always the talk was of movement in a nation that still walks pretty much everywhere.

The lodge was owned by one of the wealthier Sherpa families, people who had benefited most from the influx of tourists. Only a few hundred visited Namche in the early 1970s. Now more than ten thousand come through each year. In the kitchen, a young Sherpani was making tea and I asked her name. Dachhiri and the Magar looked at me, then at her and collapsed in laughter. 'Her name is Mayar,' said Dachhiri. 'That means love. Heesh-heesh-heesh.' She blushed, tutted loudly and spoke rapidly to Dachhiri in the Sherpa's own language before disappearing back into her kitchen. I decided to go for a walk.

Out on the street, two men were playing dice, smacking the tumbler down on a round leather pallet before an engrossed crowd of a dozen men. Another two picked up badminton rackets and batted a shuttlecock over the heads of chickens scratching in dirt. A sign outside the café next door to the Kala Pattar read Hermann Helmers Bäckerei und Konditorei. Inside two Japanese drank cappuccinos and ate fresh doughnuts. A horse grazed on hay spread over a mud bank opposite. Men in baseball caps, often wearing clothes with labels like Levi's and Patagonia, drifted through the streets. Sherpas are better off than the Rai and other tribes who fill the streets on Saturdays during the weekly market. Few Sherpas from the Khumbu earn their living carrying loads for trekkers, although this is what most in the West believe them to do. Sherpas still act as porters for climbing expeditions, something which is comparatively well paid, but portering along the trails is left to Tamangs and other tribes.

The fame of their association with early Everest expeditions and their proximity to the mountains are not the only reasons for the success of the Sherpas. They have an inherent ability to trade and much of their income came from this activity when they were still allowed to travel freely over the Nangpa La into Tibet, before the Chinese occupation. Tourism has filled the gap in trade left by the closure of the old trading routes. Now the Sherpas sell surplus expedition equipment back to the Europeans who brought it to Nepal, everything from camping gas and chocolate to novels and ice axes; Namche is the centre for this trade. Providing hospitality is also a long-standing tradition. The first expeditions found lodgings with villagers as other travellers would and this has simply been formalised with the construction of lodges.

I looked into a pool hall below the Daphne Lodge. A dozen young Sherpas with baseball caps on, their hair swept back into pony tails, were shuffling round the tables. There were pictures of James Dean and Elvis on the wall and bottles of Tuborg on the shelves. Some people find this kind of development corrupting, a dilution of a culture that might threaten its integrity. I found it rather groovy and a little hypocritical of those who visited Namche in the 1950s and 1960s to complain if local people absorbed some of their habits. Adverts round the village inviting me to a video evening and the few satellite dishes confirmed my view. Rupert Murdoch beaming down Star TV onto the heads of communities like that in the Khumbu was going to have a far greater influence on the expectations and attitudes of Sherpas than trekkers ever would.

Cultural influence and change were hardly new to the Sherpas. They had lived in the Khumbu after migrating from Kham in eastern Tibet – Sherpa, pronounced Shar-wa by the people themselves, means 'east people' – for roughly as long as the Spanish had been in South America. During that time there had been all kinds of upheaval from the introduction of the potato in the nineteenth century to the collapse of trade with Tibet. Sherpas once travelled regularly from Lhasa to the plains of India while trading, so I doubted whether James Dean would bring them to their cultural knees on his own.

Western culture is so pervasive in South Asia and elsewhere because it is delivered so efficiently through satellite television or fashion and Sherpas are open to these changes. Tenzing Norgay, who followed the exodus of Sherpas to Darjeeling in search of work with expeditions, once said that the Sherpas 'do not, like people with older cultures, cling to ancient traditions, but adapt themselves easily to new thoughts and habits'. But that doesn't mean that Sherpas will throw away the things they've got right. Wearing a baseball cap or wanting a tape recorder doesn't necessarily make you rude to your mother. The elders of Namche can also take comfort from the knowledge that their sons are truly awful at pool. I can beat these people, I thought. Then I saw the angle of the floor and decided against it.

Back at the Kala Pattar, Dachhiri and Rudra were drinking tea in Mayar's smoky, narrow kitchen, the wood stove roaring against a blackened wall. The completion of a substantial hydro-electric scheme at nearby Thamo hadn't yet resulted in a clean electric cooker at the Kala Pattar. Mayar was stirring a big pot of stew with a ladle. 'These are two very good boys,' she said. Rudra made another joke about Mayar's name and then they both looked at me again. Mayar waggled the ladle at them. I changed the subject, asking whether the showers were electric or not. Several in Namche are. Mayar said no, but that the water was already hot. I pondered the difficulties of explaining the environmental consequences of burning wood so that pampered westerners can wash their bodies and be clean for five minutes but accepted the offer anyway. She probably knew all that stuff and no one else was likely to use the water now it was dark. Why let it cool overnight? There was no light in the shower-room bar a candle.

In the evening I walked round to the Khumbu Lodge to say hello to Audrey Salkeld who was part of David Breashears' Everest expedition. Audrey knows more about the early attempts to climb Everest than anyone else alive and was offering his team the benefit of her historical perspective. I found her hunched over a portable computer, typing a letter to the park authority asking permission to establish a weather station on the South Col. There seemed to be no one else to go and have a drink with, so I looked round the lodge which was an altogether grander affair than the Kala Pattar. On the wall was a photograph of the well-known Sherpa Pasang Kami with President Jimmy Carter and Sir Edmund Hillary, each with a stack of white scarves – kathas – round their necks, given on greeting as a mark of respect. (I assume Hillary recycles his, otherwise he would have a collection of several hundred thousand.) The kitchen at the Khumbu was spotless and, more importantly, smokeless, creating an atmosphere of clean efficiency. Posters from mountaineering expeditions lined the walls, attesting to the lodge's long-standing reputation. I was glad I'd showered.

Dachhiri had already gone when I woke next morning, so I settled in for a long breakfast. The number of guests had increased by two. A middle-aged Japanese couple had put up a tent in the lodge's backyard and were drinking tea in the dining room. They smiled and nodded when I pushed through the curtain and sat down but otherwise remained silent, even with each other. I felt, and indeed was, large and smelly in comparison but they remained polite and circumspect, without giving the remotest indication of whether they were enjoying their holiday, a discretion which was rare during my time in the Khumbu where trekkers seemed desperate to report on their condition and attitudes. The woman wore an expensive cardigan draped across her shoulders, her coiffure incongruous in the basic surroundings. They didn't look like typical trekkers and in fact they weren't, although I wouldn't discover that for several days. In contrast to the Japanese, the Israeli kept up a constant monologue of complaint. He changed his plans every fifteen minutes, driving his guide Rudra to silent despair because he was much too polite to respond in kind.

When Dachhiri returned we walked up the steep hill to the police station to register my trekking permit with them and to help in my acclimatisation. My body would require a fortnight to adapt fully to the reduction in oxygen but the extra day in Namche would help in the process. On the wall of the police station was a map of the Sagarmatha National Park. I was confused by the origin of the word Sagarmatha, which is Sanskrit for 'Brow of the Ocean' and has been used by the Nepali authorities as an indigenous name for Mount Everest. One reference to the name has been found in a half-forgotten collection of essays held in a library in Kathmandu but this seems fairly lightweight evidence to base a name-change on, not least because a perfectly good local name that was recognised on both sides of the mountain already existed.

'Where does the name Sagarmatha come from, Dachhiri?' I asked him.

'Sagarmatha is Kathmandu name.' he said. 'Chomolungma is Sherpa name.'

In truth, using the name Sagarmatha is another way for the Kathmandu authorities to illustrate their control of the Khumbu. Chomolungma, which is most often translated 'Goddess Mother of the World', seems an appropriate name and I for one regret that most of the world will continue to call it Everest. When the Survey of India calculated that the mountain was the highest in the world in 1852 it already had an official number – Peak XV. Clearly this wouldn't do and the Surveyor General of India, Sir Andrew Waugh, was determined to honour his predecessor Sir George Everest. Everest was the central force in the success of the Survey of India whose contribution to human knowledge was considerable but he was not that keen on his name being preserved in this way. He pointed out that local people wouldn't be able to pronounce the name and judging by the number of Sherpas and other Nepalis I met who call it 'Everesh' this judgement has proved correct. Brian Hodgson, by then retired as Resident in Kathmandu, told the Royal Geographical Society that it was called Devadhunga. Douglas Freshfield preferred Gaurisankar, which exists but is a mountain entirely separate from Everest. When both these names, supported by such notable experts, were shown to be without foundation, the Waugh faction claimed victory. There was, however, already evidence that the local name was Chomolungma – transcribed as Tschoumou-Lancma – as long ago as 1733, published in a map drawn from information supplied by French Capuchin friars who had established a mission in Lhasa. Other travellers later confirmed this, although the controversy continued well into this century. It is all too late now.

It may seem like an over-indulgence in political correctness to prefer the local name but I am in good company. Douglas Freshfield argued that 'it is impossible to acquiesce in the attempt permanently to attach to the highest mountain in the world a personal and inappropriate name in place of its own.' There are unpleasant colonial undertones to the name Everest, but I suppose it is better named after a geographer than a politician. Mount Gladstone or Disraeli would have been ghastly. Everest himself died in 1866, too early to be sure that his name would go down in history in quite such a memorable fashion but the Chinese were infuriated that the mountain should be known around the world as an illustration of the range of the British Empire. The current regime has resolutely stuck to its version of the Tibetan name Chomolungma, a situation which is pregnant with irony. In 1951 *The Times* published a leader on the subject following another attack from the Chinese on the use of the word Everest, although political correctness was yet to be invented, *The Times* preferring the term 'appeasement'. 'The whole question,' *The Times* concluded, 'is one which it may take a considerable time to decide; and meanwhile the individual in this country, faced with the choice of talking about Chu-mu-lang-ma [sic] and being execrated as an appeaser or calling it Everest and being reviled as a provocative war-monger with no consideration for Asiatic susceptibilities, had better shun the Himalayas as a topic for general conversation.' Perhaps the final word on the issue of Everest's name should rest with Tenzing Norgay and his mum:

Usually Chomolungma is said to mean 'Goddess Mother of the World.' Sometimes 'Goddess Mother of the Wind.' But it did not mean either of these when I was a boy in Solu Khumbu. Then it meant 'The Mountain So High No Bird Can Fly Over It.' That is what all Sherpa mothers used to tell their children – what my own mother told me – and it is the name I still like the best for this mountain that I love.

Dachhiri and I walked around the National Park Office's museum which reminded me horribly of the heritage centres or 'experiences' that blight our own mountains. Dachhiri wandered about, picking up the exhibits taken from a typical Sherpa kitchen – 'This for chilli. This for butter.' – clearly confused as to why such commonplace items were thought worthy of display. Outside, he asked me to take his photograph with the shark fin of Everest in the background. Dachhiri loves having his photograph taken and the wall of his bedsit was covered with photographs of him in the mountains with clients or other Sherpas. He would take off his cap and try to smooth his thick black hair before switching on the dazzling lights of his smile. If there was a boulder close by he'd rest a foot on it and put his hands on his hips for dramatic effect.

For me, looking up the Imja Khola from the army post was a little like looking in on a party of titanic celebrities whom you recognise from their photographs. I had stared at pictures of these mountains taken from every aspect, through every kind of lens, in every season of the year. I felt like saying to ice-clad Kangtega that she looks younger or slimmer in real life. I could see lines on the faces of some of the mountains, invisible lines which I knew climbers had followed on their way to the summit. I could see areas threatened by stonefall or avalanche, places where a base camp might be made, or whether a ridge was too narrow or cor- niced to be climbed. I imagine a geologist does something similar, looking for hints in the landscape that betray the movement of the earth's crust, or a farmer looking at the fields and their boundaries and knowing instantly where the soil was good and what might grow there. Expertise tempts you to dissect landscapes.

Whether or not this landscape is beautiful I cannot say. The writer Charlie Pye-Smith didn't think so, describing it as 'disorganised and terrifying' and the mountains as having been 'carelessly chucked down from a great height'. From this angle, the searing peak of Ama Dablam certainly appears to have been badly dropped. Its summit block seemed to overhang so much that the suggestion I heard in Kathmandu that the mountain will fall over will take a lot less than a few million years to be proved correct. Ama Dablam means 'Mother's Amulet for the Deities' but there's little motherly about the mountain. She's more of a tart viewed from the Imja Khola, ridges spread like legs in a blatant attempt to get your attention. It doesn't surprise me that, after the giant 8000-metre peaks, more climbers attempt Ama Dablam than any other mountain in Nepal. An investment management company called Perpetual use her to promote their image as a reliable company with strong growth. Do they know she's on the verge of falling over? Do they realise just how promiscuous she is with her favours?

We picked our way down the steep hill back to Namche. Children were coming home from the school in Khumjung, racing down the track and kicking up clouds of dirt and stones as they shouted and laughed at each other. I watched all those tiny knees and ankles twisting and flexing, oblivious to any notion of injury. Even Dachhiri couldn't keep up with them.

Branching off from the main path, we contoured round Namche's amphitheatre to the town's gompa. An old woman showed us inside and then quietly withdrew. After the shrieks of the children and noise from the town, the silence was almost unnatural. There were no monks to be seen and Dachhiri thought that they only made an appearance during festivals. We sat in the gloom. The illustrations painted on the walls and the decorated wooden book covers were more soothing than exotic, like the smell of hymn books or the feel of a hassock beneath your knees.

Needle-thin shafts of sunlight picked out the smoke from four or five butter lamps and bundles of joss sticks, the pungent and sweet together. An old man appeared from behind the heavy rug hanging in the doorway. He nodded and smiled. Staring out from cabinets along the walls were icons of Chenresig, the patron deity of Tibet, the Buddha Sakyamuni and the Guru Rinpoche who brought Buddhism to Tibet with his Indian features and fabulous moustache.

Walking back through the town to the Kala Pattar I stopped at the office of the Sagarmatha Pollution Control Committee (SPCC). The room was quiet and the only official barely looked up from his desk as I entered. I looked at some wall-charts about the park and picked up a leaflet about minimising my impact. This initiative to clean up the park had been started in 1991 by the Worldwide Fund for Nature, the park authorities but most importantly by the Sherpa community and Ngwang Tenzin Jangpo, the abbot of the monastery at Tengpoche, initially under his direction. Reports of the pollution of the Khumbu region had been published all over the world, focusing on the streamers of toilet paper that proliferated by the trail and the huge quantities of rubbish and human waste left by climbing expeditions at Everest Base Camp. Things had got so bad that Ed Hillary had called for the mountain to be made off limits while the mess was cleared up. Images of rubbish below and on the highest mountain on earth were held up as another example of how the paradise of Nepal has been lost. 'If tourist numbers declined because of the talk of garbage, Khumbu's economy would be devastated,' Jangpo said at the time.

The project began with eighty local volunteers walking to the foot of the mountain and bringing down five hundred yak-loads of garbage, around thirty thousand kilograms. Since then teams have made regular inspections, not just at Base Camp, but all over the trekked area of the Khumbu to check on garbage disposal and sanitation standards. Western tourists may find these standards to be low, but the SPCC's work has made a profound difference to the superficial environmental quality of the Khumbu. The SPCC has also dug pits and burnt waste where possible. It isn't perfect and there are areas where it isn't working, particularly just below Everest Base Camp at the village of Lobuje but, given the SPCC's limited resources, they are doing a good job. The committee plans to extend its work by developing a training scheme for lodge owners that will cover everything from food hygiene to fuel wood conservation.

One thing that struck me about the organisation is its discretion. The SPCC does publicise its work but compared to the attention given to the environmental efforts of westerners, you wouldn't know it existed. Every 'garbage hobbyist', as *Himal* magazine once memorably called them, who thinks that solar toilets or portable furnaces are going to solve the problems of the Khumbu has his picture in the paper. In contrast, the SPCC also relies on very basic technologies and is prepared to compromise. Americans and others used to 'packing out' garbage from their national parks have suggested a similar approach in the Khumbu but local understanding has proved more reliable. Garbage could be removed all the way to Kathmandu if enough money was poured into the problem but then much of it would just be added to the garbage problem in Kathmandu, which is considerably worse than that below Everest. It offends some that rubbish should be dumped in crevasses or buried on site, but it seems the neatest solution. In truth, there seems to be an Everest-sized mountain of hypocrisy over the issue of garbage. Trekkers and mountaineers want the advantages of a western lifestyle in an environment that can't deal with its detritus and then they feel guilty about the consequences.

Over the last decade scores of expeditions have arrived in the Khumbu intent on solving the garbage crisis without realising that they are part of the problem. A German team was in the area even now, wanting to 'educate trekkers and local people about the disposal of garbage in mountain areas'. They planned to hire twenty-five porters to ferry loads from Everest Base Camp to

Shyangboche and then fly the garbage back to Kathmandu where it would be sold to recycling agencies and the proceeds given to street children. The whole project would cost $70,000. Of course, the porters would be defecating by the trail and the German tourists spreading the gospel would be eating from tins and using batteries for their cameras, all of which would compound the problem they had flown halfway round the world to solve. It's hard to see such actions, however well-intentioned, as being anything other than patronising and obstructive. It would have been so much better to give the $70,000 to the SPCC, but then the environmentally concerned German trekkers wouldn't have had a holiday. The Nepalese government has been just as guilty of failing to address the problem and has on occasion shown a staggering level of cynicism. A few years ago, an American mountaineer arrived in Kathmandu with paying clients for an attempt on Everest and no permit. While his climbers trekked towards the mountain he stayed behind in Kathmandu and managed to negotiate a special permit normally reserved for expeditions who are intending to clean up the mountain.

Despite all these problems and misdirected funds, progress has been made clearing the trash off Everest. American initiatives led by Brent Bishop and Bob McConnell have removed a great deal of garbage, not just from Base Camp but from the mountain itself, by paying Sherpas already working with climbing expeditions to bring it down. This straightforward approach is much cheaper than mounting a dedicated clean-up expedition – although Kathmandu misses out on an environmental permit fee – and is a welcome supplement to the wages of Sherpas. Using this bonus scheme, Bishop even managed to make inroads into the mess left behind at the South Col camp by forty-five years' worth of expeditions. In 1994 and 1995 as a result of a six-dollar-per-item incentive, Bishop's initiative managed to bring six hundred oxygen bottles back to Base Camp. These were later flown to the United States and sold to raise funds. The Sherpas also brought down almost four thousand kilograms of other garbage, broken tents and empty tins. The cost for the whole of the 1995 project was only $5,500. Given that big commercial expeditions run on a budget of around $300,000, this is value for money. Bishop hopes that his incentive scheme will be copied by other expeditions visiting the mountain so that Sherpas come to expect a trash recovery bonus. Already the idea has resulted in a significant improvement at Camps 1, 2 and 3. There remain some two thousand oxygen bottles at Camp 4 but since climbers now use Russian titanium oxygen bottles which have a far greater recyclable value than the old steel models the problem won't get any worse. Over time, the remaining bottles should be brought down.

Climbing, however, is only a minor if highly dramatic part of the problem. The scale of the trekking industry makes its management more difficult. The Department of Tourism has tried to push the idea of 'eco-trekking' as a tool to develop the industry without worsening the environmental problems it brings, but it must be tempting to an impoverished government to collect the increased income without properly supporting projects to control the inevitable increase in damage. The authorities have made some attempts to stop mountaineers dumping rubbish by requiring a $4000 bond that is refunded if the expedition takes care of its litter but the scheme is impractical for trekkers. They also appoint liaison officers to ensure that expeditions stick to the rules but they are poorly trained and not local to the Khumbu. Often they want the job because of its perks and have no interest in climbing. It's not surprising that most climbers view them with deep cynicism. It's also irritating for the Sherpas who have to put up with rules made in Kathmandu, like permit fees and garbage regulations, and see much of the money stay in the capital, yet are still required to sort out the problems expeditions leave behind. One solution is for the SPCC to be paid an environmental protection fee directly by climbers and trekkers to control the problem. This would be at a fraction of the cost of equipping a liaison officer, removing another layer of bureaucracy and encouraging more climbers to come, and it would bring a contribution from the more numerous trekkers. It's unlikely to happen because the Nepalese government sees trekking and mountaineering as a milch cow from which as much money has to be extracted as quickly as possible in Kathmandu.

The worst irony of all is that because of the media coverage the subject has generated and the guilt it has provoked, garbage in the mountains is considered a huge problem. But compared to the ruination of the environment in Kathmandu it is trivial. We have already forgotten that cholera and typhoid were once our major environmental problems as well. Now that the SPCC and others have started to tackle the issue of waste in the Khumbu, perhaps the focus of western concern will shift to the more mundane issues of poor sanitation and air pollution.

CHAPTER SIX

The world on their backs

Those who only ever walk among the mountains, who are never tempted to strap on crampons and dagger their way to a summit to overlook the valleys and the brown plains, imagine that climbing is a much harder road to follow. Puffing and waddling under the weight of my rucksack up the long straight path above Namche I yearned to be on a mountain and not walking under one. On an expedition you spend most of the time lying around Base Camp reading and talking, eating and sleeping. I am designed for this indolent life, interspersed with a few days of the glaring brilliance of a steep snowslope or the intricacies of a rock wall to assuage any feelings of guilt. To be walking with no mountain to climb at the end of it was a salutary lesson. Not to live in expectation but in the moment, even if at that moment I sweated and cursed in the thinning air.

At Mong, Dachhiri handed me a glass of lemon tea and I dumped my rucksack in the dirt. The lodge overlooked a narrow col and a strong cold wind was building across it. A path led down to a river, then up to the village of Phortse. Above it, dull white clouds covered Tawoche. Looking south behind me Kangtega began to disappear behind their advance. The first flakes of snow were falling as we ducked inside.

Before going to Everest Base Camp I wanted to trek up to Gokyo in the valley to the west of the Khumbu Glacier. This was partly to see an area less heavily trekked for comparative purposes and partly because I had ghost-written a book for the mountaineer and film-maker Leo Dickinson about a ballooning expedition that had over-flown the summit of Everest. The expedition had been based at Gokyo and I was curious to see how my descriptions of a place I'd never seen compared to the real thing. Even this short distance from Namche, I had the impression of leaving the mainstream behind.

Mong lies on the slopes of Khumbila, the mountain most sacred to the Sherpa and home to the god Khumbila Terzen Gelbu from whom the Khumbu takes its name. Across the valley, above the monastery at Tengpoche, is the mountain Thamserku where Khumbila's wife Tamosermu lives. This windswept collection of houses was the legendary home of the holy man Chendin who used to entertain Khumbila in the days when the Sherpa first arrived from Tibet. Chendin was the father of Sange Dorje who lived here also before studying for many years at the Rongbuk monastery on the northern side of Everest. His devotion was eventually rewarded with the power of flight and so he flew over Chomolungma, landing at Phurte between Thami and Namche, to see how his family and people were progressing. He found them suffering under the tyranny of the evil ruler Dzongnangpa who had outlawed the Buddhist faith and ordered Sange Dorje to be killed. The lama fled, first to Phortse and then Tengpoche where, on the rock where he rested, the Sherpas later built a monastery. Sange Dorje hid in a cave for three years above Dingboche but when Dzongnangpa finally discovered him, he flew to Pangboche and another hermitage. There, with the help of the people not just of Pangboche but Phortse as well, he built the Khumbu's first gompa. When the lama died, after returning to Tibet, his body dissolved into the light of a rainbow, leaving only his heart, eyes and tongue for the people to keep as relics.

Dachhiri and I sat inside the kitchen watching the young Sherpani move about, keeping the fire stoked and the kerosene burner roaring away. She had an extravagant gold-capped tooth but her apron was black with grease. She kept her bundle of rupees in a Nescafé can on the shelf above the fire. I was glad to be warm for a while, despite the smoke. Suddenly a rush of snow squirted under the curtain as the lodge door opened and closed. Two Japanese men clomped around the living room shouting for tea. I looked out to see one of them dressed in a fat down parka the colour of duck eggs, a cigarette hanging from his lips. They had come down from Dole, through deep snow, and now proposed to spend the night in this wind funnel. It was still morning and Namche was only forty minutes downhill in the lee of the hill. The other man sat on a bench and massaged his feet. He was wearing light trainers whose laces were encased in ice.

Soon after we left the col, the wind died away and we were able to walk softly up the white track, fat flakes dropping silently around us. Dachhiri took out a vast red sheet of nylon and wrapped his rucksack and himself in it. I listened to Schubert's String Quintet as I walked through this soft, closed world and imagined myself in the woods above Chamonix, or walking in the Bernese Oberland above Grindelwald with the prospect of returning for coffee and a good dinner. With the jagged white leviathans circling the valley hidden in cloud I was forced to focus more closely on the scent of the fir trees, sweet and sharp, and Dachhiri's steady gait. At one point he stopped and pointed down the hillside towards the distant roar of the river at a group of deer.

'Blue sheep,' he said. I knew that I shouldn't take this at face value. Dachhiri called most things that weren't a yak or a dog 'blue sheep'. I knew there were musk deer in these woods but even through binoculars I couldn't be sure that these were musk deer. I carried a range of books in my rucksack detailing all the possible birds, plants and animals I might meet but it made no difference. I was incapable of differentiating one species of beast from another. What I really needed was a book whose title might read *'Two kinds of bird, three trees and a deer that even an idiot like you won't fail to spot'*. In moments of adventuring incompetence like this I usually turn to W.E. Bowman's satire on mountaineering expeditions *The Ascent of Rum Doodle*. His narrator, the fantastically pompous Binder, was as ignorant as I of flora and fauna and relied heavily on the botanists on his expedition:

> I am no naturalist myself, but I tried to show an intelligent interest in the others, encouraging them to come to me with their discoveries. I am indebted to them for what small knowledge I possess in the field. The lower slopes were gay with Facetia and Persiflage, just then at their best, and the nostrils were continually assailed with the disturbing smell of Rodentia. Nostalgia, which flourished everywhere but at home, was plentiful, as was the universal Wantonia. The fauna, too, was a constant delight. The scapegoat was, of course, common, as were the platitude and the long-tailed bore. The weak-willed sloth was often met, and sometimes after dark I would catch sight of slinking shadows which Burley identified as the miserable hangdog. One afternoon Shute, in great excitement, pointed out to me a disreputable-looking creature which he said was a shaggy dog. Burley swore that it was not a shaggy dog but a hairy disgrace . . .

What I had seen was almost certainly a hairy disgrace. Finally, as the afternoon faded into evening, I entered the lodge at Dole, tired and a little cold and sat down by the usual cylindrical stove, its metal chimney piercing the roof. The lodges on the trek to Gokyo are less established and this one had not been open for long, following the winter. It was built entirely from wood with huge windows and bare floorboards. On the shelves were barrels and crates from long since departed expeditions. One read '1985 Norwegian Everest Expedition', the trip Chris Bonington had joined and during which he had briefly become the oldest man ever to reach the summit. On the wall hung a calendar with a picture of an attractive Sherpani with a katha around her neck and wearing a colourful apron.

I didn't need to look at the caption to know who she was. There was only one Sherpani in Nepal famous enough to be the subject of a calendar and that was Pasang Lhamu. She had become the first Nepali woman to climb Everest on April 22nd, 1993, almost forty years after the first ascent. But returning from the top she became progressively slower and finally ground to halt just below the South Summit where she and her two male companions, Pemba Norbu and Sonam Tshering were forced to bivouac. Out of oxygen and with no shelter, they were lucky to survive the night. Pemba descended to the South Col for fresh oxygen supplies but before he could return the weather worsened and he was forced to abandon his rescue. After the second night there was no question of finding the two Sherpas alive. When Pasang Lhamu's body was finally located under a metre of snow and recovered for her funeral at Swayambhu, Sonam Tshering's rucksack was wrapped around her legs in a pathetic attempt to give her shelter from the savage winds.

No mountaineering story since the success of Tenzing Norgay had caught the imagination of the Nepali people like the tragic death of Pasang Lhamu, made even more poignant by the presence of her husband Lhakpa Sonam Sherpa at Base Camp. The news dominated the Kathmandu media for a month and if it was generally recognised that Pasang was not a great climber, then her tenacity and courage earned her the respect of other Nepalis. There was a feeling that climbers native to Nepal had been ignored by the western media which preferred to overlook the contribution made by Sherpas while over-blowing the achievements of visiting climbers. Critics pointed to the coverage the English climber Rebecca Stephens and an Indian women's team had received for what was by 1993 a fairly standard achievement. Pasang Lhamu, on the other hand, was a heroine for a modern Nepal that recognised its ethnic minorities and could applaud the achievements of a determined woman. Thousands crowded the streets of Kathmandu to see her body carried on the back of a truck to Swayambhu. The government awarded her the Nepal Tara, a medal reserved for national heroes like Tenzing Norgay. When

Tenzing decided against returning to Nepal, preferring to stay in Darjeeling and work for the Himalayan Mountaineering Institute training Indian climbers, his reputation suffered. Pasang Lhamu's 'success' was welcomed almost as a catharsis.

The truth, as with so many recent achievements on Everest, was less heroic. Pasang Lhamu was not just a mediocre climber, she was dangerously slow and unconfident. She had tried to climb the mountain three times before succeeding, on one occasion being banned from going higher than the South Col by the French leader of her expedition because of her slow pace. Pasang had later accused him of discriminating against her as a woman and a local climber. Other expeditions she ran benefited from having the peak fee waived by the Department of Tourism but she then invited foreign climbers to join her on the mountain and charged them a percentage of the royalty. In 1993 she had been offered a place on the Indian expedition but when she was refused the job of assistant leader, she formed her own team. Pasang Lhamu took the example of western climbers and sought sponsorship and courted the media. She and her husband ran a trekking agency and the publicity she won for her climbs reflected well on her business – another example of climbing Everest as a career move.

Pasang Lhamu was under great pressure in 1993. The Indians had included another Sherpani among their number, Nimmi Sherpa from Pangboche who was stronger and at least as experienced as Pasang Lhamu. There were two other women on her own expedition. When Nanda Rai dropped out of contention early on with altitude sickness, Pasang Lhamu instructed the second woman, Lhakpa Phuti Sherpa, to help her down. She then organised her Sherpas and oxygen supplies so that she would be the first of the Nepalese women to attempt the summit. She set out for the top with five others at the end of the third week of April, an abnormally early date in a season that had left a lot of deep snow high on the mountain. It took her five hours to descend the section of ridge from the summit to where her body was found. Most competent climbers in good condition would take one hour.

Sonam Tshering who died with Pasang Lhamu was widely reported as being her climbing companion but in fact he was an employee, working for his living just as he had been on his previous four ascents of Everest. When Pasang Lhamu had insisted on going to the summit, he suggested trying with both fit women climbers and two Sherpas leaving two in reserve in case of emergency. Pasang Lhamu vetoed this. Sonam Tshering left a widow pregnant with their fourth child. His body was never found.

I thought of John Ruskin's perceptive attack on the mountaineers of his day: 'You have made racecourses of the cathedrals of the earth,' he complained in *Sesame and Lilies*. Sometimes it seemed to me that we had learned nothing since. I couldn't blame Pasang Lhamu. She had seen western climbers grow rich on exaggerating their achievements, claiming virtue where there was only greed and ambition. She knew the fame that other women had gained in their respective countries, the sense of national pride. Sometimes what is in your heart can kill you as easily as an avalanche or a fall of rock.

The door of the lodge opened and a man in his later forties entered and stood by the table opposite me. He wore a pink anorak, a green sweatshirt and blue tracksuit bottoms, all of which are filthy. Most of his teeth were missing and his upper gums misshapen. He took off a grubby white rucksack, the sort children carry to school, and took out of it a roll of paper wrapped in Chinese gift-wrapping. There followed a pencil-sharpener, a pencil, two pieces of string, two rolls of tape, a pair of sunglasses, a bottle of ink and a pen. He opened the pen, examined it, tapped the nib. He put it back in his rucksack and then sat down. After pausing for two or three minutes to stare intently at the table, he started to shuffle through the pieces of paper. He sat back and raised his eyebrows, leant forward again and ran his fingers through his long, unkempt hair. Then he simply looked at the blank piece of paper in front of him. For twenty minutes. Finally he started taping the edges of the paper, some with yellow tape, some with white. He took up his scissors and started trimming the edges.

By now I was sure he was mentally disabled in some way and I took up Dachhiri's invitation to be beaten at cards. After another half an hour I looked up and saw he had covered his head with a red and black scarf. I also realised that he had started drawing. He was working very quickly and I saw that he had already drawn a border and was adding a stylised backdrop of mountains in pencil. I'd seen drawings in a similar style in Namche. Without looking up he said he was drawing the gompa at Khunde. It was hard to judge from what he'd done whether the picture would be good but that hardly mattered. Later, as the snow fell heavily outside, the lodge-owner ladled chang from a plastic barrel, and told me the man was his nephew. I have the impression that his handicap was the result of an accident but however it was caused, it made no difference to his uncle and his cousins who sat round the fire with us. They treated him with a reserved kindness and listened to most of what he said. It felt stupid and embarrassing to have dismissed his drawing so readily and in doing so to have dismissed him as well. Where had I learned to close my mind like that?

At first light I got up to discover the lodge was covered in a foot of snow and the trail was a narrow depression in it, stretching across the walled fields behind the lodge. Dachhiri ate his usual noodle soup for breakfast while I sipped lemon tea, almost the only thing I had taken since falling ill in Phakding three days before. I was surprised at how easy it was to go without food. The combination of whatever bug it was I'd picked up and the effects of altitude left me with no appetite. The Japanese couple who had stayed with us at the Kala Pattar in Namche appeared in the kitchen, ready to leave. I hadn't seen them arrive the night before but this was the only lodge that was open in Dole. They smiled and bobbed their heads politely, before backing out of the front door into the snow. They would be ahead of us, breaking trail. "S good,' Dachhiri said through his soup. Half an hour later, as the Japanese disappeared over the rise, we followed them out. The lodge-owner's son was shovelling snow off the roof, Tawoche leered over us in a new overcoat, the ethereal Kangtega glistered at our backs in the morning sun. Dachhiri wore plastic bags over his socks in a vain attempt to keep his feet dry and we shuffled off into the day.

At Lhabarma the boy running the lodge leaned against the door frame with his arms folded, watching us approach through the snow. He wore a purple silk scarf and sunglasses. When he brought our tea he asked Dachhiri if I was Israeli. He seemed very tense. Dachhiri said I wasn't. He then began to talk with barely concealed rage about an Israeli who had seen the Sherpani at the lodge breast-feeding and started videoing her, calling to his companions that they were missing a great opportunity for a photograph. This was beyond comprehension. What would happen, I wondered, if a Nepali man started taking pictures of a woman breast-feeding in a London restaurant. It would depend on which part of London, I suppose, but would probably end either in arrest or physical assault. What were such people doing here? I had naively assumed that anyone who was prepared to put up with altitude, cold, poor food and spartan living conditions to trek in the Khumbu would have some affection for the mountains and their people, some sensitivity to their culture. In one regard, this was worse than drunken English football supporters rioting through a European city. This was an intimate violation by a sober individual who saw another human being as an object, to be collected and stored as a souvenir like tickets to the opera or dried flowers from a beautiful garden. It would have been inappropriate behaviour anywhere, but here, where there is a real hostility, especially among women, to being photographed by strangers, it showed an indifference to another people's wishes and attitudes that bordered on racism. In my more cynical moments, I felt that the only reason some trekkers came to the Khumbu was to collect enough evidence to impress on their friends that they actually had been there.

Leaving Lhabarma I noticed the Japanese sitting outside another lodge. They nodded and smiled and I smiled back, inwardly cursing. Thanks to their efforts, the trail up to this point had been reasonable, although Dachhiri had very wet feet. Now we found ourselves floundering in the deep snow, wading up to our thighs, sometimes to our waists. In his light boots Dachhiri suffered most, although he remained unswervingly cheerful. We were now at an altitude comfortably over 4000 metres and I was relieved after two hours of this struggle to reach the next collection of houses at Luza. Two Germans were sitting outside a lodge, on their way down from the next village, Machermo, which meant that the trail beyond would be easier. They recommended we try the coffee, so we sat for a while to recover from our effort. The mountains now seemed to surround us, crowding round ahead of us and moving up behind to seal our exit. The snowy bulk of Cho Oyu to the north and its rocky cousin Gyachung Kang dominated the head of the valley, still three or four days to the north. To our left and now slight behind us, Khumbila was steep and elegant like one of the aiguilles above Chamonix. On the other side of the valley the complex ridges and serac bands of Tawoche and Cholatse towered above us, and to the south, with the Imja Khola now invisible, the bulk of Kangtega seemed to have edged closer. In the valley itself the coda of yesterday's forest reached and narrowed up the river's bed until it disappeared altogether. Everything was covered in the new snow, adding brilliance and lustre. Dachhiri's smile was more dazzling than ever as he turned to the points of the compass to absorb the scale and expanse of the towering mountains. On the fringes of the azure sky, the day's first clouds were beginning to gather and, when we continued, the mountains started to disappear one by one, until we were left alone in the whiteness with just the impression of two pairs of boots and the walled fields to break the white monotony.

Each upland area, like that at Luza, is owned by families in the main villages to the south. Each village has its own upland district. With the mountains hidden, they looked like farms in Derbyshire, with their white limestone walls and low, one-storey buildings. The walled fields and houses in the uplands where livestock is held are called *phu*, or *chusa*, meaning cattle places. Like those in the upper reaches of the Gokyo valley, *phu* used in summer are also called *yersa*. The number of words concerned with husbandry and the precision of their definition, the way in which a community's rituals are bound up in land and animal husbandry illustrate the complexity of farming in the Khumbu. The problem of being a transitory visitor is that the richness of all this is missed.

One easy example is the yak. These feature strongly in the consciousness of trekkers since they're hard to miss coming at you down a trail and they are often employed carrying your luggage. Domesticated yaks, as opposed to their wild progenitors which are near extinction, are found throughout the upland areas of western China, Mongolia and Tibet, from the Khumbu to the fringes of Siberia, even in Afghanistan on the edge of the Pamirs. They are superbly evolved for coping with the extremes of the Central Asian climate, and through interbreeding with cattle have become an essential resource for the people of the Khumbu. Barbara Brower, whose book *The Sherpa of Khumbu* is an accessible but comprehensive view of the lives of ordinary Sherpas, describes the yak's advantages thus:

Its skin is thick, with few sweat glands, reducing transpiration losses. The thoracic cavity, like the thorax of high mountain populations, is unusually large to accommodate the larger lungs. The red blood cells of yak are half the size of other bovines and three to four times as numerous. The scarce and poor quality feed available to the yak in much of their native range through most of the year has fostered other specialised adaptation. The upper lip is thinner and more mobile and, according to Sherpas, the tongue is also specially designed for cropping very short material. Presumably to make travel over rough terrain easier, the yak's feet are short, the stance solid and the hooves unusually large and hard. A yak in motion is nothing like a cow. There is a fluidity, more like a running bear or badger, that makes a pure yak easy to distinguish from a cow or hybrid.

The Sherpas use interbreeding to bridge the gap between the yak's strengths at altitude and its shortcomings at lower elevations, like their temperament and vulnerability to disease and their poor milk output. The ignorant like myself call all these animals yaks, but it is far more complicated than that. Male hybrids are called *zopkio*, females are *dzum*. A *zopkio* whose mother is a cow is a *urang*. If the mother was a yak, more accurately a *nak*, then he is a *dimzo*. *Zopkio* are sterile, which ends one source of further confusion, but not so *dzum*. An immature *dzum* is a *zopruk*, but when they can breed, the progeny of a *dzum* and a yak is a *kokoyak*.

The uses these animals are put to show considerable imagination. Sherpas are prohibited by their Buddhist beliefs from killing yaks but will happily eat their meat should they meet with an accident. On rare occasions, yaks are encouraged to have accidents, but by and large Sherpas adhere to their code. When the border with Tibet was open, low-caste Buddhists from Tibet would arrive in the autumn to slaughter unproductive animals. Now, with an increased influence from Hindu Kathmandu, the killing of female hybrids is prohibited, leading to an increase in unproductive animals competing for resources. I would guess that the number of 'accidents' has increased as a result. Sherpas have their animals bled – another skill given over to Tibetans – to prepare them for breeding, or for travelling to a higher altitude. The blood is caught and eaten.

Milk is another crucial product, used for making butter and cheese. Butter is central to Tibetan culture and so by extension to the Sherpas. It is burnt in votive lamps, used in cooking and in making the salty butter tea that Tibetan people adore and most westerners gag on, although this is not drunk as widely in the Khumbu as it is in Tibet. Sherpas also make a soft cheese called *somar* which is well rotted and has a powerful, smoky flavour. The best I found came from Thami but I ate it more or less everywhere throughout the Khumbu, usually in cheese pastry turnovers or in omelettes. The long guard hairs of yaks and the soft inner coat, called *pu*, are both spun and yak hides are used for making shoes. Even the tails are important, used in ritual and sold to tourists as curios. I have read that yak tails were once exported from Tibet for the Santa Claus beard industry. Yak manure is equally important, mixed with mud as plaster, dried and burnt as fuel and put on crops. In some villages, especially those that are more progressive or have felt the influence of tourism more keenly, there has been an increase in the number of zopkio which are suited to load-carrying. Sherpas looking for ways to invest the money earned from climbing expeditions, buy zopkio to ferry equipment and supplies for trekking parties and expeditions. Consequently the number of zopkio at Namche has roughly doubled in less than twenty years, while numbers in Phortse are static.

At Machermo, at the end of our day's walk from Dole, Dachhiri and I sat in the kitchen of lodge eating noodle soup. The Sherpani owner's son – also called Dachhiri – picked up my guidebook and examined the pictures, calling the names of places he recognised and even the faces of well-known Sherpas. His mother came over and peered over his shoulder, identifying Guru Rinpoche and Dawa Tenzing. 'Chomolungma,' she said as the little boy turned the page to reveal Everest's squat summit pyramid. Then the sun burst through the clouds again, and the Sherpani dragged a mattress outside and laid it behind a wall of dried yak pats. All four of us spent the rest of the day lying on the mattress half-asleep. Dachhiri lay on his back, snoring intermittently, his hands folded across his stomach, his baseball cap pulled down over his eyes. 'Tomorrow we must get up early,' he said, as though it were I who had lazed in bed that morning. Sometime during the afternoon, as we dozed beneath the glowing western slopes of Tawoche and Cholatse, I asked about the yeti.

Machermo is a well-known spot for yeti-hunters. These men, and they generally are men, arrive periodically in the Khumbu from the West with huge resources and bizarre surveillance equipment to track down an example of the yeti. I have never seen a yeti-hunter but I am assured they exist. Quite what would happen if one of these exotic creatures ever manages to catch a yeti I can't imagine but presumably the yeti-hunter and his sponsors would look for a considerable return on their investment. And I'm sure the yeti's solitude would be ended forever, since a successful yeti-hunter would breed more yeti-hunters very quickly. My only hope is that if the elusive beast is tracked down, then it eats its hunter, camera and all, to dissuade further visitors.

As for the yeti itself I remained sceptical. Machermo was the site of the most quoted yeti sighting of the modern era. The version of the story I heard goes like this. In the summer of 1974 a Sherpani called Lhaupa Dolma from the village of Khumjung was tending her parents' herd of yak and dzum above the chusa of Machermo. It was the middle of the monsoon and raining hard and Lhaupa was anticipating the return of her brother who had been working as a sirdar, or lead Sherpa, on Everest. Hearing a whistle – yetis are good whistlers, apparently – the girl took it to be her brother and she sat down by a stream to wait for him. With no warning she was suddenly hurled into the stream by a seven-foot yeti which took a dzum by its horns and snapped its neck. Next it tore open the animal's stomach and pulled back the hide to expose the entrails. A calf who suddenly appeared with its mother interrupted the yeti which – or who? – picked it up and hurled it twenty feet, killing the poor animal in the process. The yeti then attacked the calf's mother, snapping its legs to suck the marrow from its bones. After attempting to hide the carcass for later consumption, the assailant then loped off up the mountainside, leaving poor Lhaupa Dolma in a terrible state. Only the powerful intervention of a lama at Khumjung saved her from depression and the curse of the yeti. After a period of what we would call post-traumatic stress she recovered and is, apparently, married with children and still living in Khumjung.

I didn't know what to make of such stories. I found it impossible to suspend my desire for concrete evidence and just believe. I'd read the accounts of various Everesters like Eric Shipton and Michael Ward, seen photographs of footprints in the snow with the head of an ice axe held against them for scale, but so what? I'd seen footprints enlarge and alter shape before my eyes in the heat of the sun. And climbers, Shipton included, are often practical jokers.

On the ballooning expedition I had described for Leo Dickinson, he had dressed up one of his team in a gorilla suit and sent him off up the hillside to wave at the unsuspecting film director travelling with them who, when he finally spotted what was clearly a man in a gorilla suit, believed wholeheartedly in the existence of the abominable snowman. You have to want something to exist before it truly can.

The Sherpas I spoke to about the yeti seemed convinced of it, to a lesser or greater extent, but in a more spiritual sense than the yeti-hunters who set out to prove only its literal existence. Other predators in the region, like the wolf and the snow leopard, are invested with a similar spiritual dimension by the Sherpas, as though they were physical manifestations of something evil and destructive. It is the same for the yeti.

The Sherpani at Machermo was certainly convinced and told me that a yeti had been heard at Dole three or four nights before, calling out from the hillside above. In the middle of the night I awoke, not to the distant call of a mythical animal but to a piercing headache. It felt as though a knitting needle had been driven through one side of my skull. It required four ibuprofen tablets and a quick wipe with ibuprofen gel across my neck to get rid of the needle and allow me to sleep. In the pitch dark I had the compelling but groundless belief that I was developing cerebral oedema, an increase of fluid on the brain caused by a too rapid gain of altitude. Of course, it was nothing of the kind and had more to do with sleeping on a rock hard pillow. But in the middle of the night, high on a mountainside, fear hovers at the back of your mind waiting for its chance. In that context, yetis make perfect sense.

In the morning Dachhiri examined me with some concern. I had barely eaten for almost five days, was troubled by deep blisters on the heels of both feet and had now resumed my deathly pallor of the previous week.

'It's not a problem,' I told him as I hobbled slowly around the lodge collecting my possessions. 'Pale and interesting is terribly fashionable in London these days.' I thought of the articles I had written recommending caution at altitude, of taking things slowly. As though reading my mind Dachhiri lit up one of his smiles and said, '*Bistwaari bistwaari jaun.* Let's go very slowly.' We followed the Japanese couple slowly up a long slope above the tiny village and after that I began to feel stronger, walking slowly along a flat moraine bank that had long been left behind by the retreating glacier ahead of us. At the snout of the glacier, on either side of the river, were a collection of tiny hamlets, one of the far out-reaches of summer grazing in the Khumbu. With the weight of snow still lying on the ground so late, I wondered if the migration up the valleys would be delayed this year.

As we approached the few houses that make up Pangka I saw six men grouped around a tarpaulin outside a ruined lodge. They began to walk slowly away from the broken walls of the building towards a rise in the moraine bank where several undamaged lodges stood. From the care they took with their load across the difficult terrain, I knew that the tarpaulin contained a body. Dachhiri stopped and looked with an expressionless face at the group still some fifty yards away. 'Sherpa, I think,' he said. The Japanese had stopped as well and suddenly I understood why they were there, why they had seemed incongruous in the Kala Pattar. Why they were so reserved. Dachhiri and I walked across to the lodge on top of the moraine bank. The lodge-owner hurried across the snow to us.

'No pictures,' he said. I hadn't gone near my camera, but, given the reputation of foreign trekkers, I could appreciate his concern. We stood together and watched the group struggling under the weight of the tarpaulin as they walked across the rise and down the slope to the river. Two more men followed them down carrying a pick and shovels. There they worked to dig out a hollow for the body.

The lodge had been destroyed by an avalanche while a Japanese trekking group had been sheltering from an unexpected storm that had struck most of Nepal and dumped feet of snow on the mountains. This had happened at the start of November, at the height of the trekking season during a period when the weather is most usually clear and settled. There was no warning of the storm's approach, a matter for some debate after the more immediate emergency had passed, and many were caught high up when the snow started. British trekkers who had visited Cho Oyu Base Camp at the head of the Ngozumpa Glacier were walking towards the tiny yersa at Gokyo when the snow started and by the time they arrived it had become heavy. Nevertheless, the Japanese, who had climbed the small hill above Gokyo that morning, elected to descend to Pangka. The snow continued to fall, forcing one of the British trekkers to abandon his tent after it collapsed under the weight of snow. The thirteen Japanese, with a dozen support staff made up of Sherpa, Rai and Tamang, arrived in Pangka and called at the lodge I was standing at now. According to eye-witnesses, they asked the price of accommodation there but decided it was too expensive and elected to spend the night at the lodge at the bottom of the moraine bank, at the base of a broad, shallow slope. Sometime in the night the slope had become overloaded and it avalanched, sending tons of snow crashing onto the lodge at its base. All thirteen Japanese were killed, along with ten of their staff and those who lived in the lodge. The two survivors, a Rai and a Sherpa, had been standing on the roof of the lodge, trying to clear it of snow which had threatened on its own to destroy the building. After the avalanche struck, the Sherpa had managed to dig himself out and rescue his companion.

The Japanese couple sat outside the lodge and stared at the ruined building. I could see the slope above and the broken walls beneath but could not comprehend the amount of snow that must have fallen that night. There would have been doubt, even fear in the lodge, but also a sense that in stone walls there was security. Then the roof buckled slightly, perhaps snow was pouring through gaps in the wooden shingles. I imagined the reluctance of those sent out into the storm to clear it, swearing in the cold, then the roar in the blackness, the weight of the snow pushing over the walls and settling like concrete around the soft bodies of the dead. The Japanese woman was wiping tears from her eyes.

'Your son?' Either she didn't understand me or else I spoke too softly because she made no response. I thought of her life in Japan. From the way she dressed and moved, I guessed she had little experience of mountains. I knew plenty of climbers who spoke little to their families of what they did for fear of alarming them, but this group was trekking, not climbing. I imagined her son told her all about his time up here, the freedom it brought. From my own experience, I knew she would have trouble reconciling that freedom with its price. To lose a child. The darkness of that was worse than a sudden rush of snow and the oblivion it carried.

When the authorities realised the scale of the disaster brought by the storm, not just to Gokyo but all over the Khumbu and beyond, helicopters run by the new privatised helicopter companies started flying rescue missions. I had heard from several sources that demands for up to $400 were made for the five-minute flight to safety at Shyangboche and that these demands were often met by westerners anxious to escape the snow. Nepali co-pilots were seen pocketing this money. One trek leader stranded with thirty trekkers at Na, close to the houses at Pangka, refused to pay but demanded that her whole group, westerners and local staff, be evacuated anyway. The eventual charge made by the airline was $90 a head. Her responsibility was not matched by others. Two European climbers abandoned their staff at Ama Dablam's Base Camp, paying the profiteering rate for their own rescue but not for the people who worked for them. At least a dozen porters, guides and cook staff suffered terrible frostbite. Most of these had limbs amputated as a consequence.

In total, over five hundred people were airlifted to safety following the storm of November 9th, half of them tourists. Given that the ratio of clients to staff on organised treks can be as high as one to four, it is clear that many porters were left to fend for themselves. Substantiating rumour in Kathmandu would tax the patience of Job, but I was told by several sources that in the Kangchenjunga region to the east of Everest, one helicopter landed and took off again with no one on board after realising that none of those he had gone to rescue were foreign tourists. 'There are only Nepalis here,' the pilot was reported as saying.

What is certain is that, if a storm strikes unexpectedly during the trekking season, then porters will die. There have been many substantiated reports of porters abandoned by trekking parties who have frozen to death on high passes or suffered severe frost-bite or snow blindness. At Kunde hospital above Namche Bazar, fifty porters sought treatment for the latter after the storm which killed the Japanese. Porters are simply not equipped to face the consequences of sustained bad weather and few trekking companies are prepared to shoulder the cost of doing so if such a requirement makes them uncompetitive. Most porters cope most of the time and if there are occasional losses then the fatalistic Nepali response of 'Ke garne? What's to be done?' is all that's said on the matter.

People often die young in Nepal and if there is an opportunity to make good money, then the risk is probably worth it. Portering is a fact of life across much of Nepal and most of it has nothing to do with the trekking industry. The lack of roads and the remoteness of many villages means that everything has to be carried, from foodstuffs to building materials. The rates of pay for this work are considerably lower than the $2 a day paid by trekking agencies.

The physical demands of such work are staggering. There has been surprisingly little research done in this area compared to the massive effort made to study mountaineers at altitude, but one study by Nancy and Kim Malville of the University of Colorado of porters working between Jiri and Namche Bazar gives some insight into the physical demands of carrying loads for a living.

Much of their work focused on the load weight in relation to body weight of porters, who are just as likely to be women. The trail takes ten days out and four days back and porters, or *dhakreys*, carry loads supported by a band called a *namlo* across the forehead as they have done for hundreds of years. This puts a terrible strain on the neck. Nancy Malville reported that the youngest porters, aged between eleven and fifteen, carried around 135 per cent of their weight, while men in their sixties were still carrying 116 per cent. Those carrying the heaviest loads, men in their late twenties, averaged 182 pounds or 135 per cent of their body mass. The heaviest load they recorded was carried by a forty-four year old Rai called Bhim Bahadur who stood four feet nine inches in his flip-flops and weighed 104 pounds. His load weighed 238 pounds or 228 per cent of his body mass. To put this in perspective, the world weightlifting record for the snatch in Bhim Bahadur's division is 290 pounds. And weightlifters don't have to walk anywhere.

You would expect that such severe physical exertion would lead to similarly severe health problems in later life, but what research there is suggests otherwise. At a party in Kathmandu I found myself talking to a neurosurgeon called Upendra Devkota who had studied a group of porters in their forties for signs of spondylosis, or wear and tear of the upper spine. Given the tremendous pressures transmitted by the namlo onto porters' necks you would expect them to have suffered considerable damage. In fact, the reverse was true. Just over twelve per cent showed signs of spondylosis compared to an average of twenty-five per cent in sedentary populations.

Other research has illustrated the extraordinary fitness of porters. Nancy Mulville measured the heart-rate of a thirty-three year-old Magar porter carrying a load up the hill that leads to the 11,300-foot Lamjura Pass on the trek from Jiri to Namche. This is perhaps the most demanding climb on a round-trip that totals 21,000 feet of ascent and 16,500 feet of descent. The porter carried an 190-pound load, more than one and a half times his weight. He would stop roughly every two minutes and slip a sturdy

T-shaped stick called a *tokma* under his basket – his *doko* – and rest for up to a minute. During these short rests his heart-rate fell from a maximum of around 165 beats per minute to 120 or even 110 beats per minute. This heart rate at such an altitude and the speed of recovery would impress a world-class athlete.

Unlike athletes, however, porters don't put their bodies through this kind of punishment because they want to; they do it for money and I've no doubt that if there were alternative sources of income they would hang up their namlos for good. Dachhiri had certainly done so. He'd carried loads from the age of ten, after quitting school, working the same route that Nancy Mulville had studied. He told me stories of delivering his load in Namche and drinking rakshi as they walked all night back to Jiri because they didn't have enough money to stay in a lodge. He shook his head at the memory of those days. 'Sheesh. It was very difficult. I not be a porter anymore.' As a Sherpa, Dachhiri at least had the option of picking up guiding work. Working for an agency he was covered by insurance and picked up generous tips from clients. Most of his equipment had been given to him by grateful trekkers. Working privately, as he was for me, Dachhiri could make seven times the portering rate.

The continuance of the portering industry after it has faded elsewhere in the Himalaya is a result of economic failure. There is simply no other way for many people to make a living, decent or otherwise. Reporting on the first conference ever held on the subject in August 1995, Kanak Dixit termed it thus: 'The carrying of other's people's loads for an income is more than anything else a manifestation of hill poverty and the failure of the Nepali state to be responsible for its underclass.' What is worse, the opportunity for subsistence families to supplement their income through portering is at last being eroded by improvements in communications. Russian Mi17 helicopters, suddenly available after the collapse of the Soviet Union, can lift three or four tons and deliver a load to the Khumbu from Kathmandu in half an hour. The gradual spread of the admittedly limited road network has also had a major impact. There has long been the complaint in Nepal that the elite in Kathmandu has exploited the masses for its advantage but at least portering has some economic benefit for local people. If helicopters or trucks take over the bulk of distribution in Nepal then even that will have gone.

All of this is the complex background to the exploitation of porters by the trekking industry and, ultimately, by tourists. It is shocking to think that local people serving the needs of western trekkers should lose their lives or their ability to earn a living because they were inadequately equipped. Some trekkers are equally shocked that this back-breaking work only brings them a couple of dollars a day. Much of the political debate in Europe and North America is about an improvement in the living standards of the poorest in society and an end to the exploitation of low-paid workers. To go on holiday and be reminded that most of the world's population would love to have our problems unsettles those who are sensitive enough to think about it.

The British mountaineer Doug Scott has long argued for a minimum portering wage for the trekking industry, a view that Brot Coburn had dismissed in such passionate terms at the party in Kathmandu I went to just before leaving for the Khumbu. There's no doubt that a minimum wage would have an inflationary effect as trekking agents won't absorb that increase from their profit margins. It's possible that fewer tourists would come as a result. It's also clear that the Tamangs and Rais, who do much of the portering for trekking groups, resent the disparity in incomes between agents, Sherpa guides and themselves. Given the rigid structure of Nepali society, they do not have the opportunity to establish their own agencies and earn the kind of income that agents and Sherpas do. As far as I'm aware none of the economists modelling the doubtful future of the Nepalese economy in their offices in Kathmandu have tried to determine what effect such a minimum wage would have. Perhaps they should.

The moral squalor that allows poorly clad lowlanders to freeze to death on a high mountain pass, abandoned by their employers and with no provision made for their families, can and should be addressed as soon as possible. Even if those who are responsible for regulating the trekking industry are indifferent to the human tragedy, it won't be long before some enterprising journalist arrives in Kathmandu with a television camera intent on illustrating to the viewers of Germany or the United States how people have their feet amputated as a result of working for western trekkers. This kind of coverage does not sell holidays. An insurance scheme like that which exists for those working on climbing expeditions should not be difficult to organise. Independent trekkers manage to pay a park permit fee, so it is likely that they would understand a requirement to pay for their porters' insurance. They should also be made aware that they have a responsibility to ensure that their staff are properly equipped.

None of this would have made a difference to those sheltering in the lodge at Pangka, Sherpa and client alike. I could not think of anything to comfort the Japanese couple who had travelled so far to see the ruined walls and broken roof. Mountains, especially high ones, are inherently dangerous. There is no legislation or control that can alter the fact. That is their harsh and honest appeal.

CHAPTER SEVEN

Dark side of the rainbow

Gokyo was deep in snow, the lake frozen, its legendary Brahmin ducks honking sadly as they waddled across the ice. The clouds had smothered the mountains and the shadows were gone. There were more than a dozen trekkers staying in the tiny village, hardly Torremolinos, but after Dole and Machermo, Gokyo was verging on fashionable. Most of the trekkers were holed up in the conservatory of the Gokyo Resort run by a Sherpani and her Indian husband. The conservatory, more a greenhouse manqué, had been built as a meteorology hut for Leo Dickinson's balloon flight. Its windows were now cracked or broken and snow drifted through the gaps as the wind strengthened outside. Americans, Germans and Japanese wrapped themselves in down parkas and read. It was like being in a library at the United Nations with the heating off in the middle of winter.

Dachhiri had stopped at another lodge closer to the lake, so I tried in his absence to make conversation with a tall American. Half a dozen faces glanced severely at me, so I gave up and instead scanned the lodge's menu. They served potato croquettes. These made a change from rice and lentils or the cheese omelette and chips that I usually preferred, but were three or four times more expensive. How many croquettes could Dachhiri eat each day and in how many days would he bankrupt me? I reckoned on three or four hundred and about forty-eight hours. One of the Americans sitting on the bench next to me was writing in her diary. She was, she wrote, cold and unhappy and when she looked up to catch me peering over her arm at what she was writing, she looked even colder. A German, who seemed to be wearing every item of clothing he'd brought to Nepal, opened the conservatory's rather loose door and let in even more snow. I took the opportunity to slip out.

Dachhiri was sitting in the kitchen of the lodge at the bottom of the slope above the frozen lake with two Sherpanis, the first in her late thirties and her sister who was a little older. Both were from Khumjung. There were pictures on the wall of the Mani Rimdu festival and other celebrations as well as photos of their children who were staying in Khumjung until the summer. Plastic barrels crowded on the shelves, there was a small sink by the window, the milky light seeped in. Compared to the Resort, this lodge was basic but had plenty of character. Both Sherpanis complained that while character was good, paying guests were better. The elder sister also ran a lodge but that had even more character, so she had given it up and moved in with her sister. The heavy snow lying around the lake had been widely reported and there were fewer trekkers than usual. The kitchen was quite large with a sizeable bed next to the fire. Dachhiri and I climbed on to it to play cards and wrap ourselves in blankets. The older Sherpani demanded she join us but refused to play any of the games I knew. Within fifteen minute she had won $20 off me and we gave up.

Dachhiri then said that when we got back to Namche he was going to call his girlfriend. He and his girlfriend had become very close and Dachhiri was in some kind of crisis over what to do next. Or rather, not about what to do, more whether she'd agree to do what he wanted. We ran through the next ten days on our fingers, each finger a village, huddling under the Sherpani's greasy blankets. We calculated we would reach Namche again on a Saturday and so catch the weekly market, something Dachhiri seemed keen on. The women teased us and at one point the elder of the sisters jumped on me and grabbed my thighs, rubbing them vigorously. Seeing my obvious terror that she might take things any further, she slapped me on the back and resumed her seat. Dachhiri patted the mattress where the Sherpanis would sleep and said, 'You stay here tonight. Heesh-heesh-heesh.'

In the middle of the floor was a mouse, a ball of fur that sat cleaning its face. It had prospered and grown fat in this lodge. The elder Sherpani picked up a potato and hurled it at the mouse which barely moved. The potato missed by a foot and skidded under the shelves. The mouse waddled after it. Its mate appeared from by the fire and looked up at the younger Sherpani. She placed her foot over its head, her heel on the floor, and threatened to squash it. If mice yawn then this one probably did so now. Another potato flew across the kitchen and the second mouse jogged awkwardly after it. The only way the Sherpanis would kill these mice was by over-feeding them.

The door of the lodge opened and from behind the curtain that screens the kitchen from the gloomy and frigid living room, the American I had met at the Gokyo Resort called out. '*Tato pani chha.* Hot water, man. Get me some hot water.' The curtain was pulled back and he stepped into the room, taking off his hat. He was tall and I imagined under all those clothes was rather thin. The Gokyo Resort had left him both impressed and alarmed. 'Wow! What a place. What a *place*.' He and the elder Sherpani sparred in a ribald kind of way and I was glad he'd arrived to take the pressure off me for a while, since he seemed to deal with it so much better. ('What a broad!' he'd say.) We talked about the success of the Resort. The younger Sherpani was in no doubt why it thrived and her establishment struggled. 'Sherpa people are not good bizzee-ness people. The Indian man, he knows.'

'What about Ang Tshering?' I said, thinking of his airline.

'Okay, okay,' she said. 'Some Sherpa good bizzee-ness people. Not me.'

The American and I promised to sneak up to the conservatory in the middle of the night with axes and do the place in.

'They're charging 300 rupees a night. Three hundred. What is it here? Fifty? Those guys were serving potato croquettes, did you see that? Potato croquettes!' The Sherpanis admitted they had no idea how to make potato croquettes but did have a can of tuna. They set about cooking some rice to go with it. I also swapped some dried noodles for chocolate. Since throwing up in our saucepan I had lost interest in cooking what little food we had brought. This was the first substantial meal I'd eaten for a while and I viewed it as a test run for my bowels. The American had giardia and we compared notes. There are few pleasures in life that compare with a detailed conversation about the minor illnesses one is suffering from.

'How many times are you going to the john?'

'Well, I'm not. I haven't eaten for five days. Are you farting?' Sherpas believe that Europeans fart too much.

'Sure. Wow. It's a good thing I'm not staying the Resort. Those guys would not be pleased, no way.'

He lived in a remote part of Northern California working on a forestry project. 'I came to Nepal before when I was seventeen in 'eighty-three or so. Man, it changed me. Nothing was ever going to be the same after that. I couldn't do the mortgage and kids thing after what I went through.' I asked him what has changed since then. 'Oh, the pollution in Kathmandu. The town is so much bigger and uglier. And the people of course.'

'What, the Sherpas?'

'No. *Noooo*. Not the Sherpas, man. Us! The tourists! We've changed. When I first came here people were into it. They tried to learn a few words of Nepali and talk to the people, tune in to what was going on. Not anymore.' I thought of those sitting around the walls of the conservatory cocooned in their down jackets and not looking, not talking.

In the depths of the night I woke to an urgent need to visit the outhouse. There wasn't even time to dwell in the warmth of my sleeping bag and resent it. Pulling on my boots, I shuffled out of the lodge, laces trailing through the snow behind me. The Sherpani had cleared a path whose banks reached my shoulder. Afterwards I wrapped my arms around my chest and looked into the sky. The clouds had fled leaving the black dome curving over the mountains smeared with incandescent streaks of light. Looking towards Cho Oyu I saw a comet fixed in the north, its tail streaming behind it as though caught in a distant cosmic wind. My head drained itself of home thoughts, the orange sky that frames the night, the moon blood-red through the fumes rising off the city, the rivers of cars, the towers of glass reflecting their flaring brake-lights. The black rocks on the sky-line edged against the indigo sky, the houses shrank into their beds of frozen snow. I shuffled back to bed in shit-stained boots for my stock of pills and to let the world start again.

By half past six, Dachhiri and I were at the base of the small hill above the lake that reaches perhaps 17,000 feet. It was going to be a busy day. There were two Japanese ahead of us, then the American, then us, then another Japanese and three more Americans behind. For two hours I wheezed up the slope, my bottom plugged by Lotomil and antibiotics, my blistered feet strapped and padded. High-altitude rambling seemed considerably harder than I had given it credit for. Ordinarily at this stage of the season, Gokyo Ri is clear of snow, a pile of loose black dirt and rocks framing the turquoise lake but the monochrome landscape had a surprising depth to it, a purity. Dachhiri waited patiently when I fell too far behind but I managed to keep going and after two hours of steady effort we reached the top. The Americans were close behind, shouting and cheering as they crested the ridge, jumping in their steps and slapping each other's hands high above their heads. Their enthusiasm and delight were strangely touching. It was a morning full of promise.

Around us the mountains circled, the black wedges of Everest and Makalu massive and dull, attempting to prove that unembellished size really does matter. Cho Oyu blocked the valley to the north at the head of the Ngozumpa Glacier – don't ask *me* how to pronounce it – its east ridge extended like an arm to Gyachung

Kang. I imagined traversing it, a tightrope between two giants, praying they didn't wake. Cholatse twisted in the foreground, Kangtega and Thamserku filled the end of the valley. Wherever I turned there were mountains, an endless frozen swell across the curve of the horizon.

Dachhiri and I ran down the hill, skidding in the snow, sliding on our arses. The water around the stepping stones at the end of the lake had melted and the ducks sat in it quacking up at us happily as we crossed back to the lodge. We sat in the sunshine eating noodle soup watched by the Sherpanis who shaded their eyes against the light as they talked. The gloom of yesterday had evaporated.

In the late morning we shouldered our packs and started off back down the valley towards Pangka, edging down the right bank of the glacier's end as stones skittered from beneath our feet and from the slope above our heads. Just before the village the American caught us to say goodbye and we crossed the river to a tiny hamlet called Na. Looking back I could see him struggling up the moraine beneath the lodge, not far from where they had buried the dead Sherpa. By the time I reached the lodge at Na my energy was spent and I lay down on a damp mattress in the draughty dormitory. 'Not so good place,' Dachhiri said handing me foul-smelling tea. He was reluctant to stop with so much of the day left and the thought of lying ill here was too depressing. It should only take three hours or so to get to the next lodge at Thare. I dragged my rucksack off the floor and followed him.

As the afternoon wore on, the clouds returned and the brilliance of the morning was extinguished by the damp mist. Then the snow started again as well, and I drew my head back into the hood of my jacket and stumbled on, wearied to tears, the heels of my feet throbbing with each step. Dachhiri stopped each time he drew too far ahead to be able to see me and waited as the snow fell softly on his thick hair. He never once appeared impatient with my slow progress. I felt foolish to be so weak and, as the afternoon gave way to evening, desperate to reach the lodge. At last, as darkness gathered, I heard a bell in the distance. We passed two yaks tethered against a wall looming out from the grey mist and the juniper trees. Seeing them, I knew it was almost finished and soon after I stumbled into the soft light of a single-roomed lodge. Two young Sherpanis were sitting by the fire and I collapsed on their bed.

'*Chiya. Lemon chiya chha? Chini?*' I asked, flapping my arms pathetically.

Dachhiri said something to the Sherpanis that I didn't catch. They all laughed. 'Heesh-heesh. I say you are like old woman.'

'And you have the face of a monkey,' I replied.

Dachhiri rubbed the peeling skin from his cheeks and laughed again. '*Bandar*,' he said. 'I am monkey-face.'

I sat by the fire and ate some soup before crawling exhausted into bed. As I drifted into sleep I could hear Dachhiri talking and laughing, Then the Sherpanis began to sing. My last memory before the darkness closed in was of their ethereal voices and the crack of damp juniper as it was pushed into the fire.

When I finally woke I felt instantly that the fever of the day before had gone. I stretched inside my sleeping bag and shuffled across the bed to avoid a jet of snow that had been squirting through a gap in the door and straight down my neck. Dachhiri's hand appeared clutching a cup of tea. Finally I struggled out of bed and padded across the damp earth floor to the fire. Taking off my socks the last of my plasters fell away from my feet. There were two deep holes across both achilles tendons. Blisters are infuriating. Nobody ever died of a blister – my hypochondria hadn't stumbled on the notion of blood-poisoning quite yet – but they can be agonising. What is worse, they are often an illustration of incompetence which was certainly the case here. Now I was reduced to strapping lint over them with electrician's tape and praying that the doctor at Pheriche, still two days' walk away, would sell me some dressings.

Dachhiri sat next to me and pulled a face at this procedure. He was always getting blisters but his seemed to heal without ever causing him any trouble. When I finished, we sat on the Sherpanis' bed and drank tea. He took out a picture of his girlfriend and himself taken in Kathmandu. They both sat stiffly in front of the camera, serious beyond their years. Dachhiri had made a brave attempt to control his wiry hair while Pussi frowned severely. She looked robust with her hair scraped back from her forehead and her best apron tied neatly round her torso. Dachhiri smiled sadly and handed the photograph to the two girls sitting by the fire. They made appreciative noises and handed the picture back.

'We get married,' he simply said.

'Congratulations, Dachhiri. That's great news.' I couldn't think of anything else to say.

'I ask at Namche.'

'You mean you haven't asked her yet?'

'No. I telephone at Namche.' He put the picture back in his wallet and he suddenly seemed very serious, looking blankly into the embers of the fire.

We set off through the mist but there was little to break the flat monotony of the light, except the sharp stab in my ankles. I still felt desperately weak and was grateful when Dachhiri stopped for his morning noodles at Konar at an even more basic shack than the one we had just come from. I sat on the doorstep and the old woman who was making Dachhiri's breakfast joined me. She offered me a packet of cigarettes and since eating was no longer the pleasure it had been I took one. Her granddaughter sat down next to me and we both looked out at the dismal morning, companionably sullen. I became aware of someone eating behind me.

'Dachhiri, ask her how long it is to Pangboche.' I was already thinking about the end of the day before it had hardly started. There was a brief exchange.

'She says that for her with load it takes maybe four hours. So I think maybe it takes us four hours. Heesh-heesh.'

I would sooner have extracted my teeth while dancing naked in a snowstorm than walk another four hours. There was no view as we trudged on, nothing but the dripping trees and my condensing breath to break the white silence. I found a couple of humbugs in my pocket which seemed appropriate.

'Sweeties!' Dachhiri said. My one consolation was that he at least was happy.

At last the mani stones and chorten that signalled the boundaries of Phortse emerged from the gloom. The trees thinned out to be replaced by fields. A little boy looked up and saw us. '*Namaste!* Hello!' A woman was crossing a snowy field to her lodge, her back bent under a load, her hands under her basket. The village was beautiful and again I was reminded of upland Derbyshire. Farmers there would know exactly how it felt to be carrying fodder to animals on a morning like this. Seeing Phortse somehow lifted my mood and as we left the village I resumed staring at the track with renewed enthusiasm. I started seeing fresh boot tracks. They were large, around size eleven, and judging by the crisp imprint the soles were new. Then I noticed another set of tracks, smaller, perhaps size seven. I decided that they were girlfriend and boyfriend and with feet that big were either German or American. When we caught them at the top of a steep rocky climb I took much childish satisfaction from being proved right. They were from Munich and the boyfriend seemed irritated to have been overtaken by a walking corpse, although the corpse, now surviving purely on a diet of mint humbugs, was starting to feel quite good. The track became straighter and with fewer climbs and descents to slow us and irritate my festering blisters. Long before we had walked four hours, the prayer flags and diminutive stupa of Pangboche emerged from the mist. At over 12,500 feet, Pangboche is the highest settlement in the Imja Khola that is occupied for the whole year, and the upper part of the village we were now walking through felt substantial and well appointed in comparison to the small farms and lodges I had grown used to over the last few days. The lodge Dachhiri chose, the Tashi Delek, seemed luxurious after the earth floors and damp mattresses of the night before.

I immediately set to work on cleaning my feet. Three Americans now entered the lodge, two middle-aged men and a woman who took an immediate interest in my predicament. It would have been easy for them to have done nothing and, given the level of reserve and indifference I had seen in many of the trekkers I met in the Khumbu, it wouldn't have surprised me. The three had brought with them what amounted to a small field hospital but better even than this was their sympathy.

'Gosh, that looks painful,' they would say at regular intervals as they bathed and swabbed.

'Well, it's not so very bad,' I would reply trying to look manful. Dachhiri sat some distance away drinking his tea, looking on in disbelief as so much fuss was wasted on something quite so trivial. At the end of it all, I was left with two disinfected feet, strapped and padded so effectively that I was able to walk for the next fortnight with no discomfort at all.

All three, I discovered, had trekked throughout the Himalaya and Karakoram over a number of years. Zeno had studied ethnology and anthropology at Berkeley and trekked in the Khumbu in the mid 1960s. I was curious about the changes he, like the American at Gokyo, had seen. He too felt that Kathmandu had changed beyond recognition, indeed had seen an even greater contrast. I remembered Kanak Dixit's view that Kathmandu had been relatively intact until the early 1980s. It clearly saddened Zeno but he seemed more sanguine about the changes than some. Perhaps such destructive upheavals were the inevitable consequence of development, that no amount of planning could have altered the way things had happened. In the Khumbu, he thought, the changes were less painful.

'There's a big difference in the level of affluence and scale of things,' he said. 'I mean in Namche in 'sixty-five there were still wooden shingles on the roofs. But the people don't seem to have changed their outlook that much. Their culture seems pretty strong.'

It is easy in the West to assume that an economic transformation will necessarily mean a cultural one. People coming to the Khumbu to judge the impact of the changes in the last thirty or forty years often carry that preconception with them and, seeing the predilection among younger Sherpas for western-style clothes or music, think they have evidence for such a cultural shift. But the Sherpas are a people used to adapting to fit new circumstances, indeed their cultural values sustain them in this ability to change. Dachhiri's fondness for the *masala* movies produced in Bombay, his obvious delight when I gave him odd pieces of equipment, didn't alter his sense of belonging to a family and a clan, of developing his relationship with Pussi in a way that any Sherpa could recognise. He loved being in Kathmandu as well as the mountains, but in the city he kept the same social connections and practices that he would in his village. Perhaps it was simply that the old way of life in the Khumbu was never so hard that the Sherpas abandoned it altogether when an alternative came along, but was hard enough to make them create a robust and supportive culture.

There was little to be done or seen outside and, after the last few days of illness and effort at altitude, I was grateful for the opportunity to sit and talk. Deborah was a psychoanalyst living in New Mexico and had a great interest in the motivation and psychology of climbers. All three had read a great deal of climbing writing, including that of several British authors, and were curious about whether their mental impressions of them matched reality, or at least, my interpretation of reality. Gossip is such a pleasure. They had trekked to K2's Base Camp in the Karakoram with a number of European climbers I knew slightly. They seemed to share my opinion that far from having some extra quality denied to the mortgage-paying masses, some full-time mountaineers have something missing from their lives, some shortcoming that makes the expedition life, hard and dangerous though it often is, preferable to dealing with problems at home.

My stomach felt more stable than it had since falling ill in Phakding and a mood of gluttony fell on me as I worked through the lodge's menu and started on some of the delicacies bought or retrieved from departing expeditions. The lodge itself had made a conscious effort to present Sherpa culture with a booklet describing local customs and behaviour and postcards sold for the benefit of the monastery at Tengpoche on the other side of the valley. I thought about the Alps and how local people had taken advantage of the region's exponential growth in tourism since the first mountaineers had arrived in the early nineteenth century. As in the Khumbu, a few dedicated climbers and travellers had promoted a pristine mountain environment with such success that thousands and then millions of people wanted a piece of it. From being an economic backwater, the Alps has become one of the richest parts of Europe.

This process is unlikely to be repeated in the Khumbu. The idea of extending the road from Jiri to Lukla or Namche has been suggested but would be too expensive to build and maintain and the altitude of the Khumbu would deter many people, even if the problems of poor sanitation and basic accommodation were overcome. The two things that have devastated the environment in the Alps are the skiing industry and traffic, neither of which are likely to trouble the Khumbu in the immediate future. Whether the park authorities are able to manage what growth in tourism does come remains to be seen.

One difference between the Alps and the Khumbu that encouraged me was religious. The relationship between the brand of Tibetan Buddhism practised in the Khumbu and the landscape is fundamentally different to the relationship between Catholicism and the environment. It would be a mistake to over-romanticise the link the Sherpas have with the land; they have made mistakes and caused damage, just as we have in our mountains. But there is a cultural and religious stake in the landscape that is illustrated by the mani stones and chorten that appear all over the Khumbu. The landscape was never such an important force in the spiritual well-being of Alpine people.

After the three Americans had gone to bed, I joined the card game Dachhiri and their Sherpas had been playing all evening. A huge kettle of chang was being handed round. One of the Sherpas was especially handsome, with a cool sneer permanently on his full lips. He wore black and white check trousers, a purple and green down jacket, a blue silk bandanna. Remarkably, the ensemble worked.

'His name is Pasang,' Dachhiri whispered to me. 'He was at Pangka, you know, during the snow.' Pasang seemingly spoke no English but his friend Namgyal, who was thankfully more approachable, spoke it well. Through him I asked Pasang whether it was true he had been in Pangka at the time of the avalanche. He replied that not only had he been there, he had been working for the thirteen Japanese who had died in the tragedy. He was the one Sherpa who had survived. I asked him how he came to be outside the hut when the avalanche struck and he replied that another avalanche had come down just before, burying the lodge. This was when he had gone outside to clear snow from the roof. When the main avalanche swept over the hut he had thrown his arms in front of his face to create a breathing space, allowing him to escape after he was buried. It was he who had freed his Rai companion and then dug into the ruined lodge and found the leader's radio to call for help. The next day a helicopter from Kathmandu arrived and took him off. After he finished his story, Pasang leaned forward and took my wrist.

'For me,' he suddenly said in English, 'this is a second life.'

Telling the story made Pasang more forthcoming. His good looks had apparently given him plenty of opportunities to have affairs with western trekkers. Pasang described how one woman, considerably older than he, returned year after year to go trekking with him and continue their affair. 'She calls me her black beauty,' he said with obvious satisfaction.

'So affairs like this are common?' I asked, without thinking.

Namgyal looked at me rather aghast. This kind of thing, he told me, went on *all the time*. Wasn't I curious about Sherpanis? Would I like him to sort me out a date in Lukla? I tried to think of a way to explain how married Englishmen were positively discouraged from acting out of curiosity but the task proved beyond me.

The evening was far advanced and one or two had left the circle around the stove in the middle of the room and were now asleep on the benches around the walls of the lodge. A single candle stuck in its own wax on a table was the only light and the shadows seemed to contract around the group of half a dozen faces caught in its yellow flame. An old man who seemed to be related to the lodge-owner rocked in his seat repeating a mantra over and over again while flicking beads around his rosary.

Pasang told about a recent yeti attack in Machermo. This was different from the 'hearing' in Dole a few nights before. In this instance a Sherpani heard the yeti on the roof, trying to prise off the corrugated iron. She lit an incense stick and prayed and the yeti retreated. All five Sherpas huddled round the fire in the Tashi lodge believed in the yeti. I wondered whether it was a good thing to have your demons made flesh and bone.

Namgyal and Pasang both wanted to do more work for climbing expeditions. Friends in their village near Lukla had climbed Everest and been paid up to $3000 for doing so. I asked them whether they were interested in climbing for itself and they said no. Judging by the way they were dressed, they were materialistically inclined but they also said the Buddhist faith was strong and important to them. They didn't seem over-impressed by much of what the West had to offer, and were more concerned that they should be respected in their own society. Finally, the chang ran out and we crept to the sides of the room to sleep. In the night I woke to hear the old man still whispering his mantras, even in his sleep.

When I woke next morning to find the lodge flooded with sunshine I felt I could almost guarantee that by the early afternoon the clouds would build again, but while it lasted I could not imagine a more perfect day. In sunshine Pangboche appeared even more beautiful and I stood by the stupa on the edge of the village and looked down across the fields where Sherpanis were already at work and then up the other side of the valley to the backdrop of Thamserku and Kangtega. Back at the Tashi Delek the three Americans and their Sherpas were preparing to leave for the gompa. The day before they had arranged a puja, a prayer cere-mony, and welcomed Dachhiri and me to join them. A monk had walked over that morning from Tengpoche to officiate. Sitting in the dusty gloom of the monastery was very restful as the monk took down one of the beautiful wooden covered books and began to read. He kept the rhythm by banging a drum suspended from the ceiling and at climactic moments in the course of his reading crashed a cymbal as well. Sometimes his attention would wander and he would lose his place or the rhythm and have to recover quickly. At intervals rice was handed round and at the appropriate moment we threw it into the air in a fine white spray. It landed with a rattle on the rough floorboards of the gompa. The monk would also regularly pour chang from an old Bell's bottle as a libation. After ten minutes or so, two Sherpas came up the stairs and Dachhiri waved frantically from the low bench we were all sitting on. They exchanged pleasantries while the monk continued with the puja. It was like being at a Greek Orthodox service. They stood politely in silence for a while and then the whole process of farewells began before they tramped downstairs again.

As the puja continued, I got progressively colder and looked at the few shafts of sunlight piercing the room with increasing longing. I became mesmerised by the curl of smoke reaching towards the low ceiling and by the worn frescoes and garish stat-uettes and almost missed the final great flourish of rice-throwing and cymbal-crashing that completed the puja. The monk shuffled his book together. After we made an offering to the gompa and he smiled and namasted very graciously, we took our numb limbs down the narrow stairs and out into the warm day. It was like coming out of a country church on a bright winter Sunday morning. Zeno and I stood around and chatted in the sunshine for a while and then took a few photographs. Behind the stupa three women were digging in a small field, the lime-green cap of one catching my eye. We moved inside the lodge for breakfast and then said goodbye. The Americans headed for Dingboche on the other side of the valley while Dachhiri and I prepared for the short walk to Pheriche.

As the trail above Namche gets closer to Everest the bed of the river rises from the depths of its gorge until it holds the broad curve left by glaciation rather than the deep notch of the Dudh Kosi further downstream. The walking was easier than it had been for days, as we tramped passed the mani stone walls along the muddy track carved up by yak hooves. Rejoining the main trail to Everest made an immediate and obvious difference. Trekkers and climbers were everywhere, some striding past in matching anoraks, t-shirts, even boots. It once denoted organisation, now it seemed rather grotesque. 'This is my army,' it seemed to suggest. 'We are here to conquer.' Some of the trekkers had resorted to wearing plastic mountaineering boots on a path that was considerably easier than the one up Snowdon.

Just to prove that the other extreme existed, a Japanese man rode by on the back of a yak, still dressed in the jeans, although not the trainers he was wearing when Sherpas found him stumbling across the Khumbu Glacier just above Everest Base Camp. I was told that he would lose several toes to frostbite, but he seemed insanely happy, nodding and laughing as we passed. He was probably just happy to be alive.

After the wooded charm of Pangboche, Pheriche seemed grim and desolate, not least because of the strong wind that scours the town during the afternoon. By an accident of geography, winds travelling up the Imja Khola veer west through Pheriche, leaving the village of Dingboche just to the east more or less alone, despite there being only a mile or so between them. The village is a yak-herding settlement and has been for centuries but it carried the impression that it exists only to service the needs of trekkers and climbers reaching towards Everest Base Camp. When Eric Shipton arrived here in late September 1951 it was deserted.

Dachhiri led the way through the walled village to the Himalayan Hotel where a dozen or so climbers were sprawled in the living room wrapped in down jackets against the cold and immersed in improbably fat novels. 'Your pleasure is our business,' read a handwritten sign on the wall. At the back of the room I spotted the British mountaineer Mal Duff who I knew was leading a commercial expedition to Everest. Many of the climbers in the room were members of his team. The notion of paying somebody to help you climb Everest is quite a new idea, even to climbers, and those that do are often thought not competent to climb the mountain themselves, an idea supported by reports of potential Everesters being taught to use crampons and other equipment after they arrive at Base Camp. Many of these 'commercial' expeditions, however, are made up of those with sufficient experience but who lack the time or simply can't be bothered to organise a trip for themselves, or who are capable of climbing the mountain, given good leadership. Most of Mal's team seemed more than capable of reaching the summit.

The walls of the lodge were smothered with stickers and postcards from previous expeditions. I saw pictures of people I knew, some of them now dead, one of them dying on the expedition being advertised by the poster he appeared on. The fatality rate on expeditions to the highest peaks of the Himalaya is between two and three per cent, but it varies from season to season and from mountain to mountain. That feeling of not knowing before a climb how it will finish, of whether the odds will apply to you is extra baggage you don't want or need, especially for those who haven't experienced it before. Fifty to one. You wouldn't back a horse on those odds, but would you put a gun to your head? The feeling of anticipation among Mal's team during the two or three days I saw them was palpable.

In the afternoon I walked over to the medical post, built by the Tokyo Medical College after a number of trekkers died from altitude sickness, and now run by the Himalayan Rescue Association. It offers advice and treatment to trekkers and mountaineers concerned about altitude sickness, and other ailments but, depressingly, the worst cases it now sees are often porters from lower altitudes who have gained height too quickly while carrying loads. A female porter with a South African expedition had been treated the day before for cerebral oedema. She had been put in a nylon bag – called a Gamow bag after its inventor – that can be pressurised with a foot pump. The device has saved many lives in recent years and after fourteen hours of effectively breathing at a lower altitude the porter recovered sufficiently to be escorted down. Most of the time, people are treated for non-emergency conditions like bronchitis or diarrhoea. The doctor on duty was called Larry Silver, an anaesthetist in his late thirties from Lake Tahoe with a particular interest in wilderness medicine who had volunteered to help run the post for the season. His office was full of small reminders of home, photographs and books. Silver was a little like a missionary, come to the wilds from civilisation to cure ignorant trekkers and spread the good news of appropriate acclimatisation.

Each day he gave a lecture to anyone who wanted to listen among the transient tourists of Pheriche about how to recognise altitude sickness and then treat it. The mechanics of altitude sickness are complex but Silver gave a concise explanation of how our bodies respond to altitude. In short, there is half the amount of air at Everest Base Camp as there is at sea level. The percentage of oxygen in the air is the same, there's just less air. Oxygen is forced into your bloodstream because the pressure of oxygen in the lung's alveoli, the tiny capillaries in the lungs, is higher than that in the bloodstream. When air pressure drops, the concentration of oxygen in the blood drops also. If the respiratory system cannot respond to a drop in air pressure then climbers would experience the same levels of hypoxia, or shortage of oxygen, at 5,500 metres as they do on the summit of Everest. But since there are communities in Nepal, but especially in Tibet, who live at over 5000 metres for much of the year, then clearly the body can respond. For non-acclimatised trekkers or climbers the initial response is to breathe more rapidly and for the heart to beat more. This response is called the hypoxia ventilatory response and some climbers have a better HVR than others. But the consequence of this is to increase the levels of carbon dioxide in your bloodstream and so increase its alkalinity. Over a period of weeks your body starts producing more haemoglobin and breathing rates return to normal when resting. Blood alkalinity also returns to normal. Sherpas naturally have more red blood cells and more capillaries in their muscles to provide more oxygen when working, giving them an inherent advantage when climbing at altitude.

After around six weeks, you can acclimatise fully to an altitude of around 5,500 metres. Above this altitude, however, air pressure is so low that the body can no longer make sufficient adjustments. As a consequence breathing and heart rates increase along with the alkalinity of the blood. The higher you go the more pronounced these changes become. Were Everest a few hundred metres higher it would be impossible to climb without carrying bottled oxygen.

The increase in the blood's alkalinity also worsens as altitude increases and the body adjusts to make room for more oxygen. The consequence of this is to affect the body's biochemistry and the functioning of major organs. At heights of above 8000 metres this process is fatal within days. This is why such extreme altitudes have been called the death zone. Spend too long up there and you grind to a halt, sit down and eventually die. Rescue, even by those using bottled oxygen, is difficult and unlikely. Those climbers like the Italian Reinhold Messner with a superb HVR are able to climb faster and more safely at extreme altitudes because there is more oxygen reaching their muscles and brain. As a consequence they spend less time in this so-called death zone. It's easy to see why average climbers prefer to supplement the existing oxygen from a bottle. Nor is a shortness of breath the end of it. The increase in respiration and heart rate increases the metabolic rate as well, burning more calories. Altitude, however, suppresses the appetite and climbers who spend a long time high can lose stones over the course of an expedition, weakening their reserves still further.

During the process of acclimatisation, trekkers and climbers can face a number of debilitating or even life-threatening conditions. Acute mountain sickness is the most common, affecting almost fifty per cent of trekkers in the Everest region. Most of these only suffer mild headaches or nausea that are easily treated. A very few, if left untreated, go on to develop cerebral or pulmonary oedema, where fluid builds up in the brain or lungs, conditions which can be fatal. There are now drugs like acetazolamide that can help in acclimatisation, and drugs for treating oedemas, but descent remains the best option available. Climbers are most at risk, since descending difficult terrain in bad weather or for someone incapacitated by illness is arduous.

Worse, perhaps, than the threat of sudden, serious illness is the grind of high-altitude mountaineering, the myriad slight problems like defecating in the freezing cold, the chapped lips and sun-burnt nose, the incessant cough or lack of appetite that don't stop you climbing but make it harder so that turning round and giving up make perfect sense and going on mere foolishness. I could never climb Everest. Apart from not having a spare $30,000, I could never want to enough. When Larry and I stepped outside the post after his lecture, an English girl was slumped against the wall, pale-faced and blue around the lips. For the second time in two days she had tried to climb to the last staging post before Everest Base Camp at Lobuje, despite Larry's advice to descend. She wanted to reach Everest Base Camp so badly that she had been prepared to risk her life. It was always the same question up here – why? I tried to see things from her perspective, all those fit people walking round normally, eating normally, and doing the things they came here to do. Why not her? She was just as strong, just as fit. The question with those driven to reach or climb the slopes of Everest is not why are there accidents, but *why aren't there more?*

I sat down in the living room of the Himalayan Hotel with

some tea and tried to read. For the first time since arriving in the Khumbu I wasn't welcome in the kitchen. Given the constant demands for food by the dozen or so climbers and trekkers in the room, I could understand why, but I looked forward to getting away from the mainstream again. The lodge's ill-fitting door suddenly opened and a burly man with a full black beard appeared. I hadn't seen Bruce Herrod for a couple of years but he seemed unsurprised to see me. 'I had a feeling you'd be here,' he said with a smile. He dropped his hat on he table and sat down to talk. It was good to see him, if only because we were both trying to do something similar in our lives, to spend time in the mountains and simultaneously have an interesting job, he as a photographer. Bruce was part of the South African expedition which was employing the porter who had collapsed the previous day. I asked him about it and he grinned and rolled his eyes. The expedition seemed to be fraught with problems and Bruce, who had a gentle, conciliatory presence, found himself trying to bring things back together. He was also planning to climb Everest himself and while I knew he wasn't the best mountaineer in the world, he was more experienced than many of those heading for the mountain. Six weeks later Bruce was dead, missing somewhere on the highest slopes of the mountain after reaching the summit on May 25th. He was thirty-seven years old. The expedition itself ended in bitter acrimony with the resignation of half the climbing team, alleged death threats against journalists sent to cover it and, eventually, the tragic outcome of Bruce's summit day.

For the leading South African climber, Ed February, the expedition began in 1990 with a postcard from someone he had barely known and hadn't seen for twelve years. Ian Woodall had been on the periphery of the Cape Town climbing scene in the late 1970s, working in an equipment store but drifted away in 1978. Woodall was writing from Nepal to say he was back into climbing and wanted to include February in future plans. He included his address, hoping for a response, but February felt that too much time had gone by to renew a distant friendship.

The next time Woodall contacted February, he was back in South Africa and had got backing for an expedition to Everest. Woodall now wanted to meet February and sound him out about joining it, an offer February found too intriguing to ignore. Having just turned forty, he knew that not many opportunities like this would come again. After tackling Woodall about his apparent lack of climbing experience, February was assured that he and the rest of the team would be in charge at Everest and on the strength of that assurance, he recruited South Africa's top climbers, Andy de Klerk and Andy Hackland. Both men were known in the international climbing community and commanded great respect. They all understood that the first South African to climb Everest would achieve instant fame and a measure of financial security. Lacking the means to mount an expensive expedition on their own, they leapt at Woodall's offer.

Climbing Everest is a hugely expensive exercise. In 1996, the Nepali authorities were charging $70,000 as a royalty to allow seven climbers to attempt the mountain. Five additional members could be added to the list at a cost of $10,000 per person. Then there is the cost of Sherpas, oxygen, supplies and equipment. Woodall needed to find sponsors and signed a contract with the *Sunday Times of South Africa* to cover the expedition. The newspaper said the expedition was 'about us being back in the world. It's about national pride. We hope all South Africans will be rooting for this team every cold, hard and dangerous step.' Woodall's plan was also boosted by an endorsement from Nelson Mandela. The expedition was presented as a celebration of the new South Africa, the youth of the rainbow nation pulling together to overcome the highest mountain on earth.

With the financial backing secured, Woodall finalised the team. In order to reflect South Africa's multi-racial future, it was felt that the expedition should be more representative of the nation; of the climbers selected so far, all were male and all except February were white. A competition was organised to select a woman member. Cathy O'Dowd, daughter of a director of Anglo-American and born in a wealthy Johannesburg suburb, was chosen from six finalists who were assessed by Woodall on Kilimanjaro, the highest mountain in Africa. O'Dowd was already an experienced and highly ambitious climber, studying at Rhodes University for her masters degree in journalism.

A white rich man's daughter, however, didn't add enough colour to the rainbow over Everest so they decided to select not one but two winners. Deshun Deysel was a black teacher from Ennerdale in the West Rand who had been obsessed by Everest since her grandmother made her watch a documentary about Ed Hillary. Deysel was obviously determined but completely inexperienced. Woodall took her anyway. Nelson Mandela sent his rainbow mountaineers on their way with the exhortation to 'try, because even by trying you will bring honour to our nation. It is young people such as this who are the hope and future of our rainbow nation.'

But almost from the moment they landed in Kathmandu things began to go wrong. Woodall had selected Sherpa Co-Operative to act as his agents but the company had little recent experience in organising an expedition and made several errors while importing the team's equipment. As a result much of it was delayed and Woodall had to remain in Kathmandu as the rest of the team went ahead to acclimatise. Andy de Klerk discovered that his high-altitude clothing was the wrong size. Herrod tried to organise what gear they did have through the heavy snow that had plagued Dachhiri and me at Gokyo. Worst of all, it transpired that Deysel's name was not on the climbing permit and she wouldn't be allowed to climb above Base Camp.

Woodall arrived in the Khumbu below Everest to find an expedition fraught with tension and doubt. He did not handle it well. By the time I reached the Himalayan Hotel in Pheriche, Bruce was acting as deputy leader and entangled in a crisis that would ultimately contribute to his death. The crisis quickly degenerated into allegations of incompetence. When Larry Silver treated the female porter who had collapsed working for Woodall's team, he discovered anti-inflammatory drugs in her possession and assumed that the expedition's doctor, Charlotte

Noble, had mis-diagnosed her condition. In fact, the drugs had come from a second porter who had been given a leaky kerosene tank to carry. The fuel had soaked through her clothes and burned her. The anti-inflammatories had been prescribed but given away, presumably to help the ailing oedema victim. Without waiting for this explanation, Woodall flew into a rage and at a hastily-convened expedition meeting, sacked Noble in front of the team. The three most experienced climbers, February, de Klerk and Hackland, decided enough was enough and resigned, hoping to persuade Woodall to think again. He didn't.

Relations between him and the *Sunday Times of South Africa* collapsed soon after and the newspaper withdrew its support. But despite the criticism he faced and his lack of experience, Woodall remained at Base Camp, joining the other expeditions on the mountain. On May 25th, South African radio reported that he and O'Dowd had reached the summit, climbing to the top from the South Col in the fast time of nine hours. Herrod was reported to be still on the mountain but because he had been moving slowly was assumed to have gone down. In fact, he was still plodding upwards on his own. Woodall and O'Dowd met Bruce below the South Summit as they descended and Woodall has said he tried to persuade him to descend but that Bruce was determined to continue. He reached the summit after five o'clock and radioed down just as Sue Thompson, his partner of seven years, called Base Camp from their home in London. He had promised her that he would turn back if he hadn't reached the summit by midday. In his last message to Sue from the summit of Everest, Bruce said: 'Of course I'm going to get down, there are too many sobering reminders of what happens if you don't.' He was referring to the bodies of other climbers who had not returned from the mountain. Bruce Herrod was never heard from again and in the spring season of 1997 his body was discovered hanging from the fixed rope on the Hillary Step just below the summit.

CHAPTER EIGHT

The sixty-four thousand dollar question

My passion is that of a thorn, my friend,
yours is for gold and diamonds,
you say the hills are deaf and dumb,
I say they are eloquent.

Lines from *Pagal* by Lakshmi Prasad Devkota

At the foot of the Lhotse face I clipped my jumar to the bottom of a line of fixed ropes and started hauling myself up towards the South Col. The sky was a deep blue as though hinting at the black space behind it, the snow glittered beneath the strong sun. I felt strong swinging my cramponed boots into the ice, as though I was breathing at sea level. In no time I would be at the top camp and soon after the summit. It was effortless. My family had joined me at the start of my summit bid to wish me luck, although surprisingly none of them had bothered with overcoats or gloves. After two or three hundred feet of climbing, I called down to them that the end of the Western Cwm was probably as far as they should go and I would see them all again very soon. They remained at the bottom of the slope looking impassively upwards, my mother and father and sisters – although curiously not my wife – until the moment when the rope ripped out the ice screws supporting it and I fell backwards, swinging uselessly with an ice axe at the snow in front of me before I picked up speed. It seemed a good moment to wake up.

People in the lodge were already on the move, packing gear and cleaning teeth, clumping round the wooden dormitory. Dachhiri was curled up in his sleeping bag next to me, his face unexpectedly serious in the composure of sleep. Mornings are a savage business, and I debated kicking him awake to go and fetch some tea. The pressure on my bladder spared him.

The kitchen seemed quieter than the evening before and I found a position by the fire from which I could order a succession of drinks until I was sure the sun had struck the wall opposite the lodge. Then I took my glass of tea outside to watch people setting off for the day. Dachhiri emerged from the dormitory and we sat for a while basking in the warmth and putting off the moment of departure. Above Pheriche to the west, Tawoche's North-East Ridge soared steeply up, much the most impressive aspect of the mountain. Two British climbers, Mick Fowler and Pat Littlejohn, had recently climbed this ridge over a number of long and gruelling days, all of it more technically demanding than anything found on Everest. Its summit, however, is 2500 metres lower so that while passing trekkers might pause and comment on the mountain's dramatic aspect, they would be unconcerned about those climbing it. It's true to say that many more people could climb Everest than the route on Tawoche, despite the altitude difference, but Everest's supremacy has deflected the public's attention away from those breaking new boundaries in the sport.

In my work as a journalist, it has long been clear to me that the allure of Everest has little to do with mountaineering, that loveable, unwashed, fuck-you village of miscreants. People are instead fascinated by the obsession the mountain engenders, by the risk of death that others will contemplate because it is the highest point on earth. On discovering at a dinner party that their neighbour is a climber, most non-climbers will ask whether they've climbed Everest, rather than take an interest in the activity itself. The only reason that I could think of for slogging up the wretched thing would be the pleasure taken from saying yes. But then, if that was the case, why was I having dreams about climbing Everest in front of my family?

I went back into the dormitory to get the fat wad of rupees I hid in my rucksack to pay for our lodgings. Putting my hand into its concealed inside pocket I experienced the shock of not finding something you assume will be there. I checked again. It should be there. I was sure that in a moment I would be laughing with relief and holding the notes. There was still nothing there. I started going through my pockets and emptying the rucksack. Still nothing. I sat down on a bunk and counted the money in my wallet. I had lost 11,000 rupees, over $200. A year's salary for many in Nepal. There was absolutely nothing to be done about it, as the lodge-owner pointed out when I told her as she sat in the sunshine drinking tea. '*Ke garne?*' she smiled. 'What to do?' Storm around having tantrum, I thought, that's 'what to do'. I knew it was unlikely that the thief would be local or a porter since the money was in large denominations and everyone would soon be aware that a trekker had been robbed. Getting rid of large bills would be difficult for someone who would earn just one of them each month. I remembered a New Zealand trekker who had left while I was sunbathing, jogging down the track towards Namche. Jogging at 14,000 feet. On her own. I rushed to the HRA post and found Larry Silver who had access to a radio, asking that he alert the police in Namche to the arrival of a thief. Larry said yes, he could do that and what a pity I'd been robbed, but then looked at me slightly sideways as though I was behaving strangely. I suddenly realised I *was* behaving strangely. I had no evidence against this poor woman, and if I left my money in such a stupid place, then what did I expect?

Recovering my mood didn't alter the fact that I was now destitute, which meant, in effect, that Dachhiri was equally destitute. He looked sorrowful and slightly aghast that his employer could get quite so angry. I sent him down to a small trading store with as much of my gear as I could spare, perhaps $200-worth. He returned saying that I'd been offered ten which was no use at all. I had enough money to get to Namche where I might find someone I knew to lend me more, but what if I didn't? I had expected to have several more weeks in the Khumbu and the thought of returning now seemed dreadful. Dachhiri and I sat down and drank some tea while I got progressively more depressed about the thought of our loss. One of Mal Duff's team-members, a Finn called Veikka, came over to commiserate.

'How much did you lose?' he asked. I told him. 'This I can lend you,' he replied and took two $100 bills out of his wallet. It was a spontaneous and generous act for which I was and remain embarrassingly grateful. My reaction to the theft had been typically western. I took it personally, seeing it as a slight on me as much as a loss of property. It was I who had suffered as a consequence of someone else's greed. I wanted retribution, revenge even, to see the thief caught and humbled. Dachhiri and the lodge-owner found this pretty strange. To a Buddhist, the concept of merit lies at the heart of morality. Sherpas are less obsessive about it, but it is still important to them. Briefly, each individual has a stock of merit or *sonam* which can be added to by good deeds – *gewa* – or diminished by bad deeds, or *digba*. This moral ledger has a line drawn underneath at death and affects the quality of rebirth. In *The Sherpas of Nepal*, Christoph von Fürer-Haimendorf details some of the things considered sinful:

> Quarrelling, theft and cheating are sins. To talk ill and worse, falsely, behind someone's back is sin. To kill any living creature is a sin. If someone kills a cat he commits so great a sin that he cannot make up for it even by burning as many butter lamps as the cat had hairs on its body. Killing a yak or sheep is a sin but not eating them. To have sexual relations with someone else's wife is a sin, to threaten children or make them cry is a sin. Drunkenness is a sin for monks. Exorcising spirits is a sin.

There had been no cat-slayings, but even if there had, retribution for such behaviour was not my business. It was the thief's loss, not mine. My gut response was to want bad things to happen to a bad person in this world and not the next. Sherpas don't appoint themselves as moral authorities in this way. There will be no systematic hunt for a criminal and then a trial; for this reason

the gradual imposition on the Khumbu of Hindu judicial authority originating in Kathmandu is viewed with suspicion by the
Sherpas. Their inability to deal with anti-social behaviour must be
a real handicap at times, but I doubt whether any westerner is in a
position to offer advice on law and order. I hoped, at least, that
Veikka's gewa would benefit him on the mountain.

The theft left me depressed for much of the morning but
walking up the huge curved valley across the brown grass and
stones towards the terminal moraine of the Khumbu Glacier, the
scale of the landscape simply blanked it from my mind. I felt in
much better health than I had in weeks and managed to keep up
with Dachhiri until lunch. I took pictures of him against the backdrop of Cholatse and Tawoche with his hands on his hips and his
chin jutting into the sky. 'Like this?' he'd shout.

Above the lodge at Dughla, climbing up on to the level of the
glacier, we stopped at the memorial to those Sherpas who died in
an avalanche during a Japanese expedition to Everest in 1970.
While the mountain isn't visible from here, the shark's tooth of
Pumori stands behind the memorial, the names already fading in
the scouring wind. The cairns have been added to over the years,
but the site retains a sense of unity that is absent from the
climbers' memorials on the north side of Everest. There have
been more than 130 deaths on the mountain; a third of the victims
were Sherpa and I realised I could only name half a dozen of them
from memory. Many of that number died in the Khumbu Icefall,
the spill of ice that flows down from the Western Cwm in a rush
of séracs and crevasses. Sherpas move through the Icefall regularly, carrying loads to higher camps, while climbers are only
required to make the passage a handful of times. The Sherpas for
Mal Duff's expedition were already at work as we were walking up,
fixing a line of ropes through the Icefall that all the dozen or so
expeditions who were attempting the mountain would use over
the course of the next few weeks. Each expedition would use an
average of perhaps eight Sherpas each, meaning there would be
more than eighty on the mountain. Given the statistic that spun

through my head like a mantra, perhaps two of them would die. I could see nothing wrong with them being used in this way, even though they would get scant recognition for their efforts in comparison to the generally weaker western climbers. Three thousand dollars in a poor country is a good enough reason to take a risk, better than some vague philosophical urge for a simple life and a physical challenge which were the best reasons I'd ever managed for why I climbed.

At the top of the loose dirt and rocks of the terminal moraine, we traversed across to the true right bank of the Khumbu Glacier. The ground was still thick with snow which was proving a problem for expeditions bringing their supplies to Base Camp on the backs of zopkios. A group of three slithered towards us and we were forced to move out of the way as they passed, sinking up to our thighs in wet snow. Lobuje was little more than a group of shacks in a nook of boulders in the moraine above a bowl of snow. At its southern edge by the side of the trail was a mound of garbage, a few black choughs picking through it. The grey clouds and melting snow just added to the squalor. Lobuje is a place to get away from on the way to somewhere else. Perhaps that's why it isn't cared for as well as the more established places. Those looking for evidence of the despoliation of the Khumbu come to Lobuje and photograph the garbage, a tourist attraction in its own right. I left the choughs to it and followed Dachhiri into the lodge.

Mal Duff had already settled his considerable frame at a table below the window, close to the stove. While the few trekkers in the lodge seemed slightly bewildered by it all, the altitude, the grey and black rocks and white snow, Mal was relaxed, content even, ordering beers and food. He was charging $23,000 for each place on his expedition. A company called Adventure Consultants, led by the highly experienced guide Rob Hall, was charging $65,000. And that's without air fares. Hall's clients were still on their way from Kathmandu. I asked Mal about the difference in price and his answer seemed to be 'food and Sherpas'. The expensive outfits imported beer and crisps and other treats from home. They had more Sherpas which meant their clients would need to carry very little on their way to the summit. I wondered whether the higher price put more pressure on the guides to get clients to the summit. In the free-market, multi-million-dollar economy of climbing Everest, safety was supposed to come first, but who was to say what was safe? Mal had brought ten members and hired eight Sherpas. They would get a daily rate, a clothing allowance and bonuses for reaching the summit and other targets. The Sherpa in charge, the sirdar, could make extra by taking a cut of money spent buying equipment and food. And now, thanks to Brent Bishop's garbage incentive scheme, they could earn even more bringing all that western trash off the mountain after the sahibs had finished with it. Everybody was getting a cut. There was nothing personal in climbing Everest, it was just business. In Kathmandu I had interviewed the journalist Elizabeth Hawley who had worked variously for *Time* and Reuters and had for years recorded the activities of every expedition that arrived in Nepal since the early 'sixties. She had told me that she kept tabs on which economies were booming by their arrival on the mountaineering scene. The British and other Europeans appeared before she did, but over the years others had followed, first the Japanese, then other countries from the Pacific rim like the South Koreans and Taiwanese. Most recently the Malaysians had started coming along with Russians who came not to climb for themselves, but to compete for guiding work with the Sherpas, just as their helicopters were competing with porters. Mal's trip, at $23,000, perhaps said something about the British economy, not least because half his clients were European.

The afternoon drifted by with gossip and bullshit, a group of men already stinking in their polyester underwear, drinking beer and rubbing the stubble on their faces. The good humour and anticipation were engaging despite the fact that this was no group of friends who had known and climbed with each other for years. For the first time since arriving in the Khumbu, I felt I wanted to go climbing. Between Base Camp and Lukla, the season's

Everesters were strung out, some relaxed and settled, others full of doubt. Mal's Sherpas worked on the Icefall, he waited at Lobuje with his mixture of Danish, Finnish and British climbers. Outside in the snow a team from Taiwan had raised their tents. The South Africans waited in Pheriche for their gear to catch up and their arguments to be resolved, together with the Yugoslavs from the Kathmandu Guest House, whose arguments were all at home. The American expedition shooting the IMAX format film had retired to Dingboche to acclimatise, while two more British expeditions were reported to be at Namche. New Zealander Rob Hall and the American Scott Fischer were newly arrived at Lukla with their separate teams of clients. There was something compelling in so much effort and equipment being gathered up and down the valley to converge on the same place, the same objective. It was like the excitement of a circus coming back to town after a year's absence. There was no need to ask why it was there, it just was. All there was to be done was to fill my nostrils with the smell of sawdust and take a ringside seat.

Late in the afternoon the lodge door opened and three trekkers from Singapore stumbled into the room. First were two slight, fragile girls who looked exhausted. Then a boy arrived, supported by the group's guides. They weren't Sherpas but Rai and exhibited a matey assurance that seemed untrustworthy. The boy was white with a blue tinge around his lips and was struggling to breathe. Mal gave him some pills to stave off pulmonary oedema and told the guides that the boy should go back to Pheriche where there was a Gamow bag in case his condition worsened.

'He's going to feel better in half an hour when the drugs take affect,' he warned the guide who went with him, 'but don't let him come back up.'

The two girls sat drinking tea, perched on the bunks, unhappy at our pressure to get the guide to take their friend back down. They were planning on climbing the small hill called Kala Pattar overlooking Base Camp the next day. An hour later and they were back, the boy looking pinker and stronger. The guide shrugged his shoulders. The boy dumped his rucksack on the bunk next to mine and settled down to sleep. By the early hours of the morning, the drugs Mal had given him were wearing off and his condition had worsened again. He sat up in bed and switched his torch on straight into my eyes and woke me. For the next few hours he did everything he could think of to stave off sleep, eating, reading, sorting out his gear and all the while I watched, resenting bitterly that he was keeping me awake and at the same time feeling guilty that this man was in fear of his life and all I could do was feel grumpy about it. As morning filtered into the gloomy cabin, I rolled onto my back and stared at the ceiling of my bunk. Graffiti had been carved into the smoke-stained wood. It read:

Daniel James Vallin
solo, July 1995
born 9th December, 1969
Kenosha, Wisconsin

Underneath Daniel's neat inscription, someone else had added in jagged capitals the words 'ARE WE SO VAIN?' Apparently, we were. I stepped outside with a glass of tea and took ibuprofen, antibiotics, garlic capsules and a Sikhar cigarette from Mick, Mal's laconic assistant. The Taiwanese emerged from their tents blinking sleepily in the cold blue light, wrapping themselves in parkas as they went. Inside the lodge we competed for table space as the lodge-owner struggled to make breakfast and I found myself sitting opposite a young man, perhaps twenty-five, cradling a glass of milky sweet tea. He grinned and said hello, and I grinned back but it was hard to ignore the fact that all his fingers had been amputated just above the knuckles on both hands.

'You're going to Everest?'

'Ya, sure. Everesh.' He smiled again and I looked away. The surgeon had done a good job but it was difficult to see what contribution he could make on the mountain. I was told that the previous spring he had attempted to climb Denali, the highest

mountain in North America, as part of his expedition's preparation for Everest. Caught with seven companions by indifferent
weather, he had spent a night out in the open at over 19,000 feet.
A helicopter managed to reach them next day but by then one of
them was dead and two had suffered debilitating frostbite. The
leader of the expedition, Ming Ho Gao known as 'Makalu' Gao,
was helped down the mountain. He stopped all those he met
during the descent with the words 'Victory! Victory! We made
summit!' It came as no surprise to those on Everest that spring
when one of Makalu Gao's team, a thirty-six year old steelworker
from Tapei called Chen Yu-Nan, was killed. He had left his tent at
Camp 3 on the steep Lhotse Face beneath the South Col to defe-
cate but hadn't bothered to pull his outer mountaineering boot
over the smooth-soled inner. As he squatted he lost his footing
and hurtled down the Lhotse Face until he lodged head first in a
crevasse. Bruised and frightened, he was hauled out of the
crevasse by Sherpas who had seen him fall. Next day, after his
companions had continued to the South Col, Chen Yu-Nan was
on his way back to Camp 2 with assistance from the team's Sherpas
when he simply collapsed and died. I cannot lose the memory of
the round young face of his colleague, grinning up at me from the
team's breakfast table, his ruined hands clutching a glass.

Dachhiri and I left the lodge and followed the track along the
edge of the glacier towards Base Camp, padding across the frozen
snow and over banks of crumbling moraine. Eric Shipton once
described glacier areas as materially useless. What aesthetic value
they hold is debatable. The landscape around us was colossal, so
vast that in imagining it now I know it is reduced. The twisted wall
of Nuptse soared over the glacier, white and gold, barring entry
into the Western Cwm. The glacier snaked beneath, its ribbed
surface like scales as it burrowed down the valley. Like an English
cathedral, its appeal is in its architecture and not its details. Even
at 5000 metres life still struggles to raise its head above the shale
and dust. Mosses, forbs and lichens find niches of calm in this
geological frenzy and resist the cold and wind. Choughs scatter

and wheel close to the ground while an eagle jibes against the wind above Kala Pattar. But it's not beautiful. The light is too stark for too much of the time, the sheer scale too vast for that. Perhaps this is how someone who once walked on the moon must feel, looking up into the sky and remembering a stark and haunting landscape. And when you've been to another world, how could you not want to return?

We stopped for tea at the small lodge at Gorak Shep and then started walking up the few hundred feet of Kala Pattar. The name means 'black stones' which is, I am told, the response given to Colonel Jimmy Roberts when he asked his guide its name. Roberts, a former Military Attaché in Kathmandu, invented the trekking industry in the 1960s, drawing on his memories of shooting parties before the war in Kashmir. His idea of a tented progress through the mountains managed by staff and guides is still the model for much of the trekking done throughout the Himalaya. Gradually, in the more popular areas at least, trekking's popularity encouraged local people to build lodges, allowing trekkers to walk from lodge to lodge without staff and consequently at a much reduced cost. It is this form of trekking which is now the norm in Nepal, much to the old man's irritation.

Roberts' 'invention' helped to secure the reputation of the Sherpas. Their strength carrying loads on the mountain was well known, but for his trekking holidays Roberts required staff with their own initiative and idea of standards. Their adaptation to this role gave the Sherpas a head start in an area that grew exponentially over the next thirty years. When Roberts took his first clients to the Everest region in 1965 his was the only trekking agency in the world and would remain so for the next three years. In 1994, 76,000 trekkers visited Nepal, 13,000 of those coming to Everest. The company Roberts founded, Mountain Travel, still thrives in Kathmandu, although Roberts himself now lives in semi-retirement in Pokhara surrounded by his exquisite Nepali game birds and his books. He, and those like Mike Cheney who took up his mantle, have perhaps not received the recognition they deserve for offering mountain people across the Himalaya an opportunity that would not have developed so quickly or so well without them.

As I struggled up Kala Pattar, I could sense the black wedge of Everest appearing from behind the ridge of Nuptse but hesitated to break my slow rhythm and look round. Dachhiri jogged ahead, stopping every so often to beam down at me. Walking without the heavy rucksacks of the day before, we were making excellent progress. At the summit of Kala Pattar, in reality a bump on a ridge at the base of Pumori, the wind strengthened and we hid from it between lichen covered rocks and stared across the valley. The view is inferior to that from Gokyo Ri, but Everest looms larger over the shoulder of Nuptse like a big stone shark's fin, black and jagged. The jet-stream pulled snow from its summit ridge, like fingers through hair. I thought of those waiting at Base Camp and below for the approaching monsoon to nudge the winds back into Tibet so they could sneak up to the summit and back before the snows arrived in earnest. The glacier curled away like a fat grey tongue, tasting the river beneath. Nuptse's crooked thumb gave a lopsided seal of approval to the day. Moving a little higher through deep snow, we could see the South Col and the Lhotse Face.

Finally, Everest is no more than a geological consequence, a colossal lump of rock lashed by wind and snow. Its significance is our own doing. It has provided another blank page for the adventurous and the obsessed to fill. Looking across at its squat bulk I could see features and lines that brought to mind climbers and their actions. In the faces of the peak, I could see the faces of people. By becoming Everest, Chomolungma has provided a freak show of the extremes of human endeavour. Thinking as a climber, I resented the attention heaped upon it; there are so many other mountains more beautiful, more difficult, more subtle. But there are none higher and while climbing it has attracted those who collect rather than contribute, so many of the climbers I admire the most had been drawn here, again and again.

Whatever the motivation of those who come here, the mountain is irreducible except by time. If there are those who treat Chomolungma badly by abandoning their rubbish or selling its image, then that is our loss, not the mountain's. Nothing lives up there to kill except ourselves, nothing dreams up there but us. I remembered something that Kanak Dixit had said to me in Kathmandu as he mourned the loss of his city's soul. 'They can do what they like here,' he said, 'but Everest will always be the highest mountain. They can't change that.' He is wrong, of course, as I imagine he knows very well. Once, eighty million years ago, the creatures now fossilised near Everest's summit swam in the Tethys Sea. In hundreds of millions of years perhaps another ocean will wash over the mountain's worn stump and all this will be forgotten and lost. Eric Shipton was right. There is no value to these places, except what we invest.

At Lobuje, Mal and his team dozed and read in the sunshine, their thoughts were still fixed upwards on the mountain, while Dachhiri and I had turned our backs on it. Not for the first time, I reflected that chief among the mountain climber's armoury is an ability to lie down for long periods of time. In the morning we packed our gear and said goodbye to them. I hoped that Mal would finally have a chance to reach the summit. As we walked out of Lobuje a vortex of wind caught a pile of rubbish and funnelled it into the air, twisting plastic bags and paper into the sky for perhaps sixty feet. Then we ran downhill to Dughla and across the brown flat valley beneath the glacier to Pheriche. The Americans I had met on the plane to Lukla were sun-bathing outside the Himalaya Hotel and seemed more relaxed than they had been on the way in. Their rucksacks were half the size as well, as they had progressively abandoned more and more equipment they realised they didn't need.

After a short rest we climbed the zig-zag track behind the village over the foot of what swept up to become the Nuptse ridge. On the crest overlooking the Imja Khola, the geologist Roger Bilham was at the fat IMAX camera. David Breashears hovered behind his cameraman issuing directions. A group of Sherpas lounged on the brown grass and juniper scrub. A small crowd of trekkers had gathered to watch the shoot and one of them, a Russian, drifted too close. Breashears snapped at him. 'Would you mind moving back.' Dachhiri giggled once we'd dropped well down the other side toward Dingboche. "S very funny.'

Dingboche is the only place that barley is still grown in the Khumbu and at 4300 metres it is one of the highest altitudes that grain is cultivated anywhere in the world. Sherpas grow three kinds of barley but at this altitude only a black variety they call *na* succeeds. Dachhiri called this by its Nepali name, *oua*, just to confuse me still further. Ploughs were being dragged through the walled fields in preparation for sowing which would take place in the next few days. Barley is used to make tsampa flour, a staple for Tibetans and Sherpas, although eaten less widely in the Khumbu. According to Dachhiri, his mother made the best tsampa in the world, very different from that up here. Sherpas turn this flour into porridge or paste balls called *pak* by mixing it with butter tea, or else they eat it raw. However eaten, it is filling, in the way that eating a breeze block would be filling.

On the edge of the village there was a group of tents. Dachhiri recognised them as belonging to the trekking agents who employed him. We found his cousin Pasang sitting outside the mess tent issuing instructions to his staff, like a general marshalling his troops. His charges had abandoned their intention of visiting Gokyo because of the deep snow and were now walking up the valley behind Dingboche to Chukkung below the vast wall of Lhotse's South Face. After Dachhiri and I had been bounced from the inevitable game of cards, he disappeared to find another 'cousin' who might have some chang and I walked up the track to the Himalaya Lodge. In the small dirt square in front a handsome Sherpa was having his hair combed by a Sherpani who looked rather bookish behind her spectacles. It was the first time I had seen such intimacy in the Khumbu. A tape deck thumped out

Hindi movie numbers and watery pop music and the smell of juniper floated over the perimeter walls. I felt as though I had unplugged from the current that flowed between Lukla and Everest.

When Dachhiri returned, staggering slightly, he brought the sober Pasang with him and we sat in the lodge drinking tea. He told me that the same family owned the Himalaya Hotel in Pheriche. 'The old man he died maybe three years ago,' he said. 'Liver failure,' he added, waggling his hand as though it were holding a glass. Pasang was strictly tee-total and when he discovered I was planning to visit the village he and Dachhiri came from he told me that I'd better get used to the idea of drinking a lot. 'That's all they do there,' he said with some bitterness.

Pasang also told me that a Sherpa had been stabbed the night before in a drunken brawl. The victim was badly hurt and had been carried to the aid post at Pheriche where Larry Silver's French colleague had treated him. Nobody was saying who the culprit was. Murder is very rare in the Khumbu, unsurprisingly given the importance Sherpas place on not taking a life of any kind. (The exception is lice, which is quite understandable. Sherpas believe they are demons which provides their excuse, although they have a saying that for every louse you kill, another thousand will plague you in your next life.) The one example of murder I had come across involved a man stabbed to death in a gambling argument. Despite everyone in his village knowing the identity of the killer, they prevaricated so long over dealing with him that he took the opportunity to escape into Tibet. I have read that as a consequence of this episode, the Sherpas were shocked by their inaction into asking the Nepalese authorities to establish courts in the area. Whatever the truth of this, the court's authority is mistrusted and often ignored.

In the morning we walked up the valley to the lodge at Chukkung and struggled through a biting wind to the summit of a hill beneath the Nuptse wall. I was alarmed to see my altimeter reading close to 6000 metres but it was a superb point from which to view Lhotse's black and savage South Face, perhaps the most impressive mountain aspect in the entire Himalaya – over 3000 metres of snow, ice and rock on the fourth highest mountain in the world. The Italian mountaineer Reinhold Messner, the first person to climb the fourteen peaks over 8000 metres, described it as a problem for the year 2000. The Pole Jerzy Kukuczka, a mountaineer every bit as strong as Messner, died attempting the South Face in 1989 when the rope he was climbing up snapped. The cream of French alpinism tried and failed, a dozen other expeditions large and small took on the mountain's great objective dangers, but all without success.

Then, in April 1990, a Slovenian climber called Tomo Cesen arrived at Base Camp and, after acclimatising for only a week, set out alone up the wall. He carried only light rations and a thermos of coffee – no sleeping bag, no tent, no stove. On April 24th, he radioed his friends at Base Camp. 'I cannot go any higher,' he told them, 'I'm at the top.' Mountaineers all over the world were profoundly impressed. Messner called Cesen a 'mountaineering genius', the British climber Stephen Venables praised his 'phenomenal stamina and outrageous courage'. But Cesen's photographic evidence was poor and some who had followed his career and doubted some of his other ascents began to suggest that Cesen hadn't reached the summit after all. These doubts were put aside until another Slovenian identified one of the photographs supporting Cesen's claim as his own. Cesen admitted this was true.

The debate surrounding Tomo Cesen and Lhotse's South Face is arguably the most profound in climbing's history. No one of a similar reputation had ever been mistrusted in this way on a route that had been so widely attempted. The argument struck at the soul of mountaineering; endangering the code of trust to which climbers adhere. There are many, including Messner and even some of Slovenia's top climbers, who have publicly doubted Cesen's word. Others argue that his explanations should be accepted. The only man who knows the truth is Cesen himself.

Dachhiri was supremely indifferent to the achievements and petty vanities of climbers and thought the whole business of climbing mountains a little strange. Being in the mountains, on the other hand, was wonderful, and he couldn't resist running down the grey scree of the hill we'd just climbed, shouting against the wind. As we reached Dingboche a team of yaks was pulling a plough through the black soil, an old woman walking slowly behind them. In the next field a young woman looked up from the wall she was rebuilding. Her baby lay in a box nearby completely covered with a cloth, and as we passed she slipped its strap over her forehead and, rocking the crying child from side to side, continued with her work. The handsome young Sherpa looked up from the pile of garlic he was peeling as we stepped through the lodge's gate. Inside I was alarmed to discover fresh trekking reinforcements had almost filled the main living room. An Australian was reading *Rum Doodle*.

'Y'know,' he said to his companion, 'that IMAX expedition is just like this lot.' I thought of my friend Audrey and hoped she'd appreciate the joke. As the spring wore on, events on Everest had more in common with a Greek tragedy than English farce. A young Englishman, sleek in his black jacket and sunglasses, flicked through the short pamphlet on Sherpa culture, yawned, and tossed it back on the lodge's pile of magazines. A young Japanese sitting by the door took out a cigarette and went to light it.

'Don't light that cigarette!' Everyone in the lodge looked round. The complaint had come from a narrow-faced man in his early twenties. 'It is disgusting. You are up here in the mountains with the fresh air and you are *smoking*!'

'Why shouldn't he smoke?' I couldn't believe I'd said anything. Just how big was this guy? 'There are ash-trays on the tables. If you don't like it you can go outside.' Somewhere in my head someone was saying 'Shut up!' over and over again. The Japanese came to my rescue.

'No, please. I'm sorry. No trouble.' The cigarette went back in the packet and I slunk out of the door.

Outside I was surprised to find Susan, a girl I had met with the IMAX expedition. I had assumed she was one of the crew and should therefore have been staying at the deluxe lodge just down the trail. In fact, she was just tagging along with friends on the team and was operating on her own budget. 'You think I could afford that joint?' she said with some surprise. She had been living in Kathmandu for several years and it was a pleasure to talk to someone so forthright who knew the city so well. We sat in the failing sunlight looking at the pale pink walls of Ama Dablam's West Face streaked with ice. I told her about the various environmentalists and aid projects I had encountered but she was cynical about much of it. 'There's just so much corruption and so many vested interests. And those guys running the projects, some of them are making over a hundred grand a year. Where's that coming from? I'll believe in electric rickshaws when I see a hundred of them coming at me down the street.'

The blond anti-smoking lobbyist emerged from the lodge and my pulse suddenly took off again. He was a lot bigger than I'd guessed. I felt my fingers clenching into the palms of my hands.

'You know, I'm sorry I got cross in there.'

'Not a problem, mate,' I replied, grateful he wasn't going to thump me. He was an Austrian, from Vienna, on his first trip to the Himalaya. Tomorrow he and his group were continuing to Chukkung to climb a trekking peak call Imja Tse, a popular objective for companies running commercial expeditions because there was a good chance that most of the clients would reach the summit. 'It is very different from how I thought,' he said sadly. 'It is so *dirty*.'

Susan exploded with laughter. 'Hey pal,' she said, 'this ain't Vienna.'

A drop in altitude can feel like a holiday. The sun seems stronger, the air richer and at a little over 4000 metres the trees return. Dachhiri and I lay in the sunshine at Tengpoche as the last trekkers finished their lunches and moved on. The Sherpani sitting next to me ran a comb through her hair and fussed over her son, Tshering Wangchuk. I know his name because he came and sat in the dirt beside me while I was doodling in my notebook and asked me to write it for him. Then he took the pen from me and started doodling himself until his grandmother appeared with a bowl of potatoes. The five of us sat in a circle around the bowl. Every time we had potatoes Dachhiri would watch me fumbling with the skins as I tried to peel one and not burn my fingers and then erupt with frustration and take it from me. He could peel potatoes for both of us faster than I could eat them. 'He's like a baby,' he complained to the Sherpani who almost fell over with laughter.

In the afternoon we climbed a steep ridge overlooking the gompa and the Phunki Drangka below Kangtega, kicking steps in soft snow and scrambling over rough granite until the clearing in front of the monastery was a small square and the tiny houses were like toys with streaks of smoke drifting from their roofs. We could see the track to Machermo we had walked up on the way to Gokyo, the village of Phortse, now free of snow, and the sinuous track that led down to Pangboche. Far up the valley we could even see Dingboche. Seeing so much of the Khumbu at one glance made me appreciate how small its area really was, how fragile its charm. At a notch in the ridge there was a small cairn and some prayer flags and above this the rock steepened. Dachhiri waited in his t-shirt and light sweater at the notch as I climbed higher until he could stand the cold no longer and called up to me. Then we rushed down to the tree line again, and the smell of juniper smoke and the promise of lying in the sun. Everest Base Camp was a desolate place in comparison and I didn't envy Mal and his team spending the six or seven weeks there it would take to climb the mountain.

When we got back to the lodge the first trekkers were drifting in for the evening. Some Sherpas were putting up a large group of tents outside the door and their American occupants were just arriving, their shirts open at the neck, their faces red from the long climb up from the river. They were tall, mainly middle-aged people with big feet and big arses, talking loudly as the Sherpas moved quietly around them completing their duties. Dachhiri was letting me win back more of his salary over several glasses of rakshi when they came in for dinner. There were a dozen of them seated round a table ,while the other trekkers spread around the walls in discreet parties of two or three. Then the Sherpas began carrying in the food, course after course of soup and fresh cheeses, momos and prawn crackers, while the other diners picked through their rice and lentils and stared at the groaning table with naked envy.

Gradually the rest of us fell silent as their conversation grew in volume. The talk was of real estate deals in Seattle, problems in California's Silicon Valley, the difficulties of living in New York but never, strangely enough, of the day's walking. I suddenly realised that these brash and self-satisfied people couldn't possibly be happy with inspecting just the bottom of the mountain. They were too darned big for that. The door of the lodge opened and I looked up to see the unmistakable figure of Scott Fischer, a tall and craggy mountain guide from Seattle who I knew was running an expedition to Everest. These were his clients. He took a seat at the end of the table next to a younger man and I rose unsteadily to my feet and introduced myself, an action so presumptuous that it should have warned me I was hopelessly drunk. Fischer was, given these circumstances, amiable beyond expectation.

'I've been outside supervising,' he said and then leaned towards me conspiratorially. 'You've gotta look like you're in control of things.' He was curious for news of the other expeditions, so I told him about what Mal Duff had been doing and the problems of the South Africans. Fischer was charismatic and charming and we gossiped away with the younger man he was sitting next to who it seemed was one of his guides.

'I've got Anatoly Boukreev with me as well,' Scott said. Boukreev was well-known in Himalayan climbing circles for being as strong as the Sherpas at altitude. The previous year on Everest, someone had removed his ice axe from a high camp but he had gone to the summit anyway and without oxygen, waiting until the clients he was working for had been and gone.

Fischer's sirdar was Lobsang Jangbu, a young and powerful climber who had summited Everest three times before, each time without oxygen. He had only been climbing for three years but was already well known in Nepal. He wore a gold cap on one tooth and behaved on the hill with the kind of panache that a man like Fischer would admire. It wasn't surprising that the American held him in such high regard. Both men were making their reputations. Lobsang wanted to surpass the record of Ang Rita who had climbed the mountain ten times without bottled oxygen. Fischer's rich and famous clients could make him rich and famous too, if they succeeded. Fischer was charging them $64,000 for the opportunity. He'd brought extra equipment and Sherpas so that his clients wouldn't need to carry anything up the mountain but themselves. 'But,' he added with a grin, 'the truth is I charge that much because I can.'

Just as the diners were starting to drift away from the table, the Sherpas brought in a steaming apple pie. This wasn't a typical lodge apple pie, apples weren't in season anyway, but the real thing with real pastry and a whiff of cinnamon. The departing Americans made comments about 'mom' and what a great job the Sherpas had done in producing it, but when they had all gone three-quarters of the pie remained. The other trekkers sat in their places staring at the pie with obvious longing, some with their mouths hanging open. I wasn't wasting any time and got Dachhiri to ask Fischer's crew if I could have some. They beamed their approval and we set to it. Others in the room looked on with a mixture of disgust and envy.

With the Americans now gone and most of the other trekkers too, the expedition's porters came in for their dinner. We sat drinking rakshi with them until we were both far gone. A beautiful Tamang girl with feline eyes stood by the stove. I asked Dachhiri which village she came from and he punched me on the shoulder before speaking to her too rapidly for me to grasp what he was saying. She replied and Dachhiri laughed, turning to me with his little fingers crooked around each other. The girl moved from her position by the stove and squeezed in between us. She took my arm.

'Dachhiri,' I said, 'I don't want to sleep with her, I just wanted to know where she comes from.' He covered his mouth and giggled so hard that tears formed in his eyes. I looked at the girl. She smiled back at me. 'It's been lovely to meet you,' I told her, 'but I really need to go now.' And then I stood up and ran for the dormitory. There was a roar of laughter from the other porters and looking back I could see the girl looking furiously after me. I had to wait for what seemed like hours until they had all gone and I could sneak outside to empty my bladder.

In the morning Dachhiri and I stood in the door of the lodge sipping tea, watching the Americans start for the day's trek to Dingboche. They left in pairs, gossiping loudly about other members of the expedition, like a sales team on a management training course bickering about office politics. Five weeks later they were in position to climb to the summit and I was back in London. Each evening I read their despatches released onto the Internet and followed, like thousands of others all over the world, the tragic outcome of that season on Everest. The fate of Fischer's expedition, and that of his friend and colleague Rob Hall, became the biggest mountaineering story since James Morris smuggled his report of the first ascent to his editors at *The Times* in 1953.

So much has been written about the forty-eight hours that it took for the tragedy to unfold, some of it contradictory and unfair, that looking over the stack of articles and books written on the subject, I don't feel obliged to add anything more. Simply put, thirty-three people left the South Col just before or after midnight on May 9th – 10th, 1996. Five of them never came back including the leaders Rob Hall and Scott Fischer, the guide Andy Harris and two clients from Hall's expedition, a postal-worker from Seattle called Doug Hansen and Yasuko Namba, a Japanese woman who would, at forty-seven, become the oldest woman ever to reach the summit. A sixth climber, a pathologist from Dallas called Seaborn Beck Weathers, was so badly frostbitten that his right hand and nose were amputated. Makalu Gao, leader of the ill-fated Taiwanese, was also severely frostbitten after spending a night out on the mountain next to the dying Fischer.

Shortly before Hall died and marooned close to the South Summit, the New Zealander managed to speak to his wife Jan Arnold at their home in Christchurch after his radio signal was patched through from Base Camp via a satellite phone. She was, at the time, seven months' pregnant with their first child and when she took the call she knew what the outcome would be. Exposed, exhausted and dying, Hall himself had once said that rescue from a position like his would be like bringing someone back from the moon. Hall knew very well the terrible price that his sport could exact. Three years before on another 8000-metre peak in Nepal called Dhaulagiri, he had watched his friend and business partner Gary Ball collapse and die of pulmonary oedema.

When news of the tragedy reached those in Britain with experience of guiding on Everest, the only surprise was that it had been Hall and Fischer who had got into trouble. That such a disaster should happen at all had long been anticipated. Because, if you regularly put a large number of people at the top of the highest mountain on earth, sooner or later some of them are going to die. That two of the most experienced and capable high-altitude guides should be victims was a cruel irony and little more. Despite this, clients on both expeditions with strong links to the media attempted to identify the one decision or series of decisions that killed Hall and the others. Jon Krakauer, a journalist with the American magazine *Outside*, wrote a compelling and moving account of his experiences as a client with Hall's team. He criticised Anatoly Boukreev for what Krakauer and others judged to be a precipitate descent to the South Col after the Russian reached the summit, mentioning only briefly that during the night, as clients huddled together close to death on the South Col,

Boukreev returned again and again to help them back to the safety of their tents. Nor did Krakauer report how the next day Boukreev climbed back up to where his friend Scott Fischer had collapsed in the snow the night before. To go back up the mountain after reaching the summit the day before would be beyond the powers of almost every non-Sherpa in the world and many Sherpas as well. When Boukreev found Scott's body at seven in the evening, the American had no gloves on and his jacket was unzipped. Boukreev speculated that Fischer had felt warm towards the end. In his ear was an earring Lobsang Jangbu had given him, around his neck an amulet from his wife and a small bag containing locks of hair from his children. Boukreev returned to the South Col after dark, guided in by the shouts of pain from Weathers' tent, caused by the agonies of his dead hand and face. As if his guilt and loss over Fischer's death weren't enough to deal with, he had to read the criticism of other guides who were queuing up to doubt his judgement.

Krakauer also criticised Lobsang Jangbu for not fulfilling his role as sirdar on Fischer's expedition. The Sherpa, Krakauer argued, should have been at the front of his clients, fixing a rope to the Hillary Step just before the summit for the others to follow. Instead he gave all his attention to one of Fischer's clients who I had seen at Tengpoche, a journalist called Sandy Hill Pittman. She too had bad things to say about the guides working on Everest that season, despite the fact that one got her to the summit and two others saved her life when her group became benighted after they lost their way to their camp returning to the South Col. Lobsang Jangbu was forced to write to the American press to defend his reputation, but an impression that it was a Russian and a Sherpa who had caused the accident stuck in many people's memory.

I have a lot of sympathy for Krakauer who was clearly traumatised by his experience and did his best to explain why such confident outfits like Hall's and Fischer's could meet with disaster. But the obvious question that was barely asked in the tragedy's aftermath was whether it is even possible to guide inexperienced or weaker climbers to the summit of Everest. The difficulties of rescuing a stricken client are almost insurmountable close to the summit. Lower down the mountain oedemas can kill even the experienced within hours, an avalanche or sérac fall can sweep away bodies like match sticks.

The truth has to be faced that guides have treated the mountain as a resource, just as the Nepali authorities have. It's a way to cash in on the interest generated by the regular flow of books and films about Everest, a package deal to the roof of the world for anyone with enough money and an excess of self-confidence. As for the motivation of people who are prepared to spend a small fortune for a chance to be pulled up Everest, I can only guess. If it is to impress, then the huge resources and assistance required to get them to the top should temper their sense of achievement. If it is for a love of adventure, then they probably get more than they bargain for. But then why climb Everest at all? That's the hardest thing to explain. That's the sixty-four thousand dollar question.

CHAPTER NINE

Coming down is more dangerous

Listen to the conch shell trumpet blow
which the menthol river will repeat,
echoed in consolation,
in anticipation of the scented ashes.

From *The Valley of Death* by Dominic Sasse

At around half past six in the morning the steady rhythm of
drums and cymbals was interrupted by two monks in rich yellow
robes appearing at an upstairs window of the monastery. Facing
south, they chanted across the flat brown earth and olive grass of
the meadow towards Thamserku whose upper slopes were bathed
in morning sunlight. Then they turned back into the room to
collect two huge conch shells. The trumpet sound they blew was
small, unexpectedly tremulous. The few trekkers camping in front
of the gompa had been coraaled by their staff around the breakfast table. Mist clung in the green depths of the Imja Khola, con-
cealing the river in grey shadows. The golden peak of the stupa
glittered in the sun above smoke from kitchen fires. Sherpas dis-
mantled the remaining tents and herdsmen strapped loads to
patient yaks, their bells ringing dully in the cold morning air. It was
like being lifted by a wave and carried forward. It was profoundly,
impenetrably, achingly beautiful.

The head lama at Rongbuk on the north side of Everest
commissioned the building of a monastery at Tengpoche on the
south side in 1912. It was intended to be isolated, a celibate gompa
in the Khumbu where married monasteries were the norm, a place
for reflection. Now it lies on the path of thousands approaching

Everest, a staging post where tourists acclimatise and examine the view before sitting down to dinner. It's a hard business following the dharma when the twentieth century is trooping past with a camera to its eye. In the 1970s, the numbers of monks or *tawa* dipped to a low of around thirty as many left the monastery to work in the trekking industry. Some visitors saw the monks performing the Mani Rimdu festival in front of tourists and argued that the spiritual life of the Khumbu was being weakened by commercial exploitation. (As an aside, it is interesting how most tourists, myself included, intuitively assume that the Mani Rimdu festival, a nineteen-day puja characterised by a masked dramatic dance depicting the triumph of Buddhism over the Bon religion, is an ancient part of Khumbu life. In fact, it was introduced by the Rinpoche of Rongbuk in the 1920s. The Dumje festival held in June or July is much more an intrinsically Sherpa festival.)

The numbers of monks has increased in recent years and the spiritual life of the gompa and its importance to Sherpa life are still very strong. Change has also been painful for those who arrived when visitors and the monastery were new to each other. John Hunt had been mesmerised by its stillness and position when he camped here on the way to the mountain in 1953. When he returned twenty years later he was dismayed by the changes. 'Tengpoche itself,' he wrote in 1973, 'which made me gasp in wonder at the beauty of it when I first stepped out on to the meadow beneath the monastery, is fast becoming a refuse heap of plastic bags, paper and tin cans.'

Perspective can be a grievous thing. Mine was limited to the present and the broad sweep of mountains circling the copper roof of the gompa. I simply don't know whether things have improved in the twenty-three years since John Hunt mourned the loss of Tengpoche's charm. I could see a very little garbage and some evidence of deforestation, but it seemed a minor problem, not a cause for anguish. Perhaps this is how beauty is degraded or lost, by the lowered expectations of each generation. Ngwang Tenzin Jangpo, the Rinpoche or abbot at the monastery, has tried to guide his monks and the people through these upheavals but managing so many visitors has demanded initiative and caused occasional mistakes.

None was more costly than the decision to install a hydro-electric plant. It was built in 1988 at a cost of a $100,000 donated by an American charity, and the Rinpoche and those who assisted in its construction hoped it would provide a source of heating and so reduce the need to burn wood. The system could generate twenty-two kilowatts of electricity, enough, it was thought, to light the monastery at night and power a few electric heaters and stoves. But it didn't end the use of fires and, as people stayed up later under the bright new lights, some believe that more wood was burned than saved. A technical problem that had developed during the monsoon was finally repaired in December. In January, while the rinpoche and all but one of his monks were in Kathmandu, a fire started in the monastery and burned it to the ground. Trekkers camping or sleeping in Tengpoche's few lodges helped by rescuing what they could of the gompa's relics, but the majority of its books and costumes sent from Rongbuk for the Mani Rimdu festival were lost.

When the monastery was previously destroyed during the earthquake of 1934 that so devastated Kathmandu, it was a private, local affair and the reconstruction was completed in anonymity. The ashes of the monastery were barely cool in 1989 before promises of funds and support to rebuild were being pledged. Leading the way with $100,000 for building materials was Sir Edmund Hillary's Himalayan Trust. The architect was a restoration specialist from Kathmandu, craftsmen came from Bhutan to mould the gompa's clay statues and artists from Sikkim painted its murals. The reconsecration took place under the glare of television lights and was reported around the world. It's difficult to imagine anywhere else in Nepal, even in the Kathmandu Valley, attracting similar interest or support. It may have been difficult for Tengpoche to find sufficient numbers of monks when there are so many other opportunities open to

Sherpas in the Khumbu, but money for this monastery at least has been no object. It's not surprising that elsewhere in Nepal there is resentment at the attention and resources given to tens of thousands of Sherpas ahead of millions of others.

Dachhiri, largely unconcerned by the intricacies of conservation and development, was sitting in the lodge's kitchen drinking tea and listening to a vociferous three-way argument between our host, a French mountaineer and his sirdar. The Frenchman was on his way to Everest for which he had presumably paid his $10,000 share of a permit. The cost had clearly left him close to bankruptcy because he was arguing that he'd been overcharged by two rupees – around three pence – for each glass of tea that he and his staff had enjoyed. At the same time he was trying to persuade his sirdar to make sure his gear was carried to Base Camp a day sooner than is usual. The sirdar said this was fine but that the porters would still be expecting their regular fee, however quickly they carried their loads. The Frenchman paced up and down, his arms swooping into the air as he cursed and then pleaded while they set their faces against him. Without interrupting her argument, the Sherpani poured out tea and handed me a glass as I sat down. Dachhiri had his hand over his mouth and the little boy Tshering Wangchuk was giggling uncontrollably which enraged the Frenchman even more. 'You people are ripping me off,' he cried. I counted to myself the number of mountain huts in the French Alps which serve tea for a few pence. Finally, desperate to reach the mountain and hating everything that kept him from it, he gave in and sat down. He ran his hands over his forehead and asked quietly for tea. The Sherpani grinned at him. 'Tea? For you? No problem. One dollar.' I read later that the Frenchman made the summit. I hope he thought it worth the expense. As for the Sherpas, having the world's highest mountain on your doorstep must become a bit of a drag after a while, no matter how much the world's mountain conservationists want to help.

We ran down the hill to the Dudh Kosi, the sun filtering through the strong-scented fir trees. Smells have a spiritual significance for Sherpas and not just in ritual. The idea of incinerating garbage in the Khumbu has been resisted because it was feared the gods might be irritated by the malodorous fumes. I stopped to ask Dachhiri the name of a small pink flower I hadn't see before.

''S a small pink flower,' he said and smiled in triumph. Then he noticed something moving through the trees further down the hill. He pointed excitedly. 'Blue sheep,' Dachhiri whispered.

I looked at him sceptically. It seemed wherever we went we were followed by blue sheep, and I'd long since doubted his opinion. But when I tried to argue with him I quickly came up against the insurmountable problem that I was even more ignorant than Dachhiri. I later discovered that blue sheep are neither blue nor sheep and don't live in the Khumbu but in the Nepali region of Dolpo and, less commonly, Manang and Mustang. They are an evolutionary anomaly, stuck somewhere between goathood and sheepdom. The Himalayan tahr (*hermitragus jemlahicus*) is a primitive member of the goat and antelope family. This is almost certainly what Dachhiri was pointing out to me, since they are numerous enough in the Khumbu to be considered a pest. There are barking deer in the region which are identified by their reddish colour and the fact that they bark, but they live at lower altitudes, so it couldn't have been one of these. Musk deer, whose taxonomy is almost as vague as blue sheep, do live high up in the Khumbu and are found in the area between Phortse and Tengpoche above the Dudh Kosi. However, if you asked me to pick out one of these animals at a police line-up I couldn't do it, even if it had mugged me in broad daylight. Big animals that appear regularly on television or in children's books are not a problem. Tigers, elephants, giraffes I can do, but if my daughter ever asks me for a description of a Himalayan tahr I'll probably tell her that it's like a blue sheep, only less blue.

The bridge at the bottom of the hill across the Dudh Kosi was the most dramatic yet, a slender suspension of wire, wood and disbelief, smothered in silk scarves as imprecations for a safe passage.

Below, the walls of the river's gorge gaped black and slimy like some foul maw. Cold air rushed up from the water. It was a frightening place and I couldn't imagine that the spirits associated with it were good.

'Man fell in here,' Dachhiri told me as we stared at the rushing water. I imagined that it would be easy to become mesmerised by the repeating patterns in the river and topple over.

'Which man, Dachhiri?'

'Sherpa. Very famous. Climb Everesh.'

'When did he die? Recently? How long?'

'Maybe, five year.' Five years could mean a decade for Dachhiri. It was clearly long enough to have become material for myth-making.

'What happened? Did he just fall in?' It didn't require much imagination to guess what would happen to a human body immersed in freezing water and hurled at great speed against the jagged black rocks below.

'I think he was drunk. Or maybe he just fall in.' Dachhiri clearly knew more about the incident that his English would allow him to express. Sometimes we both knew that the things he was telling me were wrong but neither of us could come up with language that would grasp the truth more completely. Blue sheep were just one example of this. Later I found out more about the man who had perished in such a brutal way. Or at least, I think I did. It is a matter of record that Sungdare Sherpa of Pangboche drowned in the Dudh Kosi below his village in the autumn of 1989. Whether this was the Sherpa Dachhiri meant I can't be certain but I think it likely.

Sungdare climbed Everest five times with various expeditions. In the post-monsoon season of 1979 on October 2nd he reached the summit for the first time, climbing with another Sherpa, Ang Jangbu, a German woman called Hannelore Schmatz and Ray Genet, an American guide. Genet had started with two other expedition members but had been moving more slowly and eventually teamed up with Schmatz and the two Sherpas who were a little way behind the first group. They reached the top in reasonable time and started descending. Nick Banks, one of the climbers who had reached the summit a little before Sungdare and the others, remembers looking up from the snow-filled gullies above the South Col to see them not so far behind. He continued down, assuming they would make camp that evening, but they stopped moving soon after, some way above the intermediary camp used by Ed Hillary and Tenzing Norgay in 1953 and dispensed with by modern expeditions. Genet argued that they should bivouac, even though it was not yet dark and Schmatz seems to have supported his decision. Sungdare and Ang Jangbu pleaded with them to continue, but in vain. At around eight that evening Ang Jangbu reached the South Col to get help. Sungdare meanwhile descended to the old camp to collect some unused oxygen bottles and returned to where Genet and Schmatz had collapsed in the snow. His effort was wasted. By morning Genet was dead and Schmatz barely conscious. She managed to reach the top of the gullies from which Banks had seen her but collapsed soon after. Sungdare reached the South Col more dead than alive. Two Polish doctors managed to ease his distressed breathing and he was evacuated down the mountain. Several of his frost-bitten toes were later amputated.

For many years, climbers on their way to and from the summit passed Schmatz's body, her blonde hair bleached by the strong sunlight at altitude, until she was swept away in an avalanche. I can only guess what was in Sungdare's head as he climbed back up to her on his second trip to the top in 1981. These things aren't generally recorded in the expedition books of western mountaineers. In May 1988, Sungdare reached the summit for the fifth time, as part of a vast Japanese-sponsored exercise that brought together two hundred and fifty-four members from China, Japan and Nepal. Nine climbers and a three-man film crew reached the summit, nine from the north side, three from the south, simultaneously. Television pictures were beamed to more than two hundred million people. But the prestige and attention earned by his involvement in projects like this did not sit easily with Sungdare. While his friend Pertemba prospered from his Everest climbs as sirdar and through his trekking agency, Sungdare was drinking heavily. Alcohol is so much a part of Sherpa hospitality which is in itself central to the Sherpa way of life that it was difficult even for those who knew Sungdare to say whether he drank simply because his fame gave him more opportunity to do so or because he could not cope with the consequences of success. On a promotional trip to Hong Kong for Nepali tourism, he complained about reporters and their *idée fixe*. 'Why do they carry on? I'm sick of answering questions about Everest.'

Sungdare never discovered the knack of turning his celebrity into financial security and he died a poor man. His friend Phurba Sonam said in Sungdare's obituary for *Himal* that it was his karma to help out. 'I'd say: "If I give you fifty or one thousand rupees, you'll come back with an empty pocket."' He went on long drinking binges that almost got him sacked from one Everest expedition, but he was never violent when drunk. Those who knew him say that he remained a gentle and sensitive man who might have coped better had he stuck with his education. His English was limited to climbing terminology, not what it felt like to be an ordinary man caught up in the monied world of climbing Everest and fêted by his people and government. When people came to seek him out, all they wanted to know about was the mountain.

Finally the confusion and alcohol were too much to bear. It is widely believed that Sungdare Sherpa jumped from a bridge into the Dudh Kosi. Death must have been almost instantaneous; nothing could survive the force and weight of the river or the rocks beneath the water. For Sherpas, exorcising demons to preserve their faith is fundamental in many of their festivals and ceremonies. Every year, at the climax of Mani Rimdu, as the monks stab the demon effigies, the people shout, 'May the gods triumph!' Sungdare must have felt that the gods had abandoned him, that the only release from his demons was oblivion in the crushing green water.

Dachhiri and I sat on the veranda of the Everest View Hotel drinking coffee and watching the now distant view of Everest disappearing into cloud. I could have gone straight back to Namche Bazar and avoided the hotel but felt obliged to pay homage to one of the Khumbu tourist boom's more celebrated failures. Built in 1972 by a Japanese entrepreneur, it was an early attempt to capture the interest of 'quality tourists' or, as they are more generally known, rich people. Guests were flown in a six-seater Pilatus Porter aircraft to the bulldozed airstrip at Shyangboche to be met with oxygen and yaks to help them make the twenty-minute journey to the hotel. The business attracted some customers prepared to pay up to $200 a night but was poorly conceived from the start. The aircraft relied on good weather to fly and since weather in mountains is generally not good, tourists who thought they were getting the whistle-stop Everest experience found their stay being extended while at the same time and for the same reason Everest wasn't viewable. Then there were the problems of flying suddenly from low altitude to 14,000 feet. Many tourists found their experience marred by sickness, leaving aside the death I've mentioned already. The hotel lacked tap water and electricity and used huge amounts of wood in its construction, causing resentment in the nearby village of Khumjung. By the mid 1980s it had fallen into dereliction and was offering beds at $7.

You might imagine that this would have been the perfect moment for the park authorities to take charge, dismantle the building and give the materials back to the village. However, in 1990 a new backer was found for the project to spend the tens of thousands of dollars on renovating a building that had never made money. The hotel staggers on, or it did in 1996. Built from local timber and stone but with large rooms and an open lobby, it is just the sort of building a 1970s architect would design for the top of

a hill overlooking one of the most spectacular valleys and mountain views in the world. We left a trail of mud from the front door,
past the scowling receptionist who was most definitely not a
Sherpa, through the dining room and onto the veranda where a
miserable waiter in a dirty and threadbare jacket served us eleven-
ses. It is ironic that the hotel's chief attraction – the view – can be
enjoyed for the price of a coffee from the veranda and absolutely
free from beneath it. Ultimately, such inappropriate developments
will be limited by the amount of water available in the Khumbu,
just as it will limit the number of tourists and trekkers generally.
Meanwhile, the hotel serves as an illustration of how crass leaving
development to those with the most capital has proved.

A group of guests came down the steps to join us. I examined
them for evidence of flamboyant and excessive wealth but concluded that they looked rather like me, but cleaner. 'We've just
come for the coffee,' a woman with a northern English accent told
me in confidential tones. The waiter, looking even more morose
than before, brought another tray. Their trekking guide followed
him out and Dachhiri sat up.

'Sonar!' he called, and added *sotto voce*, ' 's from my village. His
brother . . .' he paused and then drew his finger across his throat.
'On Pisang with German peoples. Many peoples die.'

Pisang overlooks the Marsyangdi Khola, north-east of the
Annapurna massif in Central Nepal, and is another of the lower
altitude mountains classified as trekking peaks. It is popular with
commercial outfits since it's straightforward, comparatively safe
and is only just over 6000 metres. On November 13th, 1994, eleven
climbers set out from a camp just below the mountain's summit
pyramid. The team had paid to join the trip organised by the
German Alpine Club's travel agency. Eight were Germans, including the team's leader, two were Swiss and the eleventh was Sonar's
brother Chamba, hired as a local guide. Four days later a rescue
helicopter pilot spotted their bodies at the foot of the mountain's
North-West Face, tangled in their rope. It was assumed they
had fallen while descending the exposed ridge leading to the

mountain's summit. Eight of the bodies found lying in an ice gully were recovered and taken to Kathmandu. The remaining victims were discovered in an area threatened by rockfall and were deemed irretrievable. It was the worst single climbing accident in Nepal's history. The trip's organisers faced some difficult questions, principally why all eleven had died from what appeared to be a simple slip or the collapse of a cornice. There was speculation, denied by the Germans, that the team had been tied together on one rope which would have been poor practice by the team's twenty-five-year-old German guide, Stefan Hasenkopf. He had been due to marry on his return from Nepal. One of the team's non-climbing staff was reported to have said that the team had only brought three ropes and that one of these had been left at Base Camp, while another was used as a fixed line at a difficult point on the climb. Sonar certainly thought this was what happened. I asked him whether the German organisers had paid any compensation to Chamba's wife and two children.

'Yes, they give her a thousand dollars. And she get insurance money.'

'That sounds pretty good.'

'Yes, it's enough. But I am still angry. All the time the papers in Germany say ten climbers and a porter die. Chamba wasn't a porter, he was a guide. He climbed on Cho Oyu and many, many trekking peaks. But they say he is nobody.' I tried to remember how I'd written about the accident, whether I'd dismissed Sonar's brother as just another local casualty. He seemed bitter that his sister-in-law had remarried so quickly. The customs and rituals associated with death in Sherpa culture are complex and impenetrable to my literal mind but Sonar's mixture of regret and anger at the sudden and premature death of someone close was familiar beyond expression.

Namche was busier than when we had left. Day-glo trekkers armed to the teeth with survival equipment drifted past the stalls of souvenirs and supplies with fixed smiles, shaking their heads at the handfuls of jewellery thrust under their noses by anxious Tibetans. At one of the permanent stores I found a collection of books. Kurt Vonnegut seemed to be the trekkers' literary choice, along with fat airport novels and multiple volumes of Pico Iyer's *Video Night in Kathmandu*. Buying a book wasn't possible, I had to rent one or swap. All I had left was my recently finished copy of Joseph Conrad's *Nostromo*. This was an exquisite literary acid test. Just how highly was Conrad valued in Namche Bazar? I tapped the spines of various novels and travelogues and the sharp-faced proprietor shook her head while examining my battered volume with some distaste.

'It's a classic,' I told her, 'it'll walk out of here. It's a light holiday read.' Under a pile of tedious rejects, its cover half torn, was Keri Hume's *The Bone People*. The Sherpani's face lit up.

'Okay, you take this one.'

I took my new book down to Hermann Helmers Bäckerei und Konditorei, ordered fresh doughnuts and coffee and sat down to read. In a way my book was a little like Namche Bazar in its modern incarnation. Keri Hume's novel about family violence, love, redemption and Maori tradition had done little business in Britain – or in Namche for that matter – despite winning the Booker prize in 1985. It had the reputation of being difficult and peculiar. In truth it is gripping and very readable. Namche's reputation has also suffered unfairly. While the villages of Kunde and Khumjung retain much of their original character, many regular visitors have dismissed Namche as ruined by tourism. I found the town to have an energy all of its own, modern and artificial perhaps, but with hugely enjoyable idiosyncrasies. The post office was one of them. This occupied an upper storey in a dilapidated building on the edge of town. The office was manned by two officials from Kathmandu who clearly loathed their job. They lived and worked in a room which appeared as though a violent lunatic had set about it with an axe. Piles of paper were spread out across the floor, furniture was jumbled and broken. One of the men sat on the floor in the midst of this chaos franking stamps and snarling at any of his customers who dared step out of line. I handed over my letter in complete confidence that it would be yak-fodder before the day was over.

Dachhiri and I spent Saturday morning at the weekly market. My initial impression gleaned from guidebooks of this long antic-ipated event was that I would witness some ancient tradition prac-tised by many generations of Sherpas. In fact, the Namche market was established in 1965 as part of a wider programme by the Kathmandu authorities to revive economic fortunes damaged by the closure of the Tibetan border in 1959, following the flight of the Dalai Lama to India. For centuries, Sherpas had sent animals to Tibet in return for salt which they exchanged for grain with tribes from Nepal's middle hills. Before 1965, Rai and Tibetan traders would visit Sherpas in their households. In 1959, eighty thousand Tibetans joined the Dalai Lama in exile, five thousand of them coming over the Nangpa La and settling for a while in the Khumbu. They brought with them so much salt and livestock that trade with Tibet simply wasn't necessary for a while. Sheep were sold for a few rupees. When the refugees moved south to new camps in Solu, the situation in Tibet was so chaotic that a contin-uance of large-scale trade wasn't possible. Sherpas still travelled into Tibet as far as Shigatse where there was a market for light-weight luxury items, including, apparently, Swiss watches for Chinese soldiers, and they brought out religious art back to Nepal. In its absence, the market for Tibetan salt was fatally undermined by the gradual acceptance of salt from India. The destruction of monasteries following the Dalai Lama's flight and during the Cultural Revolution ended the trade for butter and paper. Now almost all trade with Tibet, or at least the Chinese within Tibet, is conducted along the Friendship Highway.

The Namche market, like others throughout Solu Khumbu, has replaced the system that made some Sherpa families wealthy. Now, instead of salt, they use cash earned from trekkers and mountain-eers to pay for their rice and grain and all the other goods that Rai traders carry on their backs from the road head. The market starts early before the sun has climbed above the mountains and the lowland traders wrap scarves round their faces and hug their themselves for warmth. I recognised Sherpas from nearly every village I'd visited. The handsome boy from the lodge at Dingboche stood on a huge rock opposite the tiered trading area, a video camera held to his eye as he panned across the market and then across the village.

'His family live there,' Dachhiri told me, pointing out a large and freshly painted structure in the heart of the village. The young man's wife was in the melée at his feet buying vegetables. Along the edges of the market a few white faces with zoom lenses tracked back and forth across the bobbing heads and waving arms. The lodge-owner from Dole stopped me on my way back to the Kala Pattar for a chat. I was pathetically overwhelmed that he recognised me at all and we managed to have an intelligible conversation about what we had both been up to and where we going before he shouldered his sack of rice and set off back to his lodge. I had expected something exotic after Dachhiri's lavish description, but it was like most markets in most places with a lot more dust and a lot less oxygen. Its attraction was the pleasure people took in meeting once a week to talk and argue and catch up on news.

I waited in the Kala Pattar while Dachhiri went up the lane to call his girlfriend again. He'd been trying ever since we got back to Namche and the only telephone in the Khumbu but without success. The night before he had become so morose at this delay in his hopes that he got more drunk than I'd ever seen him. Sitting in Mayar's kitchen, I told her about Dachhiri's frustration. She looked suddenly thoughtful and paused in her work.

'You know, Dachhiri is very good man.'

Some things you enjoy by their absence. When I saw the first pylon, its spidery wires reaching over the trees, it was a little shocking, like seeing blood on the face of a child. In the Alps, no one thinks twice about such mundane structures and the ridges bristle with antennae, pylons, cable cars and funiculars. Even in Britain, where the hills and moorland had been kept free of such detritus, vast propellers have been built to catch the wind and generate electricity. But seeing such modern excrescences in the Khumbu was shocking. The source of this power supply was a recently completed hydro-electricity scheme built in the Bhote Kosi valley that runs north to the Nangpa La and Tibet. This is the trail that Tibetan pilgrims and refugees still travel along, their numbers swelling at each new security initiative by the Chinese.

Dachhiri waited patiently as I read the inscription on the wall outside the generating plant's bottom station in Thamo. The project, it said, had been completed in 1994 but it gave no indication of the problems and setbacks its construction had faced and nor did it mention the opposition of many who knew and understood the Khumbu. The plan for generating electricity in the Bhote Kosi was first formulated in the mid 1970s and the Austrian government promised $4,000,000 and technical assistance for its construction. Work began in 1978 and was due for completion in 1982, but delays pushed the start-up date further and further back. In the meantime, Brot Coburn, with local help and $78,000 from UNESCO, installed a 'micro' hydro-electric scheme below Namche that provided sufficient electricity to light houses and power water heaters in four of the town's lodges. Sherpas in Namche were delighted but ecologists, as they had at Tengpoche, warned that cheaper lighting would allow locals and tourists to stay up later, requiring more wood to be burned for heating. Doubts had been raised at a local level about the practicality of the larger scheme by park officials and Sherpas. Construction workers and porters would use local supplies of firewood. Geologists and glaciologists expressed concern about dam construction in an unstable area like the Everest region. The economics of other hydro schemes also suggested the Bhote Kosi scheme would be a failure. In the mid-1980s small hydro schemes were recouping only one sixth of their running costs in revenues.

In August 1985, the project which had already cost $2,000,000 and was years behind schedule, was destroyed by an event the Sherpas call a *tshoserup*. An ice cliff broke off a hanging glacier on a mountain above the Langmoche valley which feeds the Bhote Kosi, dropping into a lake below left by the valley's retreating glacier. The resultant wave breached the lake's moraine banks. During the next four hours, some six to ten million cubic metres of water drained from the lake, sending a thirty-foot wave of mud and water sweeping down the Bhote Kosi valley, washing away the dam, some twenty houses and ten bridges in the immediate area and more downstream. Few people died in the *tshoserup*, purely because they were celebrating the festival of Pangyi and weren't at work in the fields or on the trails close to the river.

Despite this broad hint, work started again on a hydro scheme for the Bhote Kosi and after another nine years of construction the turbines are generating six hundred and thirty kilowatts of power for Namche, Khumjung, Kunde, and the larger villages in the Bhote Kosi valley. The inscription pointed out that the majority of the scheme's shares are owned by the people of Khumbu although whether they ever see a dividend remains to be seen. It's too early to tell whether the scheme will be sufficient to take pressure off the Khumbu's forests but, if the number of tourists is sustained or grows, then this project, or something like it, will be needed. Hydro-electric schemes, like the massive, ill-conceived and inappropriate Arun III project planned for Eastern Nepal, have got a bad name in recent years, but there's plenty of evidence that smaller schemes run and managed by local communities could transform the lives of people even in the remotest parts of the country, while at least slowing the devastating rate of deforestation. The World Bank, however, has trouble looking down from its lofty height to see anything quite so small.

Walking up the Bhote Kosi valley from Thamo we fell in behind three Tamang porters carrying loads for a trekking group ahead of us. An older man kept up a monologue in a sing-song voice for five or six minutes until Dachhiri could stand it no longer. 'I no like men who talk too much,' he said. 'Makes them sound like a girl.' We caught up with their employers, three Germans resting enormous zoom lenses on a stone wall. More blue sheep, I thought and followed their line of vision. In a field some two or three hundred feet below was a group of women digging up potatoes. Sherpanis are annoyed to be photographed in this way, concerned about how pictures will be used. The Germans had the same open-mouthed stare of children at the zoo seeing a crocodile for the first time. Dachhiri looked into the field and waved and cheered at the women who cheered back before spotting the cameras and shouting angrily. The Germans withdrew, looking darkly at Dachhiri, to follow their porters up the track.

Potatoes had become increasingly important to me as the weeks went by. I ate two plates of them every day in various forms, but most often chips. Not only were they often better fried than most chips bought in London, they tasted better and didn't come in wraps of greasy newspaper. Sometimes, when they were offered or were the only thing available, we'd eat a plate of plain boiled potatoes with salt which were delicious once Dachhiri had removed the skin for me and we'd dip them in chilli powder. Spuds flourish in the high altitudes of the Himalaya and are easily the Sherpas' most important crop. They use potatoes in many different ways, as food for themselves, for trade and as fodder for their animals. They boil them, mash them, grind them to flour, put them in stews, curry them, distil them into alcohol, parboil them, chop them up and dry them in the sun. Sun-dried potatoes may one day be fashionable in Islington.

There are almost as many theories as to how potatoes arrived in and influenced the Khumbu as there are anthropologists who have studied the issue. My preference is to go with Charles Darwin's *confidant*, Sir Joseph Hooker, who collected specimens throughout the Himalayas in the late 1840s. Four of Hooker's companions died during this perilous research project, and southern Sikkim was annexed for the Crown after he was kidnapped and held for ransom. The liberated Hooker acted as guide to the troops. (These dramatic events gave the hypochondriac and nervous Darwin all kinds of terrors.) Hooker had this to say about the introduction of potatoes to the Bhotia tribes: 'Potatoes have only very recently been introduced amongst the Tibetans, from the English garden at the Nepalese capital, I believe, and their culture has not spread in these regions farther east than Kinchinjunga, but they will very soon penetrate into Tibet, from Darjeeling, or eastward from Nepal.'

It was generally accepted, following Fürer-Haimendorf's work, that the introduction of the potato led to almost immediate prosperity and population increase, but recent research suggests that the influence was more gradual. The Sherpas have taken over a hundred years to develop and perfect a complex system of growing and storing them. The Sherpanis in the field below us were digging up potatoes buried in a hole around three feet deep and insulated by dry plants and earth to protect their crop from frost. In the spring they calculated the appropriate moment to plant seed potatoes by the intersection of the rise or fall of the sun or moon with a specific point on an intervening mountain ridge. What I found most interesting was the main variety now used by the Sherpas – *rigi ceru*, or yellow potatoes – was only introduced during the 1970s. Throughout the century the Sherpas have experimented almost constantly with new varieties, showing a typical willingness to change and improve.

We crossed to the west bank of the Bhote Kosi on a suspension bridge spanning a white granite ravine through which the emerald water roared and then slowly climbed up the steep path to emerge beneath the village of Thami Og. The path branched here, our fork leading up to the houses, the other continuing north towards the Nangpa La and Tibet.

In 1959, this was the pass that many Tibetans crossed in their flight from the Chinese. Refugees were again making the difficult journey across the ice and rocks at 18,500 feet following a new security initiative by the Chinese-backed authorities. In 1994, at the Third National Forum in Beijing, China's leaders agreed measures aimed at speeding up economic development in China and accelerating the migration of Han Chinese into Tibet. At the same time they agreed that the easing of restrictions on religion, begun in the late 1970s, had gone too far and new guidelines were drawn up to reduce the influence of monasteries in Tibet, guidelines published by the Tibet Autonomous Region under the unnerving title *A Golden Bridge Leading Into a New Era*:

> A number of religious institutions have been used at times by a few people who harbour sinister motives to plot against us and have become counter-revolutionary bases. The influence of our enemies in foreign countries, especially the 'Dalai clique', was slipping into the monasteries of our region more than ever. They assume that to get hold of a monastery is the equivalent of [getting hold of] a district of the Communist party.

In the summer of 1996 the authorities in Tibet banned the display of pictures of the Dalai Lama and sent a work party to remove pictures from Ganden monastery just outside Lhasa. The monks threw stones at the officials and the Chinese responded by sending in troops and arresting scores of monks the following day. Less than two weeks after the start of the unrest there were fewer than fifty monks left at Ganden out of a population of six hundred. Those not already arrested had fled to their villages or gone into hiding. In November 1996, the Tibet Central Committee published a report denouncing the 'spiritual garbage' encouraged in monasteries and promising to curtail religious freedoms not compatible with socialism. Tibet's Party Secretary Chen Kuiyuan announced that a 'final battle' against the Dalai Lama had begun.

Anyone who doubts that the Communist regime in China is dedicated to eviscerating Tibetan culture need only consider the grim journey made by monks and lay people affected by crackdowns like that of 1996 to escape their own country into Nepal, often dressed in inadequate clothing and risking snow blindness.

The Sherpas have a cultural and ethnic sympathy with Tibetan refugees and they are generally welcomed when they arrive in the Khumbu. Many stay for a while in the Solu's beautiful Junbesi valley to recover from their arduous journey before continuing to India. The United Nations' High Commission for Refugees reports that in recent years the numbers have averaged between two and a half to three and a half thousand, but many do not bother to register at the UNHCR's halfway house in Kathmandu before continuing to Dharamsala and the Dalai Lama's government in exile.

While the Sherpas sympathise with the plight of Tibetan refugees, the Nepali authorities have traditionally tried to balance between *de facto* acceptance of the situation while giving rhetorical support for China's position. Officially, the government has not acknowledged that Tibetans are given safe passage to India but everybody, especially the Chinese, knows this has been happening. More recently the Nepali authorities have hardened their attitudes. In December 1996 a group of eighty-two Tibetans was arrested for entering Nepal without a visa and handed over at a Chinese border post. This followed the shooting of three Tibetans by Nepali border guards at Lamabhagar, a hundred kilometres north-east of Kathmandu. The Tibetans were escorted to the city, walking for ten days despite their injuries. Doctors in Kathmandu were amazed none had developed infection in their wounds. Such hostility to genuine political refugees is depressing, but given the effective indifference of most western governments to the plight of Tibet, it is difficult to criticise Nepal's position. In 1997 there were reports, denied by the Nepali Home Office, that a Tibetan woman had been repeatedly raped by several policemen over a period of two days. She was later treated at the Kathmandu refugee centre.

At Thami Og another valley feeds into the Bhote Kosi, circled by elegant, steep mountains of granite and ice more beautiful to my eye than anything above the Imja Khola. The village itself stretches across the eastern end of the valley, its sleepy mood only broken by dogs yapping at the end of their chains as we passed. Above the village is a gompa, the oldest in the Khumbu, perched against a steep mountainside overlooking the smooth curved floor of the once glaciated valley. Its position is more than just apparently precarious. As we approached I could see that it wouldn't take much to bring some of the bulging and cracked walls to the ground. Removed from the main flow of trekkers heading towards Everest, the monastery has to rely on the generosity of far fewer visitors. Without land or income the outlook for its thirty monks is bleak. It was impossible not to think of the international friends of Tengpoche flying in to celebrate its reconstruction.

There were a couple of new lodges in the village but most visitors come only for the day to see the monastery and acclimatise. This is a shame, because of all the places I visited in the Khumbu, Thami Og's stillness and beauty couldn't be understood over a quick lunch and from behind a camera lens. Dachhiri chose a small two-storey lodge at the edge of the village, a stunted juniper growing against its southern wall, a heap of dried yak dung on the grass outside. Unlike the lodges at Namche or others along the Everest trail, the lower storey was still used for livestock. Climbing down the narrow ladder at night in the deep blackness I felt warm bovine air and heard the sonorous breathing of the family's cow. Thami Og is the village where the most famous of the Sherpas, Tenzing Norgay, grew up to work with his father growing potatoes and barley and caring for the yaks. His memories of his childhood are of a simple life, bucolic and hard.

I remember the animals in winter, when they were crowded into the lower storey of our house, and how they steamed and smelled as they came in out of the cold. Still another is the rest of us, the family, almost as crowded in the upper storey, all of us packed together in no space at all, with the noise and the stenches and the smoke from cooking, but happy and contented because we did not know there was any other way to live.

It must have been difficult for those who saw the Khumbu in the 1950s and 1960s to watch change overtake this tiny fragment of land and its people lost in the mountains. Many have continued a lifelong connection with the area from their youth and must resent that things are not as they were. There is something in the nature of studying societies or cultures that suggests stasis or nostalgia is preferable to change or development. Lying in the sunshine with my back against the dung wall, I couldn't help but imagine how this village would be in another thirty or forty years. If the spirit of Tenzing could drift along the old paths now I doubt much would surprise him. He relished the changes and opportunities his life presented him. The regret and disappointment of seeing somewhere so extraordinary absorbing what we believe to be tawdry or commonplace is more a problem for us. We want to imagine that there are havens in distant corners of the world where life is simpler, purer, without the constant grind of money or position, where we can be free. That is why we prefer to remember them as they were when first experienced, before symbols of our world began to sour the ideal. It's a false and romantic premise. People and their ways are like the trees beside the river below me growing strong and straight but brushed away like match wood as each new tshoserup comes sweeping down the valley.

In the upper storey of the house were souvenirs and salvage from many expeditions, as well as postcards from well-known climbers. The lodge belonged to Ang Phurba who had climbed Everest, once in the company of a Texan millionaire who had set himself the challenge of climbing the highest peaks on each of the seven continents. His success on Everest had persuaded many rich Americans that with enough disposable income and a positive attitude they too could climb to the roof of the world. I checked later in the Texan's account of his adventures for a description of Ang Phurba but he appears a shadowy figure, another smiling Sherpa among many, liked but barely known.

Ang Phurba sat on a bench, his daughter barely six months old in his arms. His wife worked by the fire with her mother-in-law.

The old man lay under a pile of rugs at the far end of the room, hacking from a lifetime spent in the fire's smoke and whispering his mantra. The old woman folded pungent cheese into a pancake for me and said she'd had three children who'd survived. Her daughter appeared often during the day, her stomach round and full with another grandchild while her first two shook sticks of firewood at each other at the foot of the ladder and ran in the sunshine. At the far end of the room were the customary religious objects, peacock feathers and silver bowl, photographs of family members framed by white silk kathas and the broad, toothy grin of the Dalai Lama who they would only ever see if they made the long journey to Dharamsala.

Outside, the mountains loomed in the moonlight, curling towards the village. The lights of the monastery seemed unreally high, like diamonds set in the black peak behind the village. I envied Ang Phurba, having his daughter there in his arms, surrounded by his family. But being in the Khumbu was my choice. I could decide when to go climbing and I could turn my back on the hardship and walk away should I think the risk too great. But there was something I found here, some threat or uncertainty that had been stripped out of my life at home and which would keep me coming back. Ang Phurba didn't need the exhilaration of stepping along a snowy tightrope high above the valley to be reminded how fragile life could be. He held the evidence in his hands.

CHAPTER TEN

Dachhiri

Travelling is a fool's paradise. We owe to our first jour-
neys the discovery that place is nothing. At home I dream
that at Naples, at Rome, I can be intoxicated with beauty
and lose my sadness. I pack my trunk, embrace my
friends, embark on the sea, and at last wake up in Naples,
and there beside me is the stern fact, the sad self, unre-
lenting, identical, that I fled from.

From *Self-Reliance* by Ralph Waldo Emerson

Getting here had taken three hard, long days. I sat on a fat white
rock at the river's edge and bathed my ruined feet in the icy green
water. Dachhiri leaned against a mud bank on the other side, his
rucksack still on his back, his face impassive, listening to a Hindi
film score on his headphones as he waited for me. The closer we
got to his home village, the more thoughtful he became. The
dense forest muscled round us, oaks dripping with damp moss,
groves of bamboo ruler straight. Above me the vast flank of a
mountainside rose out of the trees through thousands of feet of
terraced fields and Rai villages to the next strata where a few poor
Sherpas scratched a living. At lunch time we had stopped at a low
shack, its floor scooped from the dirt and matting walls staked
around it. A young Sherpani, with a thin, lolling infant in the crook
of her elbow, boiled some potatoes while her eldest child kept her
serious eyes on every movement we made. The early morning had
been spent on the ridge-line above, walking above a thin silver
mist, the white summits still visible at our backs and the heat of
the plains rising in the distant south. On the other side of the river
was the rest of the day, almost the same thing but in reverse order.

The morning was spent walking downhill, the afternoon walking uphill. There was no avoiding it.

I struggled after Dachhiri as we rose slowly back through the dense woods, the first few terrace fields with their deep green shoots, and then the first houses and the first inquisitive children running up to us. When we stopped to rest Dachhiri would switch off his cassette player or stop singing and we'd talk.

'What about politics, Dachhiri? Who will you vote for in the next election?'

'Communiss,' he said without a pause. Sherpas are considered to have an atomised, individualistic society which I thought might incline them to backing political free-marketeers. But then Buddhism theoretically suppresses the self, preferring to concentrate on the universal, the commonality within us and all living things.

'Why?' I asked him.

'My father is Communiss. My uncles is Communiss. They help ordinary peoples.' Dachhiri clearly didn't waste time on spurious political theory. His family's Communism seemed to spring from a sympathy for the underdog and a healthy distrust of authority and the establishment. Dachhiri had never heard of Stalin and barely knew where Russia was. 'I know Hindi movie stars,' he told me once, 'I not know politicians.' He understood unwanted interference from strangers from different tribes. On the trail outside Lukla we had met a column of troops on their way to a two-year posting at Namche Bazar. They slouched along, rifles slung across their shoulders, their shirts unbuttoned, greeting us as they passed. One even had a flower tucked behind his ear. The officer in charge was so embarrassed by his men's slovenly appearance that he bristled with anger when I said hello and ignored me.

'I no like soldiers,' Dachhiri said. 'Or police.' He pronounced the word in the same way and with the same venom that Glaswegians do.

'What's the Nepali army like, Dachhiri?'

'First you have Britis' Gurkha with much money, then you

have Indian Gurkha with not so much money, then you have Nepali army. 'S not so good.' Pemba, the Sherpa I had travelled with the year before, had told me his brother had joined the Indian army, keeping his Sherpa origins quiet. Sherpas, whose religion forbids them to take life and whose society inclines them to an individual approach, do not make ideal soldiers and are not actively recruited.

At dusk we turned the ridge-line we had looked across at in the morning and saw the village of Sotang running down the hillside towards the river at its base, caught by the warm evening light. At the head of this valley was a steep wooded hill with a few houses scattered across its flat green summit. 'That's my village,' Dachhiri said. I was too exhausted to care. All I wanted was to lie down and take the weight off my battered feet. Walking downhill for hours on end in heavy boots had stripped the skin from the knuckles of my toes and the dressing the Americans had used to cover the blisters on my heels had long since come away. My socks were soaked in blood.

'How far is the lodge, Dachhiri?' I asked pathetically.

'Soon. Just behind those houses.'

'Good place?'

'Not so good.'

He wasn't joking. The lodge was falling down, its scarred white walls bulging and cracked, the ceiling warped and hollow. The interior was lit by a few candles and in the thin yellow light two men were having a loud and very drunken argument. One of them had a horribly disfigured eye. 'He's lodge-owner,' Dachhiri said. With people of his own kind he was warm and open, here he was brisk and on his guard. We looked into the kitchen which was piled with dirty plates and bowls of stagnant water. I checked the location of the toilet and for any hazards, like vicious dogs, between it and the bedroom. I had a feeling I might need it. It was one of the most loathsome and foul-smelling holes in the ground I've ever seen with shit spreading out and up the walls. We sat in the eating area at a greasy plastic-coated table in the half-darkness and the owner's wife brought us two filthy cracked bowls of scraggy-looking meat and gritty rice. Dachhiri and I turned it over with our fingers and looked at each other. Then he put his hand on my shoulder.

'No touriss come here. Nepali place. Not so good.' I was too hungry not to eat. While I started to pick through the rice, the lodge-owner lurched round the room and his companion shouted at him.

'One thing we have to consider is our guest,' the second man said trying to catch my eye. He was just as drunk. I stared out of the door. 'One thing we have to consider is our guest,' he repeated.

'He's headmaster of school,' Dachhiri said. I pitied the children. 'When I was small I come here to school.' It was at least four hours up to his village even for a Sherpa, perhaps two down.

'You didn't walk here each day?'

'No. I stay in the village for five days, then home. School here is not so good. Now there is school in my village. Sherpa school. 'S good.'

The headmaster staggered over. He was sweating heavily into his cheap shirt and his breath stank. 'You are from where my friend?' I gave him the name of the previous night's village. 'No, I mean which country?' The lodge-owner grabbed his arm to intervene and started speaking too quickly for me to understand the gist of what he was saying.

'What are they talking about now, Dachhiri?'

'He say Nepali people are not good. They are stupid people, not like Indians. Very poor.' Before the headmaster could turn back to me I ducked through the door. Next to the lodge was a small shop, a weak bulb hanging from the low ceiling, the wooden shelves groaning with things for sale. There were cheap Chinese torches and bolts of fabric, packets of Nepali biscuits and bottles of Coke. I bought two of these and sat in the shop drinking them. I bought a torch to replace mine which I'd left in a lodge. I bought biscuits and scanned the shelves for anything else I could use. 'I'll take some soap, and a pen, and some batteries.' The old shopkeeper rubbed his hands happily. 'Shoes? You want shoes?' I considered swapping my boots for flip-flops but decided instead that shopping my way out of despair would solve nothing. I went back to the lodge to find the headmaster had gone. Dachhiri looked up and smiled. 'Lemon tea?' he asked, pushing a glass towards me as I sat next to him. I handed him our battered pack of cards and he dealt out a hand for rummy, putting the rest of the pack down. Then he looked across at the lodge-owner sitting in the deep shadows at a table across the room, his head on his arms. He was still talking but only to himself.

'Is like my father,' Dachhiri said blankly.

Dachhiri's father is a builder and was on the other side of the village's two small gompas when we finally broke out of the trees and reached the level area below the summit of the hill I'd seen the day before. We stopped first at Dachhiri's aunt's house. Dachhiri's father had married the elder of two sisters, his younger brother the younger sister. Both sisters had high cheekbones and narrow, delicate jaws which gave them an elfin quality, emphasised by their gentle, reserved manner. Dachhiri's father's elder brother was the father of his cousin Pasang. I asked Dachhiri whether he was related to Pemba as well. 'Pemba my best friend,' he replied, lighting up his biggest smile.

Dachhiri had two brothers and two sisters. Another sister had died in her early twenties the year before. 'First she well,' Dachhiri told me, 'then she sick for a little bit, then she die.' His elder brother, Temba, also worked in the trekking industry and was away with a group of Israelis on their way to a trekking peak called Mera, a little to the north. Temba had married some years before a beautiful Sherpani called Ingi who was an elder sister of Dachhiri's girlfriend, Pussi. Their house, built by Dachhiri's father many years before, was just below his house. Ingi had two boys, one of four, the other only two. Dachhiri's younger brother, Danru, was away trekking in the Langtang but his two sisters still lived with his parents. Tashi Lhamu was a little younger than

Dachhiri, about twenty, and looked very like her brother. Kilamu, the youngest at fourteen, had inherited the feline beauty of her mother.

Tight and complex family structures are reflected in the subtle nomenclature of relationships. Sherpas have a different word for nephew depending on the relationship and gender of parents and their siblings. The word for my father's sister's son is different from the word for my father's brother's son. Different terms can also apply, depending on the age of the speaker. Sherpa families are divided into around fifteen clans and marrying within the clan is one of their strictest taboos. Ingi and Pussi, two of six sisters, came from a village on the other side of the hill to marry the two brothers, since there was only one clan in Dachhiri's village. It doesn't surprise me that the Sherpa word for clan translates as bone.

Dachhiri's sudden appearance didn't seem to cause any great surprise. Dropping in on your family unannounced is only a shock if you have the option of letting them know you're coming. There were no phones in Dachhiri's village, no electricity or running water either. Local gossip came up the hill with the Rais who brought goods or rakshi to sell to Dachhiri's family and the others that lived there. Dachhiri's father had an old wireless which brought him news of events in Kathmandu. I wondered how the news of Chamba's death arrived in the village, whether Radio Nepal had reported that a Sherpa had died with a group of German tourists and Dachhiri's father had heard the broadcast in the darkness of his home. Dachhiri showed me which of the thirty or so houses spread across the hillside belonged to Chamba's wife and children.

His family may not have been surprised to see him, but they were certainly delighted. I asked Dachhiri for his aunt's name but he blushed and covered his mouth and giggled as he struggled to remember. 'She's called Aunty,' he finally said and then added weakly, 'I can't remember.'

Aunty's house was arranged like all Sherpa houses. The fire was built opposite the only door in the upper storey of the house. There was no chimney and the smoke brushed against a tarry sheet of matting fixed above it before filtering out through the roof and windows. Like many older Sherpas, Aunty had a deep cough from years of inhaling the smoke. The single room was long and narrow. At its far end on the same side as the fire, was the family's altar. Dachhiri, being the chief guest, sat closest to the fire in the position his uncle would have occupied as host. Aunty poured us chang and put on some potatoes to boil. Her house seemed different to those we had stayed in in the Khumbu but only, I soon realised, in superficial ways. There was none of the salvaged detritus from western mountaineering expeditions and the windows were wooden grills with no glass.

After lunch and already unsteady from the chang Dachhiri's aunt had given us, we walked the short distance to the gompa where his father was working. This was the new gompa, Dachhiri said, as opposed to the old gompa. New, I could tell, was a relative term. The chapel's most striking feature was a huge, drum-like prayer wheel fixed just inside the door. As it was spun, a metal clapper fixed to the top turned and struck a bell. Dachhiri set the rumbling cylinder spinning and clanging and walked past it into the gompa where his father was working. He was standing on the top rung of a short ladder, his back to us, hammering at a thin strip of wood wedged into a crack between a window frame and the wall. Looking round at the noise of the prayer well, his mouth opened and he put down his hammer to rub his eyes. Then he climbed down the ladder and hugged his son. Dachhiri explained who I was and he took my hand. I could hear Dachhiri's flat comparison of this man with the lodge-owner from the night before. The man in front of me was in his fifties with a rasping grey stubble on his cheeks and soft, heavily lined eyes. His skin was like paper but he held the attention of all those around him. It was clearly more complicated than I thought.

There would be no more work done that day or, as it turned out, for several days to come. We walked up through the terraced fields to the house where Dachhiri had grown up. Two huge poles stood in front of the white house, faded prayer flags pulling raggedly in the slight breeze. Down the hill and to one side was a one-storey house that his father had built first for himself and then moved his eldest son into when he married. His wife and daughter-in-law were waiting for us when we climbed the stairs. We sat along the bench running from the fire towards the family's altar in a very deliberate order. Dachhiri's father sat next to the kitchen area, then Dachhiri next to him and then me. As people came and went, the men would make room to their right to accommodate those of higher social standing. The women sat around the fire or served food and drink but the men sat in a line rather than round a table, so the constant flow of esprit, which ended only when the whole family slept, was as often between men and women as between men. Ingi, I noticed, despite being younger and related by marriage rather than by blood, led the way in this, responding to the provocative comments thrown out by her father-in-law and others with instant good humour. Her eyes glittered and she lifted her chin as these retorts were delivered. She clearly revelled in her ability to hold the room's attention, while Dachhiri's mother and aunt sat back by the fire and smiled.

All the conversation was in the Sherpa's own language of which I understood hardly a word, so I was thrown back on expressions and the rhythm of what was being said for clues. It required all my concentration to follow the flow of initiative around the room, a process which wasn't helped by the regular pressure on me to drink more. Dachhiri and I had been drinking chang all day, but this milk-white beer is only moderately alcoholic. Ingi, however, was serving rakshi. This is a spirit distilled from rice which to my palate tastes, in the villages at least, of alcoholic gravy. In Kathmandu it is cleaner but much stronger, like aquavit or schnapps. Ingi handed me a small silver chalice early in the evening and until I slept it was kept full no matter how fast I drank from it or how strongly I protested. One book advised that three firm refusals were the socially correct procedure for turning down an offer of food or drink from a Sherpa but Ingi clearly hadn't read it.

'*Shey, shey*! Drink!' she demanded. If I demurred for an instant she would simply take the cup from my hand and hold it to my lips. I either drank the contents or had them poured down my neck. The pressure of Sherpa hospitality would make you either drink too much or nothing at all and doing either, I guessed, would add tension to a party. Pasang was tee-total and I remembered him at the lodge in Dingboche shaking his head when he heard I was visiting his village. I didn't have a measure of his self-restraint. Like many Sherpas, I feel I need to drink at a party to forget to be shy, but this was excessive. The arrival of a vast plate full of rice and dahl and vegetables was a welcome break. After watching me eat four eggs a day for several weeks, Dachhiri had warned his mother and she cracked an egg over my dinner before handing it over.

The tempo of the evening altered at dinner, the edge was taken off it and, feeling full, I leant my head against the window frame and dozed as Dachhiri's father talked gravel-voiced in the orange glow of the fire and a single candle. Ingi's children lay on the floorboards in front of the fire, now fast asleep. Dachhiri would turn to me every so often and bang me on the knee with his fist and then ask me if I was coping. I kept my eyes narrowly open to prevent the room from spinning and as soon as I dared move crawled down the bench to my sleeping bag. The last thing I saw was Ingi, one son draped around her neck, the other hanging by his hand, being dragged towards the door.

The sun was already high when I woke. I could feel its warmth on my face building through the window. I lay very still with my eyes shut against the savage protests of my desiccated brain. I felt I was sweating rakshi. Suddenly a hand gripped my shoulder and I opened my eyes. In front of them was the silver chalice from the night before full to the brim with rakshi. Dachhiri's father beamed down at me as I struggled to free a hand to take the cup.

'Radio?' he said and pointed to the ancient equipment sitting on a shelf behind my head. I tried to smile back at him and he switched the machine on. The first words I heard were, astonishingly, in English. '. . . and the World Service is now closing down on this frequency.' Dachhiri's father pointed at the radio and grinned even more and then pointed at my rakshi. '*Shey*,' he said and then went back to the fire. As soon as his back was turned I extended my arm through the window and tipped the drink into the dust below. When I turned round Dachhiri was sitting up in his sleeping bag grinning at me.

'Too much rakshi!' he said. 'Heesh-heesh-heesh. I get some tea. No lemon. 'S okay?'

''S okay.'

I sat outside the house in the sunshine, drinking tea and reading. Dachhiri sat with his knees drawn up, his head in his hands. I gave him an ibuprofen tablet for his head and after a while he took out a slim illustrated novella he'd bought in Namche. He would whisper to himself as he read. Dachhiri had always understood that education was important but the chance to earn money and experience places beyond his village and Sotang took him away from school before his tenth birthday. The little English he spoke had been picked up trekking. He also spoke some Japanese, the race he enjoyed working with most. I thought of the Japanese couple we had shared the trail with to Gokyo, the polite discretion with which they greeted us and the blank desolation on their faces as they viewed the ruined lodge at Pangka. Dachhiri had what he called an uncle in Japan who hired him on his regular trips to Nepal and sent him presents if he decided not to come that year. Dachhiri seemed content to let these bonuses come to him rather than seek them out. He was more conscientious than Pemba, but not ambitious like Pasang. Perhaps his imminent marriage and the arrival of children would change him.

He took me on a tour of the village, starting with his father's fields. There were sugar-snap peas growing near the door which were ready to eat, sweet and deliciously crisp. In front of the house were terraces of barley. Dachhiri walked among them snapping the heads of different varieties.

'This is oua, this is gau and this is jau,' he said holding out his hand.

'Sorry. Which is gau?'

'This.'

'So that's jau.'

'No, that's oua.'

'So that's jau.'

'No, I say that's gau,' he said throwing the golden heads at me. Two hundred yards down the hill I could see his sister Tashi Lhamu in her head scarf bent double as she worked.

We visited perhaps half a dozen houses in the village, most of them belonging to Dachhiri's extended family and at each we were invited to sit and drink for a while, so that by the time we came to inspect the school we were drunk again. As we approached, the dozen or so children abandoned their classroom in mid-lesson and stood at a distance outside the low school building which was little more than two or three rooms. I looked past them into their classroom to see the teacher turning round from his slate to see where his charges had gone. The children spent their school day at low planks propped above the ground with rocks. They had small collections of pebbles to count with and a standard reading primer and pencils to write in them. The school master seemed sober in comparison to the teacher at Sotang and I could see why the villagers were so keen to have their own school where they could keep an eye on things. The children stared at me open-mouthed as I swayed back and forth. In Namche the children have long been indifferent to white-faced visitors but here I was news. The teacher invited me to say something to his pupils. An impromptu talk in Nepali on a topic suitably edifying for young children was going to be difficult.

'Nnnnghh!' I said and they smiled and nodded to each other. It seemed to be enough because the teacher then beckoned us to join him in his room. There were perhaps half a dozen books and a desk and chair. He apologised in broken English for the poor state of the school's resources. It was the government he said, there was never enough money. He wasn't asking, but I gave him some anyway, even though I knew it was the wrong thing to do.

After our school visit was over, we went back to Dachhiri's home for lunch. His father was already drunk as well and as Dachhiri started on a bowl of noodle soup, he began a long monologue that I couldn't understand. Tashi Lhamu, her work outside finished, sat by the fire making tea. I was too tired to be interested in how he moved around the room and how Dachhiri stared fixedly at his bowl. I looked at the pictures of the family by the altar, the alarming Mani Rimdu masks which had been removed from the gompa for safety. The alcohol made me feel strangely distant. When the Indian Buddhist teacher Guru Rinpoche taught the Tibetans how to make chang he included owl's eye and tiger's heart in the ingredients which is why some drinkers become sleepy and others aggressive. Too much owl's eye, I thought.

But when I focused again on the conversation I realised that things had turned suddenly bad. Tashi Lhamu was crying. Dachhiri was stuffing his sleeping bag into his rucksack, preparing to leave. I saw that he was crying as well. His father was now shouting at him. Dachhiri saw the confusion on my face and broke into Nepali, although not to me but to his father.

'Look,' he said. 'You've embarrassed me in front of my friend.' I felt uncomfortable being in the room and suddenly I understood how Sherpas could feel that just witnessing an argument is polluting. Dachhiri came over to me, his cheeks wet with tears and wrapped his arms round my chest. It was like being hugged by a small bear. He then sat down on the bench and buried his face in his hands. His father had suddenly lost his anger and his eyes filled with tears as well. He sat down next to his son and put his arms round his shoulders and spoke quietly into his ear. I crossed the room and went down the steps and out into the sunshine. Tashi Lhamu followed me and apologised for her father's anger.

'He wants Dachhiri to come back to the village when he is married,' she said. 'But Dachhiri wants to stay in Kathmandu. My father says he will build Dachhiri a house but Dachhiri still wants to stay in Kathmandu.' I thought of his passion for the garish excesses of Bollywood, his friendship with Pemba and the other Sherpas living in Kathmandu, the excitement of the city and the prospect of work. He loved more than anything to be on the move. I thought of my family at home brought together a few times a year and the arguments and tensions that arose among people who had moved in different directions, trying to square the circle of love and self-interest. Dachhiri appeared and again began to apologise. He seemed mortified that I had witnessed such a thing. I told him I regretted asking him to bring me here when it had caused so much conflict. It was nothing to do with me, I knew that, but I needed to apologise for something.

In the end, Dachhiri's elder brother, Temba, rescued things. He appeared as unexpectedly as Dachhiri had, just as the evening's drinking was getting underway. His sudden appearance was a catalyst for a resolution between his brother and father. Dachhiri moved to his left to make space for him and Ingi his wife poured him a glass of chang as he gathered his sons to his chest. The elder boy rubbed his father's cheeks three times and then held the back of his hand to his forehead while muttering some mantra that I could barely hear. Then he leant forward and kissed his father on either cheek. It was a small ritual he repeated often which delighted his grandfather. Now it helped the family recover the joy of the previous evening. Outside the light failed and Ingi's face shone in the firelight as she moved along the line of drunken men, filling their cups. Dachhiri's mother smiled from her seat by the fire, her two surviving daughters to her right, her sister to her left.

When Dachhiri next came home he would be bringing his fiancée for the first of the marriage ceremonies that are the tradition with Sherpas. The process would continue over a period of years and either party could withdraw before the process was complete. 'We drink a lot of beer,' Dachhiri said during his explanation.

It didn't surprise me that we were drunk before we could leave the village next morning. We stopped at the house of Dachhiri's older uncle after we'd packed and said goodbye to his father and mother, and then Ingi and his younger uncle ran down the track after us. They placed white silk kathas round our necks to go with those from his parents and pushed a bottle of rakshi into my hands. At least the alcohol blunted the pain in my feet as we rushed down the thin, tortuous track through the terraced fields and then the forest below, sweating from the booze and the heat. By the time we reached the river we were sober again.

Dachhiri slipped off his pack and removed the scarves around his neck and then bowed his head under a small stream that fell clear from a steep bank of mud. He took out a comb and tried to force his thick wet hair flat as I drank deeply from the diamond-clear water. Then we shouldered our packs again and stepped onto the narrow bridge suspended across the river. The wooden planks rose and fell beneath our weight until we reached the centre with the water black in shadows rushing beneath our feet and the green trees crowding the banks. Here Dachhiri stopped again and taking a scarf from around his neck tied it around the bridge's wire rail. He stood there for several minutes, his face mask-like, serious, staring at the water until I almost spoke. Then, without looking at me, he crossed to the other side, folded his arms across his chest and started up the steep dusty track to the next village.

Epilogue

The China South-west Airlines Boeing rumbled and bounced along the tarmac, struggling to take off through the thin air of high altitude. The runway at Gongkar Airport which serves Lhasa is unusually long to allow aircraft to reach the higher take-off speeds necessary but it seemed to me that in Tibet there is just less certainty as to where the earth ends and the heavens begin. Finally the jet lumbered into the air and banked south towards Nepal and the international airport on the outskirts of Kathmandu. Mountains slid past my window, unknown to me and most of the world's mountaineers, ranges as large as the Alps explored by only a handful of westerners and entirely unclimbed. Then more familiar shapes began appearing as the aircraft climbed, Kangchenjunga, third highest in the world, to the east and then the Everest massif itself. The elegant black pyramid of Makalu rose to my right, behind it the steep southern precipice of Lhotse, with deepset gullies like claw-marks. Further west were Cho Oyu and the beautiful Shisha Pangma but dominating all was Everest, holding my attention like a grossly fat man in a room of beautiful women. India was shrouded by mist, the vast cities and crowded plains unseen, the Tibetan plateau was brown and empty. Far to the west was the triangle of K2 and Pakistan and then the fringes of Europe. To the left of the white aircraft was the real China with its ever-growing population and its new cities of steel and glass.

Climbing mountains seemed trivial up here, looking across at the gabled roof-top of the world, hardly something to risk a life for. But then these vast mountains, so far from the everyday business of the world and the hordes of people, were utterly compelling, a place of complete freedom and beauty seemingly beyond the grinding control of work and duty. I could easily conceive a life of endless wandering, Eric Shipton's life of 'sunny vagabondage', but the plains and the cities and the comfort of society have their claim as well.

Perhaps the only truly undiscovered country that we ever had was the future. Sitting miles above the ground I could not foresee how the lives of those I had met around Everest would change. Lobsang Jangbu Sherpa, Scott Fischer's friend and sirdar on Everest during the tragic spring of 1996, was killed later that year on September 23rd in an avalanche while attempting the neighbouring peak of Lhotse. He was only twenty-three but had already climbed Everest four times. Killed in the same accident were another Sherpa and a French mountaineer.

Mal Duff, who had entertained and informed me on our way to Everest Base Camp in the spring of 1996, suffered a fatal heart attack while sleeping at Base Camp the following year on April 23rd. He had been leading a group of clients on the mountain. He left a wife, Liz, and many friends who, months after his death, still cannot believe he is gone forever.

By the summer of 1997, 726 people had climbed Mount Everest, with the number of ascents totalling 932 because a few westerners and many Sherpas have climbed the mountain more than once. The number who have died now exceeds one hundred and fifty, with over a hundred of these deaths occuring in the last twenty years. The rush of mountaineers to Everest and the consequent commercial opportunities have left the mountaineering world concerned and confused about its future. The accidents there have served as a tragic reminder that nobody, no matter how capable, is immune from accident or sickness in the Himalaya. If people continue to climb on Everest then a small number of them will continue to die.

Sher Bahadur Deuba, prime minister of Nepal, managed to preserve his fragile majority until the spring of 1997 before the only political combination not yet tried, the communists and the monarchists, voted him out of office. Nepal's political future is uncertain and while it remains so the condition of her people is unlikely to improve.

Tension in Tibet, already on the increase during the three years I was visiting the region, has worsened still further as the Chinese-backed authorities have tightened their grip on religious expression. Bombs were exploded in Lhasa and elsewhere in 1996 and protestors were arrested for demonstrating after the authorities banned the display of pictures of the Dalai Lama. Tibetans, in their resourceful and humorous way, began displaying empty picture frames instead. Political arrests and torture continue, as does the policy of immigrating Chinese into Tibet.

My friend and guide Dachhiri Sherpa left Kathmandu in the spring of 1996 soon after I did, to return to his village in Solu and begin the long process of marrying his girlfriend. In the autumn, shortly before my son was born, he wrote to me with news of his family and to remind me gently that when I came back he would be available for hire. I couldn't help but think of his father drunk by the fire, and he and his brothers and the other Sherpas working round or on the mountain, setting out each morning on the trail with the smell of juniper in the air and the mountains rising to meet them.

Index

pulmonary oedema, 150
Pumori, 166
Pye-Smith, Charlie, 78, 89, 102

Queen Elizabeth II, 6, 56
Queen Lakshmi Devi, 47
Queen Victoria, 49

Radio Nepal, 208
Rana dynasty, 12, 66
Rara National Park, 91
Rastriya Prajatantra Party, 37, 61
Rechungpa, 24
Reuters, 161
Roberts, Colonel Jimmy, 165
Rock and Ice, 78
Rongbuk Glacier, 34
Rongbuk monastery, 29, 32, 109, 180
Rongbuk Valley, 32
Royal Chitwan National Park, 61, 72, 91
Royal Geographical Society, 2; political clout, 4, 51, 99
Royal Nepal Airlines, 82
Royal Society, 1, 49
Ruskin, John, 8

Safa auto-rickshaws, 71
Sagarmatha, 99; *see also* Everest
Sagarmatha National Park, 89, 99
Sagarmatha Pollution Control Committee, 103, 106–7
Sakyamuni, 103
Salkeld, Audrey, 97
Sange Dorje, 109
Santa Claus, 120
Scott, Doug, 78–9, 129
Scott, Robert Falcon, 3
Seattle, 174, 176
Shackleton, Sir Ernest, 3
Shah dynasty, 64
Shangri La, 66
Shaw, George Bernard, 4
Shekar Dzong, 28
Shekar, 27, 29
Sherpanis, 74

Sherpas of Khumbu, 118
Sherpas of Nepal, 158
Sherpas, 6; use of forestry, 90–2; origins, 96; reputation of, 96; migration to Darjeeling, 97; early myths, 109; female climbers, 112–14; investing in yaks, 118–20; attitude to yeti, 122; relationship of Tibetan Buddhism to environment, 142; responses of to crime, 158–9; memorial to, 159; uses of barley, 168; reactions to violence, 169; resentment of, 182; attitudes to alcohol, 187; their cultivation of potatoes, 196–7
Shigatse, 36, 192
shinggi nawa, 90, 91
Shipton, Eric, 3–5, 121–2, 147, 164, 167
Shiva, 66–7
Shivaratri, 67
Shyangboche, 84–5, 125, 188
Sikkim, 14–15, 182
Silver, Larry, 148, 150, 153, 157, 169
Singapore, 162
Singha Durbar, 46–7
Snowdon, 9
Somers, Dermot, 31
Sonam Tshering, 112, 114
Sonar Sherpa, 189–90
Sotang, 204, 212
South Africa, 152
South African Everest Expedition 1996, 148, 151–4, 174
Specialist Trekking Co-operative, 79
Sri Lanka, 73
Star TV, 20, 96
Stephen, Sir Leslie, 2
Stephens, Rebecca, 112
Strutt, Edward Lisle, 2
Sunday Times of South Africa, 152, 154
Sungdare Sherpa, 185–8
Survey of India, 52, 99
Swift, Jonathan, 69
Switzerland, 8